4·50

GW01465127

A GUIDE TO

Barnsley Libraries

STACK

P.S.442

TEF Study Guides

This series was first sponsored and subsidized by the Theological Education Fund in response to requests from Africa, Asia, the Caribbean, and the Pacific. The books are prepared by and in consultation with theological teachers in those areas. Special attention is given to problems of interpretation and application arising there as well as in the west, and to the particular needs of students using English as a second language.

General Editor: Daphne Terry

TEF Study Guide 16

A GUIDE TO
ISAIAH 40—66

E. John Hamlin

LONDON
SPCK

First published in 1979
by the S.P.C.K.
Holy Trinity Church
Marylebone Road London, NW1 4DU

© E. John Hamlin 1979

The photographs in this book are reproduced by courtesy of
Camera Press Ltd and the Girl Guides Association (p. 46).

The design on the cover of this book is based on one of the
lions which decorated the brick walls on each side of the
procession street in Babylon. Archaeologists estimate that
there were originally 120 of these lions, each about one metre
high, enamelled in yellow and white with black markings on a
background of turquoise-coloured tiles.

The cypress tree and palm design on the title page symbolizes
the 'garden' theme which is so strong all through Isaiah
40–66. It is based on carvings which decorated the apadana
or audience hall built at Persepolis by Darius and his son
Xerxes.

Printed and bound in Great Britain at
The Camelot Press Ltd, Southampton

ISBN 0 281 03668 3 (net edition)
ISBN 0 281 03669 1 (non-net edition for Africa, Asia, S. Pacific, and Caribbean)

2 113632 01

Contents

CONTENTS

Using this Guide

This book is planned on much the same pattern as other biblical Guides in the series.

There are introductory notes explaining why it is important for Christians to study the Book of Isaiah, and showing a helpful way of doing so.

Each section of the commentary on the Bible text itself covers one prophetic poem, or group of poems, and the treatment in each section normally consists of:

1. *Background and Outline* of the passage, describing the occasion for which it was probably composed, and briefly summarizing its main theme and contents
2. *Reading Suggestions*, showing how a close study of the language and structure of the passage can help to clarify its meaning. These are intended for students who are able to spend some time in detailed textual analysis. It is important to work carefully through the introductory note on How to Study Isaiah 40—66 before following the Reading Suggestions. Readers who wish to work through the book more quickly, however, need not use them, but can go straight on from the Outline to the Interpretation in each section.
3. *Interpretation* of the prophet's message as it applied to his own people at that time, and as we should understand and apply its teaching in the world today.
4. *Notes*, where necessary, on particular words and points of possible difficulty, especially as relating to the history of the time and the condition of the Israelites in exile in Babylon, and to comparable passages and references in other parts of the Bible.

SPECIAL NOTE

Separate Special Notes deal in greater detail with the historical background, and with the question of who actually wrote the Book of Isaiah and when it was written. These will give readers a fuller understanding of the conditions in which the prophet was carrying out his mission. But the commentary itself provides some background information, and readers with limited time need not regard these Special Notes as essential to their study of Isaiah. Others may wish to read through Special Note A, or indeed all the Special Notes, before embarking on their study of the Bible text.

USING THIS GUIDE

GLOSSARY

Glossary notes at the end of the book (pp. 204–220) provide additional discussion of a number of important themes and ideas which recur in many of the prophetic poems, and in other parts of the Bible. These notes are an integral part of the Guide, and all references to them should be followed up.

STUDY SUGGESTIONS AND QUESTIONS

Suggestions for revision and further study are provided at the end of each section. Besides enabling students working alone to check their own progress, they provide subjects for individual and group research, and topics for discussion. They are divided into two main sorts:

1. *Review of Content:* These will help readers to ensure that they have fully grasped the ideas and points of teaching studied, and to check their understanding of specific words and phrases.
2. *Application, Discussion, Research:* Some of these will help readers to discover how the work and words of the prophet were understood and passed on by other Bible writers, especially those of the New Testament. Others will enable readers to clarify their own ideas and beliefs, and to relate the prophet's message to the work of Christians today.

The best way to use these Study Suggestions is: first, re-read the Bible passage; second, read the appropriate section of the Guide once or twice; then do the work suggested, either in writing or in group discussion, without looking at the Guide again except where instructed to do so.

The *Key* on p. 221 will enable you to check your work on those questions which can be checked in this way. In most cases the Key does not give the answer to a question: it shows where an answer is to be found.

Please note that all these are only *suggestions*. Some readers may not wish to use them. Some teachers may wish to select only those which are most relevant to the needs of their particular students, or to substitute questions of their own.

INDEX

The Index (p. 229) includes only the more important names and the main subjects which appear in Isaiah 40—66 or are discussed in the Guide.

BIBLE VERSION

The English translation of the Bible used in the Guide is the *Revised Standard Version* (RSV). Reference is also made to the *New English Bible* (NEB) and the *Authorized* (King James) *Version* (AV) where these help to show the meaning more clearly.

viii

Further Reading

Readers who wish to carry their studies of Isaiah 40—66 further, may find the following books useful.

INTRODUCTORY BOOKS

The Book of Isaiah: 40—66. E. J. Young, Eerdmans
Exile and After. G. A. F. Knight (World Christian Books), Lutterworth Press
God and the World of Nations. E. John Hamlin, ATSSEA Singapore
Isaiah. G. E. Wright (Layman's Bible Commentary), SCM Press
Isaiah 40—55. C. R. North (Torch Commentary), SCM Press
Isaiah 40—66. Douglas R. Jones, SCM Press
Isaiah 40—66. N. Whybray (Century Bible New Series), Nelson
Second Isaiah: Introduction, Translation and Notes. J. L. McKenzie (Anchor Bible), Doubleday

MORE ADVANCED BOOKS

Deutero-Isaiah: A Theological Commentary on Isaiah 40—66. G. A. F. Knight, Abingdon
Isaiah 40—66. Claus Westermann, Westminster OT Library, SCM Press
Isaiah 40–66, James Muilenberg, *Interpreter's Bible*, Vol. V (Abingdon).

Introduction

WHY WE STUDY ISAIAH 40—66

1. Isaiah 40—66 is a well-loved and much used part of Christian Scripture

We hear the words of Isaiah 40.1–11 each Christmas, and on Good Friday those of Isaiah 53. Handel's *Messiah* has made some of these verses familiar throughout the world: 'Comfort ye my people' (40.1); 'Every valley shall be exalted' (i.e. 'lifted up') (40.4); 'The glory of the Lord shall be revealed' (40.5); 'He will feed his flock like a shepherd' (40.11); 'He was despised and rejected by men' (53.3); 'Surely he has borne our griefs' (53.4); 'Arise, shine, for your light has come' (60.1).

Hymn writers, like Isaac Watts, have put these words in verse. Here is a verse from the hymn 'How firm a foundation':

> Fear not, I am with thee, O be not dismayed,
> I, I am thy God, and will still give thee aid.
> I'll strengthen thee, help thee, and cause thee to stand,
> Upheld by my righteous, omnipotent hand.
>
> (Isa. 41.10)

> When through the deep waters I call thee to go
> The rivers of woe shall not thee overflow;
> For I will be with thee, thy troubles to bless,
> And sanctify to thee thy deepest distress.
>
> (Isa. 43.2)

> When through fiery trials thy pathway shall lie,
> My grace, all sufficient, shall be thy supply
> The flame shall not hurt thee, I only design
> Thy dross to consume, and thy gold to refine.
>
> (Isa. 43.2; 48.10)

Missionaries, like Adoniram Judson or Hudson Taylor, have travelled long distances across barriers of sea and mountain, culture and language, inspired by the words of Isaiah 42.6 that they were God's 'light to the nations' and 'covenant of the people', to carry His salvation to the end of the earth (49.6). Many people, like Albert Luthuli or Toyohiko Kagawa have devoted their lives to bringing liberty to captives, and opening blind eyes, following the words of Isaiah 61.1–2. Ordinary Christians have learned that 'they who wait on the Lord shall renew their strength' (40.31).

1

If former generations of Christians have found inspiration in Isaiah 40—66, we of this present generation should also study these chapters for ourselves.

2. Isaiah 40—66 is essential background for understanding the New Testament

Jesus himself used Isaiah 61.1–2 as the basis for His life task (Luke 4.18–19).

The New Testament writers thought that many verses in Isaiah 40—66 were fulfilled in the life, death, and resurrection of Jesus. The following are some of these fulfilments, they say:

John the Baptist was the voice crying in the wilderness calling on the people to prepare the way of the Lord (Isa. 40.3; Matt. 3.3).

The birth of Jesus was the revelation of the glory of God to the nations (Isa. 40.5; John 1.14; Luke 2.32).

Jesus's work of healing was the fulfilment of the mission of the servant of the Lord (Isa. 42.1–4; Matt. 12.18–21).

Jesus was the 'Lamb of God who takes away the sins of the world' (John 1.29), 'put to death for our trespasses' (Rom. 4.25) in fulfilment of Isaiah 53.7,12.

The resurrection and exaltation of Christ (Acts 3.13; Eph. 1.20–21; Phil. 2.9) fulfilled the words of Isaiah 52.13.

Paul used Isaiah 49.6 to explain to the Jews the reason for his mission to the nations (Acts 13.47). The author of the Book of Revelation used Isaiah 54.11–12; 60.19; and 65.17 for his picture of the new Jerusalem and the new heaven and earth in Revelation 21—22.

Christians should study this part of the Old Testament in order to understand the New Testament better.

3. Isaiah 40—66 is also important because it grew out of the deepest crisis of Israelite history

The tiny Israelite minority in Babylonia faced temptations to despair, idolatry, and narrow nationalism, in a world which held no security for them. They had to reconstruct their traditional faith for the changed world. They had to think anew about who they were, who God was, and what they should do. God sent prophets to help them.

Christians today also live in a time of crisis, and of deep changes which are taking place every day in society, political life, village life, and personal life. Many are suffering great hardship. All face temptations as the Israelite exiles did in Babylonia. A reconstruction of traditional faith is necessary now, as it was then. We need to ask who we are, who God is, and what we must do. Isaiah 40—66 can help us if we listen carefully to the message of the authors.

4. Why do we study the second half of the book of Isaiah separately?

The reasons for dividing the book into two parts are given in Special Note B. Some scholars believe that the whole book was composed by Isaiah of Jerusalem about 700 BC. In this Guide we accept the view that one author composed the prophetic poems of Isaiah 40—55 in their present order, before 538 BC, and that one or more authors composed Isaiah 56—66 in Jerusalem after 538 BC. Other scholars who agree that Isaiah 40—55 were composed before 538 BC believe that an editor collected short poems of the author and put them into their present order after 538 BC.

HOW TO STUDY ISAIAH 40—66

1. Look for the poetic divisions

This part of the Old Testament is written in poetry. In order to understand what the author was saying, we need to find out where each poem begins and ends, and what its main theme is. But this is difficult because the poems were not clearly separated when they were first collected and written down. The chapter and verse divisions in our Bibles do not help us much in this matter. In any case, the Hebrew text was not divided into chapters and verses until many years after the time of Christ.

Some of the poems begin in the middle of a chapter. 40.12–31 is a separate poem with a different theme from 40.1–11. Chapter 43 contains parts of three different poems.

Scholars are not agreed about where the poems originally began and ended. Some think that the poems were rather short, and not related to each other. They think that the poems were put in their present order by a later editor. If this view is correct, it is difficult to get a clear idea of the way in which the prophet developed his thought for his people.

Other scholars think that Isaiah 40—55 is a series of long poems by a single prophet, and that the order in which they come in the Bible is the order in which they were originally delivered. If this view is correct, all the themes of the poems are related to each other. For example, the new Jerusalem, the salvation of the nations, and the servant of the Lord, are all part of the prophet's message to the exiles in Babylon. People today who hold this view will keep all three themes in mind as they make decisions from day to day. They will see that God's will includes people outside the Church, and that God has appointed His people to a mission of service to the nations.

In this Guide we follow what seem to be the most probable divisions (see table of Contents).

2. Look for the subdivisions in each poem

Each poem is sub-divided into groups of verses called 'strophes'. Modern translations, beginning with the RSV, show these divisions by leaving a space between the last line of one strophe and the first line of the next.

Practice: Find the four strophes of 40.1–11 by consulting the RSV or another modern translation.

Each strophe has a theme, and some have more than one theme. Example: 40.3–5 has two themes: (1) preparation, (2) the revelation of God to all people.

Practice: Find the themes in 40.9–11 and decide which you think is the major theme. Why do you consider it the major theme?

In each chapter of this Guide, we give an outline showing the strophes and themes of the poem to be studied. Not everybody will agree with these divisions and themes. Study the text for yourself to see what other divisions or themes, if any, you would like to propose.

3. Look for the actors in the poem

In Hebrew poetry there are usually three main actors: (1) God, (2) Israel or some Israelite such as a prophet, and (3) the nations or some power from the nations such as the enemies of Israel.

Here is an exercise for those who like detailed word-studies, using coloured pencils. You could use red to mark nouns, pronouns, and verbs related to God, with blue for Israel, and green for the nations.

Example: Isaiah 40.1–2. Circle in red 'my people', 'your God', 'the Lord's hand'. Underline the verbs describing God's action: 'comfort', 'speak tenderly', and 'cry'. These are God's commands to the prophet. They show what God is going to do through the prophet.

Now circle in blue 'people', 'your', 'Jerusalem', 'her', 'her warfare', 'her iniquity', 'all her sins', and draw a blue line under 'ended', 'pardoned', and 'received'.

Practice: Use this way of studying Isaiah 40.27–31.

4. Look for the important words

Verbs are especially important in Hebrew poetry. Look at the verbs you have underlined in Isaiah 40.1. They come in two sequences of three. Now look at the verbs in 40.27–31. Note that the noun 'Creator' means 'the one who creates'.

Sometimes the author repeats words to show that they are important. 'Comfort' is emphasized in this way in 40.1. The words 'faint', 'weary', and 'strength' are repeated in 40.27–31. By looking for words that are repeated we can find out what the author wished to emphasize.

Sometimes an important word is used in one strophe and repeated in another strophe. In 40.5, the prophet says that 'all flesh' shall see the glory of God in the future. This refers to their future salvation. Then, in 40.6 he says that 'all flesh' is as beautiful as the field flowers, but as transient as grass which lives only for a single season. Thus he relates present and future by the 'word of God which stands forever' (40.8). This helps people today to accept their limits and appreciate the goodness of life, while depending on the undying power of God's word.

In 42.5, we read that God gives breath to 'the people' on the earth. This refers to the original unity of mankind as a family. Then, in 42.6 God gives a mission to Israel to be 'a covenant to the people'. By relating together these two uses of the word 'people', we can see that the mission of Israel is to bring all the nations and peoples of the earth together as a family under God.

Sometimes important words or phrases are repeated from one poem to another. A good example of this is the phrase 'ends of the earth' in 40.28 and 41.5, 9. The prophet tells the Israelite exiles that God created 'the ends of the earth', and can help them wherever they are. Then, in 41.5, he describes the nations and peoples all over the earth trembling in fear as Cyrus advances. In their fear they make new idols. But in 41.9 he tells them that God took Abraham 'from the ends of the earth'. By putting the three passages together, we can see that God, who created the 'ends of the earth', chose Abraham from the 'ends of the earth', in order that the 'ends of the earth' might know the true God.

Practice: Find a phrase which is repeated in 41.1 and 40.31. Try to see what the prophet intended by this.

When you find an important word in a poem, you can use a concordance to find out where else the poet uses the same word. This will help you to follow the lines of his thought. For example, a concordance will tell you that the word 'comfort' is used nine times in Isaiah 40—55, but only twice in Isaiah 1—39, and four times in Isaiah 56—66. This shows that it is one of the important ideas of the prophet whose words are recorded in 40—55. You will also see that it appears three times in the poem 51.1–16. From these references you can make a study of the meaning of this word, i.e.:

(1) release from oppression and famine (51.12–14),

(2) restoration of an ideal society of love, joy, and peace (51.3; 52.9),

(3) for the sake of the whole earth (49.13).

Practice: Use a concordance to find in which verses the word 'Jerusalem' is used in Isaiah 40—55. List the various meanings and try to relate them.

5. Look for words with special meanings

Some words have more than one meaning. 'Jerusalem' may mean the people or the city. It may be a city of the past, or an ideal city of the future.

5

'Wilderness' or 'desert' in 40.3 may mean a waterless place. It may also mean a kind of society or existence without blessing, and without God.

Some words show that the author was thinking of a picture of the universe which we no longer hold today. The prophet says in 40.22 that God 'stretches out the heaven like a curtain'. He thought the earth was flat, and had a covering over it. This does not need to be a problem for us just because we know more today about the real structure of the earth and its place in the universe. If we look carefully at this verse, we will see that the author was not trying to give a lesson in geography or astronomy. He was writing about God, and the real meaning of his words is that God is always using His creative power to make the earth a good place in which to live.

Some words have a special reference to historical events. 'A way in the sea' (43.16) refers to the story of the Exodus. But the prophet is also pointing to God's power to make a new way out of chaos and disaster in the time of the Babylonian exile.

A dictionary of the Bible will help you to discover what these special meanings are. You can also use a concordance to see what the word means in other books of the Bible, including the New Testament.

Practice: Use a concordance to find where in Isaiah 40—55 the word 'law' is used. Then consult a dictionary on the meanings of the word, and decide which of the meanings is fitting for the verses you have found.

6. Look for the climax

Each poem and each strophe has a climax, and some have more than one climax. The climax is the most important idea of the poem or strophe. This poet usually puts it at the end of a poem or strophe. In 40.6–8, the climax is in the last line: 'The word of our God will stand forever.' It stands in sharp contrast with the transient grass which grows up and dies every season. The climax of 41.2–4 is also in the last line, which answers the questions in vv. 2 and 4: 'I the Lord. . . .' The climax of 55.1–13 is in the last line again: 'an everlasting sign. . . .'

Practice: Find the climax of 40.3–5.

7. Look for historical references

These references will help you to understand the prophet's message. Some of them are very clear. The prophet speaks twice of Cyrus by name (44.28; 45.1) and four times of Babylon (43.14; 47.1; 48.14, 20). This tells us that the prophetic poems come from the time before 538 BC.

Other references are not so clear. For example, 'warfare' in 40.2 refers to the time of exile in Babylonia. The idols on the backs of animals in 46.1–2 may be a reference to part of the New Year procession, or to preparations for the attack of Cyrus. Often we have to guess what the exact reference is, without being able to prove it.

40.1–11
The Lord God is coming to Save
March – April, 541 BC

BACKGROUND AND OUTLINE

The first four prophetic poems were probably composed in or near the city of Babylon in the year 541 BC. King Nabonidus had just returned during the previous year. The New Year celebration in the month of Nisanu (March–April) was the first in ten years (see Special Note A, p. 42). This prophet probably witnessed the festival himself, and felt the excitement of the Babylonian people.

The Babylonians believed that the gods of heaven and earth all assembled in the Esagila temple in Babylon at New Year. Their images were carried from various temples for the occasion. Marduk (also called Bel) was the chief and leader of the gods. Next to his image was that of Nebo, his son, secretary of the council of the gods. The tablets of fate were in his hands. Near him was the image of Sarpanitu, his wife.

The king entered the temple on the eighth day of the month. While he stood before the images, the priests chanted the story of creation. He then grasped the hands of Marduk. The fate of the nation for the new year was forecast, probably by examining a sheep's liver, and recorded by Nebo.

The priests then took the images of the gods out of the Esagila temple and put them on ceremonial carts for a procession along the Marduk Road, past the great temple tower of Etemenanki and on to a canal. There the priests transferred the images to sacred barges for a journey to special New Year pavilions set up on the bank of the Euphrates river. On the eleventh day of the month, the images were brought back along the river, the canal, and the ceremonial road, and placed in their own temples until the next year.

This New Year Festival in 541 BC was a suitable time for the prophet to present the idea of Yahweh's struggle for a new world. The end of Babylon seemed near. In this first prophetic poem he used themes from the Babylonian ceremonies to present God's message. In Isaiah 40.1–2, Yahweh seems to be speaking to a heavenly council, just as, according to Babylonian belief, Marduk spoke to the council of the gods. Voices (vv. 3, 6) are heard from members of the council. 'The way of Yahweh' (v. 3) may have been adapted from the Marduk Road. The tall temple tower of Etemenanki may have been in his mind when he spoke of a 'high mountain' (v. 9, Glossary, *Mountains*). The command to call out, 'Behold your God!

Behold the Lord God comes with might!' (vv. 9, 10) may have been adapted from the ceremony of the return of Marduk on the eleventh day of the festival.

The prophet was saying that the true leader at New Year 541 BC was not Marduk but Yahweh.

The outline is as follows:

Main theme: The Lord God is Coming to Save!

Vv. 1, 2: God's decision to save His people.

Vv. 3–5: His people must prepare the way.

Vv. 6–8: His word is the solid reality behind all change.

Vv. 9, 10. His people must proclaim the good news.

INTERPRETATION

1. GOD'S DECISION TO SAVE HIS PEOPLE (vv. 1, 2)

The Babylonians believed that Marduk decided the fate of his nation for the coming year. This prophet told the suffering and discouraged Israelite exiles in Babylonia that Yahweh had at last decided to save His people. History has proved that he was right. Moses told the Hebrew slaves about God's promise to bring them out of their suffering (Exod. 3.17). God used Moses to make this promise come true. Jesus proclaimed a similar message: 'The time is fulfilled. The Kingdom of God is at hand!' (Mark 1.15). His life, death, and resurrection proved the truth of His message.

When the time is right, God acts. The situation in the land of Canaan in 1250 BC was right for the Hebrews to enter and settle there. The time was right for God to act. The Roman Empire on the west, and easy communications to the east, made the time right for the message of Jesus. So, in 541 BC, when Cyrus was on his way to defeat Babylon, the time was right for an announcement of salvation.

So today, God comes when the time is right in a particular country, or in the life of an individual. A Thai proverb catches the urgency of time: 'When the water is high, fill your jars!'

Study the meaning of the three verbs in God's command:

1. For a hopeless people: acts of comfort, like release from oppression, or the opening doors of a prison. Jesus's words of comfort were also acts: 'Rise, take up your pallet (bed) and go home!' (Mark 2.11).

2. For a hard-hearted people: winning words of love and care to convince their hearts, to draw them gently back to God.

3. For a people who cannot hear because of sorrow, a broken spirit, or for other concerns: a cry to waken the dead.

Look at the verbs again. Now study the contents of the good news:

1. You are free! The time of slavery is now past. (See note on 'warfare', p. 13.)

2. You are forgiven sinnners. A completely new beginning is possible because God has wiped out your sins from His record.
3. Your suffering is a part of God's plan. It has been more than enough for your sins. It will teach you to bear suffering for others. Look at the three clauses beginning with 'that' in v. 2.

2. HIS PEOPLE MUST PREPARE THE WAY (40.3–5)

The people of Babylon, and perhaps even some of their Israelite slaves, spent much time and work preparing the ceremonial road for the New Year procession of Marduk and the other gods of Babylon. How should God's people prepare for His coming? This is a question we ask every year at the season of Advent. We think of the mission of John the Baptist 'to make ready a people prepared' (Luke 1.17).

Let us look at the climax of these verses, in order to see what the prophet wished to emphasize. Vv. 1 and 2 told of God's comforting action for Israel. In v. 5, the circle is widened to include the whole human race! The prophet wished to stretch the vision of the exiles out from their own concerns to understand God's purpose for the whole earth. Christians today still need this double focus. Too often we concentrate on the narrower circle.

The word 'Glory' as used here, means God's grace and power made visible in His people (Glossary: *Glory of the Lord*). This is God's way of becoming visible to the people of the world. The only way they can see God is to see His glory in His people (Glossary: *People*).

The way of the Lord begins with God's people. He comes to them so that they can be prepared to show His glory to others. But the way leads out to the ends of the earth.

The way of the Lord is *in the wilderness* (see Glossary). This does not mean an actual desert, though it may be a way of recalling the experience of the Israelites during their Exodus through the wilderness. More probably, it refers to a 'wilderness world' where social order has broken down. Babylon in 541 BC was that sort of world. According to Isaiah 14.17, the whole of western Asia was a wilderness world. Many people today also live in this sort of world. People who live in a wilderness world may be more ready to recognize God when He comes, than those who live in security and prosperity. When God comes, He will make the wilderness world into a garden.

Part of the work of preparation is to bring down *the mountains and hills* (see Glossary). By these pictures from the physical world, the prophet probably meant the pride and selfishness of individuals or social institutions. One example is racial prejudice. Individuals may be prejudiced. To shake the 'mountain' of their security through some difficult experience may be sufficient to change their attitudes. But sometimes not only individuals but the institutions of society such as schools,

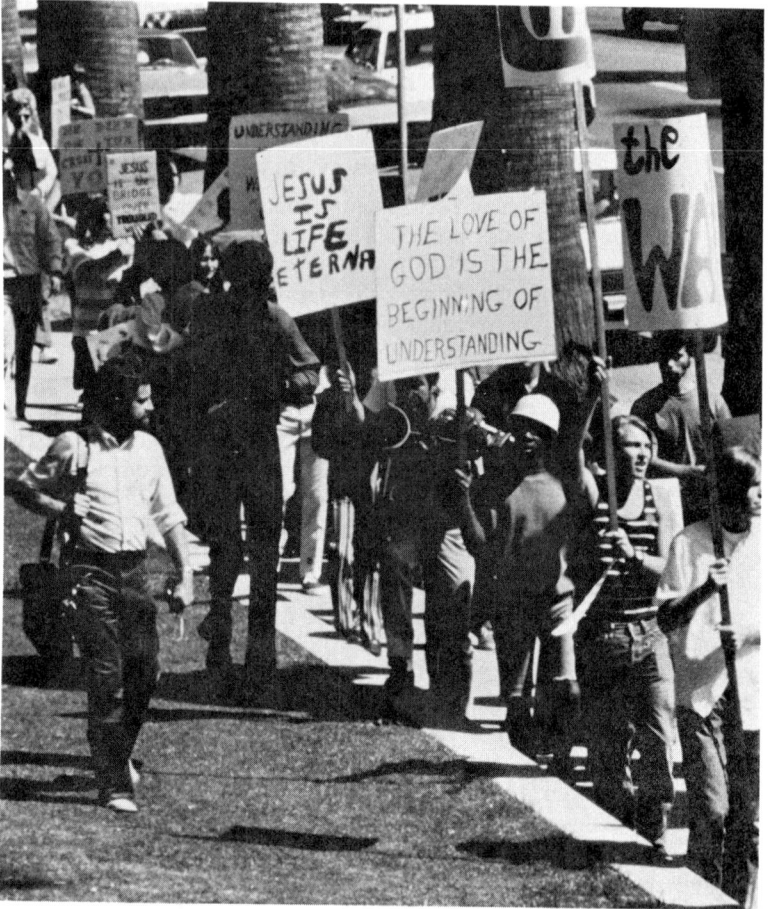

'The way of the Lord begins with God's people. He comes to them so that they can be prepared to show His glory to others' (p. 9).

A group of young Christians in the USA 'show God's glory' by carrying banners in procession through the streets.

In what chief ways do the members of your Church show God's glory to others today?

government, mass media, and the family may be strong centres of prejudice. Preparing for God's coming means to work for a change in these institutions.

Another part of that preparation is to *raise up the valleys*. Since valleys are the opposite of the mountains, it is likely that the author wanted his hearers to think of people living in hopelessness or despair. These people would be in the valley of deep shadow (Ps. 71.20), a sort of living death (Isa. 29.4). One example of people living in valleys is the slaves in Egypt, who were not able to hear Moses 'because of their broken spirit and their cruel bondage' (Exod. 6.91). People living in 'valleys' today might include refugees from war, slum dwellers, poor people without land, those sick with an incurable disease, a girl who has been sold into prostitution. Those who prepare for the coming of the Lord will work to help make a better life for such people, and encourage them to turn to God and depend on Him to help them come up out of their 'valley' and stand on their own feet.

3. HIS WORD IS THE SOLID REALITY BEHIND CHANGE (vv. 6–8)

In these verses the prophet poses a question which is very common to us all, and finds an answer. Perhaps we can see behind it his own struggle for certainty.

Two pictures come to mind: (1) the massive tower representing the 'world mountain' (Glossary: *Mountains*, before which the New Year procession passed, and (2) an old man carrying a bundle of dry grass to burn for fuel.

In the first picture we can see the arrogance of the Babylonians who thought their empire would last for ever (Isa. 47.7). In the second, we see the real nature of that empire, soon to be a heap of ruins. Assyria had been like that grass, too. So had the kingdoms of Israel and Judah. We think of the ruins of many other ancient civilizations now being uncovered by the archaeologists. They had their time of flowering, but then they faded away like dry grass under a hot wind.

So, many people ask today: will liberation movements lead to new slaveries? Will development be able to close the gap between rich and poor? Will a change of government solve the problems of corruption and injustice? Is there anything we can really depend on in a world that is changing so much and so quickly as ours?

The answer which came to that prophet is also true for us today: All things are indeed changing. But beneath the change there is the one dependable reality: the active word of God (Glossary: *Word of God*). God has a plan (His 'counsel', 46.11) which He is working to carry out. He has stated His purpose to reunite all nations in a covenant family (45.23). His word is like rain in the dry field (55.10–11), which will bring food for the present time, and seed for new beginnings in the future.

4. HIS PEOPLE MUST PROCLAIM THE GOOD NEWS (vv. 9, 10)

The priests called out the arrival of Marduk, the God of Babylon, along the Marduk Road at New Year 541 BC. With that picture in his mind, the prophet gave the small group of Israelite exiles a divine command that they should proclaim the coming of Yahweh, God of the whole earth. Those who hear the good news must be its herald.

'You have heard, now see this;
    and will you not declare it?
From this time forth I make you hear new things,
    hidden things which you have not known' (48.6).

'What we have seen and heard, we now proclaim to you.' (1 John 1.3).

This prophet tried to prepare His people to be heralds. To be a herald is to be an evangelist. The Hebrew word *mebasereth* means 'one who proclaims the good news', that is, the *evangel* or Gospel.

What do these verses tell us about evangelism?
1. The herald is the people (Glossary: *Jerusalem-Zion*). Evangelism is the responsibility of the whole people of God, or at least of all those who will listen to His voice.
2. The place of proclamation is the beginning of God's new creation (Glossary: *Mountains*). To put it another way, wherever the Gospel is proclaimed, there is the beginning of a new earth.
3. The people whom the herald addresses are: (1) the other Israelites ('the cities of Judah, see note on 40.3), (2) those living in the wilderness world of that time (Glossary: *Wilderness*), and finally (3) the whole divided family of mankind (40.5, 7 'all flesh', 'the people', Glossary: *People*).
4. The good news is that God is coming to rule and to save. His arm (Glossary: *Arm of the Lord*) will overcome the proud arrogance of the strong, and tenderly care for the weak, like a shepherd or any farmer who tends animals with care.
5. The response of the hearers who live on the 'mountains' of pride (Glossary: *Mountains*) is to repent; and those who live in the 'valleys' of despair and oppression must rise up and walk.
6. New members from the broken family of nations will join the procession led by God. These are God's 'recompense' (see note on 40.10) to His people for the losses they suffered at the time of the destruction of the Israelite kingdoms of Ephraim and Judah.

NOTES

40.2. Speak tenderly: This means 'to speak with love in order to gain a response of love'. The prophet must love the people with God's own love. This same expression is found in 2.14.

40.1, 2. My people . . . Jerusalem: The Israelite exiles in Babylon are God's people. The covenant relationship was expressed from God's side as 'my people . . . your God'. When the Israelites broke this relationship, they became 'not my people' (Hos. 1.8). But God promised that a day would come when 'not my people' would become 'my people' (Hos. 2.21–23), and He would make a new covenant with them (Jer. 31.22). The good news was that that day was now at hand.

Warfare: Means 'term of service', or time of forced labour. It refers to the period of Babylonian captivity.

Double for all her sins: Probably means 'paid in full', but there may be some reference here to the words of Isaiah 53.5: 'he was wounded for our transgressions . . .'. According to this idea, part of Israel's punishment was for the sins of others.

40.5. All flesh shall see it: According to the description of the great flood which was probably well known among the Jews of the sixth century, God who was 'the God of the spirits of *all flesh*' (Num. 16.22; 27.16; Jer. 22.27), had permitted (or even caused) a physical disaster which brought destruction on 'all flesh' (Gen. 6.12, 13, 17, 19; 7.21). This was of great interest to the Jews of the sixth century BC, because the Assyrian and Babylonian empires had been like a flood which swept over 'all flesh' in the seventh and sixth centuries (Jer. 25.31; 45.5; Ezek. 21.4–5). But the story of the flood also told of a new beginning for *'all flesh'* (Gen. 7.15–16; 8.17; 9.11–17). The author of Isaiah 40—55 was expressing the same idea when he wrote that God's action in the sixth century would be a revelation of His glory to and for 'all flesh', so that a new beginning could be made.

40.6. Cry . . . What shall I cry? The author here makes his first and only reference to himself, showing his own discouragement when he was called to speak for God.

Its beauty: A better translation would be 'reliability' or 'loyalty' or 'kindness'. The Hebrew word is *chesed*, used most often to mean 'steadfast love', which was expected from people in covenant with God. The author here says that faithfulness in human relations is found among 'all flesh' as a part of the natural goodness of man.

The flower of the field: The beauty of these flowers was noted by Jesus (Matt. 6.28). The author shows an appreciation for human virtues and the accomplishments of culture, even though they may exist in the midst of idolatry and cruelty.

40.7. The people is grass: This does not refer to the people of Israel, but to 'all flesh', i.e. the whole human race, originally joined together as one family (Glossary: *People*).

40.9. The cities of Judah: Before the destruction of Jerusalem, the neighbouring cities were known as her daughter towns, because they depended on her for trade and protection. No one was living in these ruined cities during the time of the Exile, as far as we know. Probably the prophet meant either: (1) other groups of Israelites living in such places as Egypt, Arabia, Syria, or upper Mesopotamia; or (2) the future inhabitants of the cities around Jerusalem; or (3) future 'daughters' of 'Mother Zion' from the other nations (Glossary: *Jerusalem*).

40.10. His reward . . . his recompense: There is no clue in this passage to help us find out what these words mean here. However, with the help of a concordance, we find one clue in 49.4. A discouraged Israel says, 'my right is with the Lord, *my recompense* with my God'. Israel hopes for some compensation from God for what has happened in the past. A second clue is in Jeremiah 31.15–17. In this passage, the poet imagines he hears Rachel weeping because her children are dead. Rachel was the mother of Joseph, and the grandmother of Ephraim and Manasseh, the largest tribes of the northern kingdom (Gen. 46.19–20). Rachel is a poetic name for the northern kingdom which was destroyed by Assyria in 722 BC (2 Kings 17.6). 'Children' of Rachel means the people of the towns and cities of Ephraim who were killed during wartime. Then God promises *a reward* to Rachel: her children will come back. If we look at Isaiah 49.12, we see the children of Zion coming from every direction. Following these clues, we can say that God's recompense as mentioned in 40.10 will be new children for mother Zion, to take the place of those who were lost at the time of the destruction of Jerusalem.

STUDY SUGGESTIONS

REVIEW OF CONTENT

1. What parts of the Babylonian New Year Festival may have given the prophet the framework for his message in 40.1–11?
2. In what way were the messages of Moses and Jesus similar to the message in Isa. 40.1–2?
3. In what ways is the 'Way of the Lord' different from the 'Marduk Road'?
4. Where does the 'Way of the Lord' begin? Where does it lead to?
5. What is the meaning of a 'wilderness world'?
6. What is the difference between people who have 'mountain' experiences and attitudes, and those who have 'valley' experiences and attitudes?
7. In what way was Babylon like 'grass'?
8. What is the responsibility of those who hear the Gospel?

APPLICATION, DISCUSSION, RESEARCH

9. The author of Isa. 40.1–11 used the events of the Babylonian New Year as the form of his message. What festival that you know might provide a form for proclaiming the Christian message in the place where you live? How could it be used?

14

10. 'God used Moses to make the promise come true.' Do you think God uses His servants today to make His promise come true? How might God use someone to lift up those in the 'valleys' of despair or oppression, or to bring down those on the 'mountains' of pride?

11. Three kinds of communication are suggested in vv. 1 and 2: (a) an act of comfort, (b) a winning word of love and care, (c) a cry to wake the dead. Give an example of the one you prefer, and your reasons for preferring it.

12. The prophet called for a 'double focus' on the grace of God for His people, and the revelation of His glory to the wider world ('all flesh'). Do you have this double focus in your Church? If not, how would you improve the balance in worship, evangelism, and service?

13. Find a picture in a newspaper or magazine that illustrates the prophet's statement that 'all flesh is grass'.

14. Read the Glossary note on the 'word' of God. Which of the five meanings given is appropriate for each of the following statements?
    (a) The Bible is the word of God.
    (b) God does not seem to have a word for us in our time.
    (c) In this school we teach people to love God's word.
    (d) The Word was made flesh.
    (e) The word of God will stand forever.

15. Study Hosea 4.1–3. How does this passage illustrate the meaning of the 'wilderness'.

16. Read the Glossary note on the 'glory' of God. How do the following verses show us the fulfilment of Isa. 40.5?
    John 1.14; John 17.22; 1 Cor. 11.7; 2 Cor. 3.18; 1 Pet. 4.13.

40.12–31
The Creator's Power and Wisdom
March–April, 541 BC

BACKGROUND AND OUTLINE

New Year is a time when people think of beginnings. They like to go back to the origin of things, and get ready for a new start. Christians may read Genesis 1—3 and John 1.1–14 at New Year. According to some tribal customs, a religious leader will recite legends about how human beings came to be on the earth, and how the tribe began.

The Babylonians shared this custom. In the New Year festival the priests chanted the story of the fierce struggle between their god Marduk and Tiamat, the chaos monster. After his victory, Marduk split Tiamat's body in two like a shellfish. The upper part became the sky, and the lower part became the earth. He gave the gods the task of taking care of the earth, wind, and sky, and put some of the gods in the sky as stars. Then he formed mankind from the blood of Kingu, the demonic commander of Tiamat's forces, in order to serve the gods. Finally he built the city Babylon and the temple tower of Etemenanki (Glossary: *Mountain*) as a gathering-place for the gods.

This story of beginnings made the Babylonians feel good. It told them that they were at the centre of the world, close to the power and wisdom of Marduk, the creator.

The prophet used this opportunity to encourage the small, suffering group of Israelite exiles to think about the true meaning of creation.

Main theme: The Creator's Power and Wisdom

Part 1: The hidden creator (vv. 1–20)
V. 12: Whose power?
Vv. 13–14: Whose wisdom?
Vv. 15–17: Not the power or wisdom of the nations.
Vv. 18–20: No clue from the idols.
Part 2: The revealed creator (vv. 21–31).
Vv. 21–24: The first revelation: Our God is the gardener of the world.
Vv. 25–26: The second revelation: Our God created the stars.
V. 27: The key question: Why do you doubt the power and wisdom of our God?
Vv. 28–31: The third revelation: The creator's power and wisdom can be yours.

READING SUGGESTIONS

Some things to look for as you read this poem for yourself:
The *questions* in vv. 12–14, 18, 21, 25–28.
The *statements* about God's creative work, in contrast to the idols' inactivity.
The *similarity* between vv. 17 and 23, 24.
The *repetition* of key words: 'who', 'understanding', 'nothing', 'power', 'strength', 'faint', 'weary'.

INTERPRETATION

THE KEY VERSE

From v. 27, we learn that the Babylonian New Year presented a problem to the Israelite exiles. They had their own story of beginnings. But their

'Scientific studies have taught us about galaxies of stars' (p. 18).

This spiral galaxy was photographed through a new Anglo-Australian telescope in New South Wales. Scientists call it NGC 1365. They know how far away in space it is, what it consists of, and many other facts about it.

How far does this knowledge help us to answer the question in Isaiah 40.26: 'Who created' the universe?

nation was in ruins. Some of them thought that their God was too weak to defend them from the Babylonian armies. Marduk seemed to them to be stronger than Yahweh. They began to doubt Yahweh's power and wisdom.

The subject of creation is a problem for Christians today also. Scientific studies have taught us about galaxies of stars millions of light years away from the earth; about how people in power can use religion to oppress other people; about the ability of people to construct myths from their own thoughts; and about many different cultures and world-views. All of this new knowledge makes people have doubts about the power and wisdom of a creator god. Some say, 'We can explain everything without God. We do not need to believe in a creator.' They think that the stories of creation in the Bible are interesting, but not very relevant to people today.

THE PROPHET'S USE OF PICTURE LANGUAGE

In order to understand the message of this prophet, we must look at the picture language he uses. He shows us a picture of a gardener at work. Perhaps he was trying to explain the words in Genesis 2.7: 'The Lord God planted a garden in Eden'.

First the gardener prepares the water (v. 12) and puts it in the clouds ('bucket', v. 15). He measures the width of the garden space between his thumb and little finger ('a span', v. 12), he puts his soil in a basket ('measure', v. 12), and weighs it to be sure he has the correct amount (v. 15; Glossary: *Mountains*). He puts a ridge around the edge of the garden ('isles', v. 15; Glossary: *Coastlands*) to keep out the salt water of the ocean; and stretches out a sky cover ('tent', 'curtain', v. 22) to prevent flooding. (In ancient times people thought that there was a huge body of water above the sky; they believed that the sky was a hard dome that kept this water in place.) The gardener has a whole company of helpers to keep the garden in working order ('host', v. 26).

The gardener then plants his crop (v. 24), and keeps careful watch over it ('sits above the circle of the earth', v. 22) to ensure that it produces fruit according to his purposes. When the fruit is not good, he holds back the water, and sends a hot wind to wither up the plants, so that he can start another planting (v. 24).

The first part of the Apostles' Creed is this: 'I believe in God the Father almighty, maker of heaven and earth'. By this picture the prophet tells us that the maker of heaven and earth is like a gardener. The earth is His garden.

WHOSE POWER? (v. 12)

Read the question in v. 12 again. The prophet wanted his hearers to think about the invisible creator. Here are two suggestions. Perhaps you can think of others.

1. A creator who is powerful enough to hold the mountains in his

'hand', and put the earth in place must be larger than the earth, and the sky, and the whole universe. This means that he is not a part of the universe he has made. Marduk was a sun god. He was a part of the universe. Some scientists believe they can explain the universe without reference to any outside power. Other scientists more recently have come to believe that we cannot explain the universe without an outside power. Could this power be God?

2. It is important to know *who* the creator is, because that will help us to understand the purpose and meaning of the world, mankind, and the whole universe. If Marduk is creator, what kind of a universe is it? If there is no power outside the universe, is all development and evolution a matter of blind chance? If there is an outside power, what kind of a power is it?

The prophet suggests by his question that the creator keeps himself hidden so that he cannot be seen directly in what he has created (45.14).

WHOSE WISDOM?

Read vv. 13–14 again. According to the Babylonian epic of creation, Marduk could not construct the world by himself. He had to rely on Ea, his father, as 'counsellor'. Marduk had power, but not wisdom. Again, the question causes us to think for ourselves. Here are some suggestions:

1. The *power to create* (symbolized by the 'hand' of God, see Glossary: *Hand*, and by the 'Spirit of the Lord', v. 13, as in Genesis 1.2) and the *wisdom to create well* must go together. Power without wisdom would result in an unworkable universe. Wisdom without power could never accomplish anything. The creator must have both power and wisdom. The Babylonians, like their god Marduk, used their power to oppress others, that is, without wisdom. Scientific discoveries have put great power in the control of modern nations. But how will they get 'understanding'?

2. There is a *design of creation* ('the path of justice, the way of understanding'; Glossary. *Justice*). This *design* of creation means the right way of working in the whole set of relationships within nature, human society, and between nature, mankind, and God. It is important to know the 'designer' in order to learn about the design.

NOT THE POWER OR WISDOM OF THE NATIONS (vv. 15–17)

Read v. 15 and look for for two pictures. Remember that the 'bucket' probably means the rain clouds. Perhaps the 'drop from a bucket' is a poetic way of describing the irrigation system of lower Mesopotamia. The second picture shows us a gardener weighing out the soil, and putting ridges around the edge of the garden to keep out the salt water.

The prophet used these two pictures to tell his hearers about the 'nations' (Glossary: *Nations*). He wanted to say two things:

1. The 'nations' have a part in God's design in creation. Their irrigation systems are necessary for the earth to produce vegetation for food,

clothing, and buildings. Their laws and social customs keep out chaos (symbolized by the turbulent ocean). They are the garden land, where people 'may blossom from its cities, like grass in the field' (Ps. 72.10). Paul wrote to the Christians in Corinth, 'You are God's field' (1 Cor. 3.9).

2. The 'nations' have an important, but limited, part in the whole work of the creator. We see this today in the efforts of social groups such as governments, voluntary agencies, etc., to produce more food, clothing, and building material, to work against the powers of corruption, oppression and destruction, to provide an environment that will allow people to 'blossom like flowers'. All these are acts of co-operation with the creator according to the design of creation.

The problem is that human beings, both as individuals and as groups, want to exceed their limitations. They pretend to be the centre of the earth, where all the powers of the universe (gods) live. They say 'I shall be mistress forever' (Isa. 47.7). In fact, Babylon was 'a mighty tyrant' (49.24–25), a 'furious oppressor' (51.13), who 'made the earth like a desert' (Glossary: *Wilderness*) and 'overthrew its cities, and did not let its prisoners go free' (Isa. 14.17). In other words, Babylon refused to accept its part in the design of creation. It had power, but not the wisdom to know its limitations. That, said the prophet, is the way that 'all the nations' (v. 17) behave. That is why they become 'nothing and emptiness'.

Colonial nations thought they were a part of the design of creation when they brought 'civilization' to underdeveloped peoples and prepared them for living in the world of today. Perhaps they were partly right. But they often forgot their limitations, when they used the lands and peoples in their power for their own profit and well-being.

NO CLUE FROM THE IDOLS (vv. 18–20)

The position of the passage after v. 17 shows that the prophet wanted to relate the idol (vv. 19–20) to the 'nations'. He wanted to say that the workman who made the idol was really working for the 'nations'. He thought of the idol as a symbolic expression of the spirit and history of the 'nation'. But an idol like this did not give any clue to the power or wisdom of the creator. In the same way, a cathedral, or shrine, or image may be a symbol of a nation or a tribe. But as such, it can give no idea of the purpose of the creator, or the design of creation.

More than this, the idol is meant to be a 'likeness' of the unseen God (v. 18). In some forms of magic, a person will try to obtain an image or a picture of his enemy, in order to get control over him. In the same way an idol may be the means by which a 'nation' tries to gain access to the power of the creator in order to increase its own strength. The idol was the means by which a 'nation' thought it could go beyond the limits set by the design of creation. The prophet said that the idol had no such supernatural power to give to those who worshipped it: 'It will not move'.

THE CREATOR'S POWER AND WISDOM

Some scholars think that this prophet was not fair in his criticism of the idols. They say that the Babylonians did not worship the idol itself, but thought of the idols as symbols of the gods they represented. For example, the image of Marduk was only a reminder of the 'reality' of the god Marduk.

However, the prophet was probably thinking of the god and the idol together. Perhaps he knew that there were different versions of the creation stories. In each version the hero was the chief god of the nation. In the earliest stories, the hero was Enlil, the god of the storm. In the Assyrian version, the hero was the national god of Assyria, named Asshur. Marduk was originally the name of an unimportant god of a spring or stream. The priests of Babylon raised him to the position of sun god, and made him hero of the Babylonian version of the creation story. So Marduk as a god was really 'constructed' by the nation, like an idol.

THE CREATOR REVEALED – FIRST REVELATION:
OUR GOD IS THE GARDENER OF THE WORLD (vv. 21–24)

Every verb in the four questions of v. 21 is important. Two words, 'known' and 'understood' are related to v. 14. By comparing the two verses we can see that they mean a knowledge of the hidden design of creation. This knowledge comes directly from the Creator Himself. He 'told' it, His people 'heard' it. The clue to the power and wisdom of God does not come from the expansion of national or institutional or personal power. It does not come from mathematical or scientific research, or from rational proofs. It comes from listening to the hidden creator.

When the prophet said that this secret had been 'told you from the beginning', he was probably referring to the story of the garden of Eden in Genesis 2—3, and of the creation of heaven and earth in Genesis 1.1— 2.4a. In vv. 22–24 he gives his own further interpretation of the secret design of creation:

1. The creator is intensely interested in what is happening on earth. From His great height he can survey the entire surface of the earth. He is always protecting the earth from disaster (the heavenly 'tent') by His loving action.

2. The creator's purpose is that the earth should be a garden of life ('to live in', v. 22, 'to be inhabited', 45.18).

3. Political structures ('princes and rulers') are his planting (see pp. 19, 20, para 1 on v. 15), to make the earth fruitful, to preserve order, and to support life.

4. When these political structures fail to work properly, that is, when they make the earth barren, or are unable to bring order, and crush out life, then God brings them down, and 'plants' other structures.

THE CREATOR REVEALED – SECOND REVELATION:
OUR GOD CREATED THE STARS AND ALL THE
POWERS OF NATURE (vv. 25–26)

Did you ever look up at the skies on a clear night and ask this question: 'Who created these?' (v. 26)? Even when telescopes and rockets probe deeper and deeper into space, the mystery still remains. Astronauts Edward Gibson and Jack Lousma, looking at the earth from the window of their skylab in outer space in 1973 and 1974, said that they 'gained a whole new feeling for the world. It is God's creation put before us, and whether you are looking at a bit of it through a microscope, or at most of it from space, you still have to see it to appreciate it . . . there is no noise, no vibration; everything is silent and motionless.' For people living in a space age, as we are, the question about the power and wisdom of creation is urgent.

Here on earth, there are many people who believe that the stars are 'astral powers', which control the lives of everyone on earth. These people think that it is important to know the day and month on which a person was born, so that the person can learn what each day has in store for him or her. Horosocope columns in the newspapers carry this kind of 'information'. For these people, too, the question is relevant: 'Are these stars independent powers? Are they simply part of an impersonal 'nature'? Are they and the other powers of nature under the direction of a powerful and wise creator?'

As with vv. 18–20, the position of vv. 25–26 following v. 24 shows that the prophet thought of Babylonian astrology in relation to the breakdown of Babylonian society. In 47.13 he described the mathematical observations of the court 'counsellors' to learn from the stars about the future. In 47.14 the prophet said that the astrologers were like 'dry stubble' (the short useless stalks left after the corn has been cut, which a farmer burns off before ploughing his field for the next crop). The prophet used the same word in 40.24 to describe the political leaders. He was telling his hearers that the court astrologers and the rulers of Babylon would be destroyed in the fire of war which was coming.

The stars, and all the powers of nature, said the prophet, are in the service of the creator who is 'strong in power'. They are a part of His design of creation. The important thing for the scientist or the person interested in astrology to ask, is whether they are living according to the purpose of the creator. If they are not, nothing can save them. If they are, the heavenly gardener will nourish them.

THE CREATOR REVEALED – THIRD REVELATION:
THE CREATOR'S POWER AND WISDOM CAN BE YOURS (vv. 28–31)

This is the climax of the whole poem. It is one of the most beautiful passages in the whole Bible. It is a good passage for fellow-workers in God's 'garden' to memorize.

Look at the picture of God:

1. He is the God of Exodus and Covenant (the Lord, or Yahweh).

2. He is the everlasting God, who does not pass away. He is living and active from age to age.

3. He is the one who is at work creating the whole earth from one end to the other.

4. He is the all-powerful God working with unwearying and limitless strength to make the earth a 'garden'.

5. He has wisdom ('understanding') beyond anything which human beings can understand.

6. He is ready to give of His power and wisdom to His people.

The prophet had already told his hearers that the way to understand the power and wisdom of God was to listen to Him (v. 21). Here he gives his final word: men and women, social institutions, and nations, can find the power and wisdom of the creator by *waiting on the Lord*. This is a combination of patient waiting for God to speak, and a joyful hope that God will act. It requires some personal or corporate discipline. People of different cultures and traditions have various ways of 'waiting on the Lord'. Perhaps it should include the following:

1. Forget your concern about how difficult your life is (v. 27), and look for 'the way of the Lord' (40.3), or the 'way of understanding' (40.13).

2. Forget your concern with what God owes you (40.27), and try to fit your life in with God's design of creation ('the path of justice'; v. 13, Glossary: *Justice*).

3. Listen again to what God has told us in the Scriptures (Have you not heard? Has it not been told you?).

4. Hold in mind the love of 'the Creator of the ends of the earth' for all parts of the earth including 'nations' and non-human nature. Then prepare yourself to 'mount up on wings' to go to very distant places, or to 'run' to nearer by places, or to 'walk' to places close at hand with the news of the hidden design of creation, and the creator who is both powerful and wise.

STUDY SUGGESTIONS

REVIEW OF CONTENT

1. Explain why verse 27 is the key verse to this poem about creation.

2. What verse in Genesis may have been the inspiration for this prophet's picture of the gardener?

3. What is the meaning of 'the bucket', 'a drop from a bucket', and 'isles' in v. 15?

4. Why is it important to know 'who' the creator is?

5. What is the meaning of the 'design of creation'?
6. What is the purpose of the 'nations' in God's design of creation?
7. What was the 'history' of Marduk as the god of Babylon?
8. What is the creator's purpose for the earth?
9. What is the most important question for a person interested in astrology or fortune-telling to ask?
10. What two things must the people of God do in order to learn the secret of the creation, and receive power from the creator?

APPLICATION, DISCUSSION, RESEARCH

11. Find a New Year custom or legend which has the meaning of 'going back to the beginning'.
12. Give three reasons, from your experience, why the idea of a creator God is either (a) a problem, or (b) irrelevant, to your friends. How would you go about explaining to them what you have learned from Isa. 40.12–31?
13. The picture of a gardener in this chapter is especially meaningful to agricultural peoples. How would you explain the idea of the power and wisdom of the creator to people who live in cities, or on house-boats, or to some other people who are not agricultural?
14. Which of the following pictures would best help you to explain how God is related to the world? Give reasons for your choice.
    (a) A radio station broadcasting to many receiving sets in various parts of the world;
    (b) A computer storing and sending information;
    (c) A communication satellite;
    (d) A gardener;
    (e) A king's son acting for his father, but in disguise;
    (f) A radio beacon for guiding aircraft.
15. Studies in mathematics and science have enabled men and women to 'decode' the secrets of nature. Do you think this is a good thing or a bad thing? Is there more to the 'design of creation' than a knowledge of nature? – if so, what is it?
16. Give two ways in which Christian people can be partners in the creating work of God?
17. 'The power to create and the wisdom to create well must go together.' (p. 19).
    Give illustrations of this statement from three different sorts of activity, such as construction, education, nation-building, city-planning.
18. Consider the contrast between what the Babylonians pretended to be, and what their nation actually was. Give two examples of this kind of contrast today.
19. Look for a building, an image, a song, or something else that is a

symbol of the spirit and history of a nation or a people. Think about it after you have re-read the discussion on pp. 20, 21, and Isa. 40.18–20. Does this symbol have sacred power by itself? Would you call it an idol? Give reasons for your answers.

20. Think of an image used in a religion you know about. Do people believe that it has sacred power in and of itself, or is it merely a symbol of the power? Is it a means to gain supernatural power? Give the evidence for your answers.

21. According to Isa. 40.21, God 'told' Israel about the secret 'design of creation'. Do you think He told the whole secret to them? Did God tell anyone else about this secret? (For example, the 'Buddha' means the 'enlightened one'; what do you think this means?)

22. How should a Christian look at astrology, or fortune-telling? Base your answers on Isa. 40.12–31 as well as your own ideas.

23. Write a proposal for an individual or a group wishing to practise 'waiting on the Lord' (Isa. 40.31), explaining what they should do.

24. Write a poem or a hymn based on Isa. 40.28–31.

41.1—42.4
Who Controls the Future?
March–April, 541 BC

BACKGROUND AND OUTLINE

In the last chapter we saw that the New Year is a time to return to the beginning, and search for the power and wisdom of the Creator. But New Year is also a time to look ahead. We say, 'I wonder what this year will bring?' Our greeting to each other is 'Happy New Year!' But we all know that a new year may bring sadness and disaster as well as happiness and prosperity. Many people are afraid of the future. Others will try to do as many good things as possible on New Year's Day so as to bring good luck for the year.

Today people have many reasons for being afraid of the future. Some fear communism. Some white people fear black power movements. A weak tribe may fear a strong tribe's aggression. Landowners may fear land reform movements. Small nations may fear attack by powerful nations. Those in government jobs may fear a revolution or a *coup d'état*. Factory or office workers fear to lose their jobs; farmers fear a bad harvest; a boy fears he will fail in his exams, a girl that her boyfriend will get tired of her; parents may fear the day when their children grow up and leave home.

In the Babylonian New Year ceremony of 541 BC, the priests tried to learn about the future (see p. 7), much as people do in various ways today. In that year many were worried about the future. The situation in Babylonia itself was very serious. There was conflict between different groups in the land, trade was bad, and famine threatened (see Special Note A). More important, King Cyrus of Persia had conquered all of Western Asia from the border of India to the borders of Asia Minor – all, that is, except Babylonia. There was every reason to expect that he would not be content until he had conquered that too, the most powerful empire of all. So, at New Year, 541 BC, people in Babylonia were afraid of what the coming year would bring. Besides the Babylonians themselves, and the Israelite exiles, there were slaves and traders from almost every nation or people of Western Asia. This poem was the prophet's message for them, as well as for the Israelite exiles.

The prophet composed his poem in the form of a debate. Using picture-language, he said that God called all the nations of the whole earth to attend an assembly for a debate about the question, 'Who controls the future?'.

Main theme: Who controls the future?

Introduction: God's call to the nations (42.1)

Part 1: Who is giving victory to Cyrus? (41.2–10)
Vv. 1–4: I, Yahweh!
Vv. 5–7: Not the idols!
Vv. 8–10: Strength to my Servant for the future.

Part 2: Coming events (41.11–20)
Vv. 11–13: The coming liberation from oppression.
Vv. 14–16: The coming harvest: seed for the future.
Vv. 17–20: The coming garden in the wilderness.

Part 3: Who controls the future? (41.21—42.4)
Vv. 21–24: Not the gods of the nation.
Vv. 25–29: The powerless gods and the Lord of the nations.
Vv. 42.1–4: The Servant of the Lord of the nations.

READING SUGGESTIONS

Here are some things to look for as you read this poem for yourself:
Note the *words* which the prophet used *three times*. Try to understand his reasons by looking at each case. Some of these words are 'coastlands', 'servant', 'chosen', 'justice'. You can find others.

This is a poem about the *nations*. Make a list of the number of words referring to the nations. Some of them are 'peoples', 'coastlands', 'those who are incensed against you'.

There are several terms relating to *agriculture*, continuing the themes of 'grass', 'wilderness', 'chaff' from the previous poems. Make a list of these terms, and write down what you think the prophet meant by them.

Find the *climax* of each 'strophe' or group of verses, and write each on a piece of paper. They will give you a clue to the prophet's thought.

INTERPRETATION

CYRUS, GOD'S VICTOR (41.2–3, 25)

Look at the two pictures of Cyrus. In v. 2 he is described as being like a strong wind driving the nations before him, and the nations as like dry stubble. Compare this with 40.6–7 and 40.17, 23, 24. The prophet was telling his hearers that God was using Cyrus to clear the earth of corrupt and decadent political structures. But we learned from the previous poem that the divine gardener will plant a new crop. The emphasis is on the future, after the old structures are gone.

In v. 25 we see the picture of a potter or a potter's helper who is trampling the clay with his feet to prepare it for making some kind of vessel. Cyrus was like the potter. The political structures ('rulers') of the nations were like the clay ready for the potter's hand to shape. In Isaiah 45.9–13, the prophet described God as a potter, making new sons and daughters out of the clay. We should think of these verses as related to 41.25. Cyrus was like a potter's helper, preparing the clay for the hand of God (Glossary: *Hand*).

THE LEAGUE OF IDOL MAKERS (41.5–7)

The 'nations' (Glossary: *Nations*; *Coastlands*; *Ends of the earth*) were afraid of change. They did not dare think about the future when their traditional customs and ways of government would be destroyed or very much changed. Because of their fear, they formed a league of 'neighbours and brothers' (v. 6), not in order to prepare for the future, but to preserve the decadent past. They built bigger and more stable idols than those mentioned in 40.18–20. This time they fastened them with nails.

We do not know whether or not the prophet was describing an actual alliance of the nations. In any case, he was describing the people's tendency to hold on to old habits and customs which no longer supported life according to the design of creation (see p. 19). When forces for change threaten them, they make their 'idol' even stronger. So the force required to topple the idol has to be more violent and destructive.

THE POWERLESS GODS (41.21–29)

Try to picture in your imagination what is described in vv. 21–29. All the images of the gods of the nations are seated or standing on a broad field.

Behind them are the anxious peoples who have constructed them. The debate which began with vv. 2–4 now continues. God challenges these gods to present evidence to prove that they are in fact worthy to be called Gods. They remain silent, without a word. Read the verdict of the debate in vv. 24 and 29, and compare these verses with 40.17, 23. The prophet used the same words to describe the gods and the nations. He wanted to say that the gods were no different from the nations, because they had no lasting strength in themselves. They too would pass away, like the nations, as mere 'empty wind' (v. 29).

The test of whether a 'god' could be called 'God' was this:

1. Can that god direct the course of events in the whole world of nations, across all generations from beginning to end, according to his purpose? This is the meaning of the challenge, 'Tell us what will happen?' (v. 22).

2. Is there any record of that god speaking a word in the past, which has been fulfilled already? 'Tell us the former things . . . that we may know their outcome' (v. 22).

3. Can that god continue to direct the course of events in the future for the whole world of nations, *after his nation has been destroyed*? 'Tell us what is to come, that we may know that you are gods' (v. 23).

Some people may think that this prophet was not fair to use this kind of argument. A representative of another religion could set up a test to prove that his or her own religion was the only true one. But we must remember that the prophet was not trying to prove which religion was true or false. He was using the form of a debate to ask the nations to think about the question: 'Who controls history?' The rise of Cyrus and his conquest of all the nations he fought against (41.2–3) did present them with this challenge. The basic question is whether history has any meaning larger than any one nation. Or is it just a blind and meaningless struggle between powerful contenders? The defeated nations could give no answer.

Many people today think that this is a very important question. They ask 'Is there any law or power higher than the power of a strong nation or combination of nations? Do the weak always have to be oppressed by the strong? Is there anything beyond national self-interest?'

LORD OF THE NATIONS

Read Isaiah 41.2–4. Think what it must have meant in a time of fear and anxiety about the future when the prophet composed these words.

Now read the second part of v. 4, which forms the climax of this strophe. Think what this tells you about present-day movements like communism, socialism, nationalism, liberation movements, dictatorships, democracy, social change in the country where you live.

Review the important events in the history of your nation or your people. What does this verse tell you about them?

'Who controls history?' (p. 28).

Some people would answer: 'The politicians of our country', or 'the military leaders'; or 'the rich bankers and industrialists'; or 'the scientist checking switches at an Atomic Energy Establishment' – like this one near Bombay in India.

How would you explain your own answer to this question?

Finally, say to yourself, 'This is my God, the Father of our Lord Jesus Christ'.

The main argument of this debate was as follows:

1. No god or religion that belonged to any one nation could give any meaning to the coming of Cyrus. Cyrus was the *conqueror* of nations and national gods. Only the 'Creator of the ends of the earth' (40.28) and the Lord of the nations was great enough to give meaning to this world-shaking event.

2. The coming of Cyrus brought new possibilities for the nations to begin again, with the old 'stubble' blown away, and the peoples in a soft, pliable condition ready for new customs and ways of life. This was because of the active purpose of the Lord of the nations at work among them. Cyrus was being used by the Lord of nations to do His work. But His purpose was larger than Cyrus.

When the prophet said that God had 'declared it from the beginning' (v. 26), he did not mean that any prophet had actually predicted the rise of Cyrus. He meant that Cyrus was a fulfilment of God's purpose in the sixth century BC in Western Asia. Remember, from 40.21, that God had declared His hidden design of creation to His people 'from the beginning'. The prophet believed that God was using Cyrus to help make the earth like a garden of life once again.

THE SERVANT OF THE LORD OF THE NATIONS

God works not only through victorious leaders and conquering armies or movements of social change, or revolutions or reforms. He also works through His Servant community (Glossary: *Servant*). The Servant community in any age have, in the first place, *a special relationship to their Lord*. They receive strength (40.31; 41.10) and help (41.10, 13, 14) from Him to endure all sorts of opposition and suffering (41.11–13).

But the Servant community also have *a mission to perform for their Lord*. They live among the peoples who need to find new strength of their own (the 'bruised reed' and 'dimly burning wick', 42.3), and need to find new strength for living (41.1). The members of the Servant community are the descendants of Abraham (41.8). This means they must carry out his mission of blessing to all the families of the earth (Gen. 12.3) and gather the nations into a covenant family (Gen. 17.5).

Look at the last strophe of this poem. After the final verdict on the powerless gods of the defeated nations (see 41.28–29), the Lord of the nations speaks directly to the nations and says, 'Behold, my servant' (42.1). The obedient faithful work of the Servant is essential to God's plan to make the earth once more a garden of life.

Now look at the three word-pictures of the Servant community at work:

1. *The harvester* (41.14–16). In this picture, the Servant is God's helper in the harvest. He threshes and winnows the 'mountains and hills'

(Glossary: *Mountains*). These are symbols of the old nations that must pass away (see 40.17, 23–24). The purpose of the harvest is to gather seed. This means that the Servant will look in the ruins of the defeated nations for something of value for the new garden of life. When he finds it he will be very joyful.

2. *The garden in the wilderness* (41.17–20). In this picture we see the Servant walking on a path in the wilderness (Glossary: *Wilderness*), almost dying of thirst. Suddenly God makes waters flow and beautiful trees spring up. This is a sample of the garden of life which is God's will for the whole earth. It is for all to see and recognize as a work of the Lord of the nations.

3. *The gardener among the nations* (42.1–4). In this picture we see the Servant working quietly and faithfully among the nations, showing them how to build up a new way of life according to God's design of creation. This picture seems to be related to 41.17–20. As a result of the Servant's work, there will be fountains of water and green trees according to God's design of creation. The Servant will be God's gardener among the nations.

In some parts of the world today, the Christian community is very small, less than one per cent of the population. In other countries, which arc traditionally Christian, the group of *faithful* Christians is small. They are like the 'tiny worm' of Isaiah 41.14.

People living in this kind of a 'minority' community tend to turn inward and think only of their own survival. But this is not what God wants of His Servant community. The Servant community has both a close relationship to God, *and* a mission to perform for Him as the Lord of the nations.

Look at the word-pictures again. In a society which destroys some people, the Servant community is looking for those who can be potential leaders ('seed') for a new and better society. In a society, or home, or institution that is like a 'wilderness', the Servant community will look for 'streams of water' that nourish life, and help people to grow like green trees. Wherever the Servant community live, or wherever they go, God wants them to work quietly, unselfishly, patiently for a healthy and creative relationship between God, human society, and the non-human world of nature.

NOTES

41.1. Let them renew their strength: This shows God's loving concern for the renewal of the defeated and captive peoples. Israel knows the secret of this renewal (40.31).

Judgement: This is the same Hebrew word as that which appears three times in the final part of the poem, translated 'justice'. This word thus draws the poem together (Glossary: *Justice*).

41.2. Stirred up: This verb suggests God's way of acting. He does not control every action, but stimulates, and opens doors.

One from the east: The prophet did not say clearly who this was. Not all scholars agree that the prophet was referring to Cyrus. Some think he meant Abraham. However, if we consider all the poems as a unity, and compare these verses with 45.1–6; 45.13; 46.11; and 48.14, it will be clear that the prophet wanted his hearers to think about the victories of Cyrus, who did come 'from the east', that is, from Susa, the capital of Anshan, east of Babylon, and 'from the north' (Isa. 41.25), that is from Ecbatana, capital of Media, to the north of Babylon.

41.18. Springs of water: The word used here means literally a gushing forth of water. The same word is used in 42.1, 3 to describe the mission of the Servant to 'bring forth' 'justice' to the nations. The author was trying to suggest in a poetic way that the Servant people would carry on the work of God in the wilderness of the nations (41.18) by making 'justice' available for all alike, poor as well as rich, in fulfilment of the prophecy in Amos 5.24.

41.19. The cedar: There are seven sorts of trees in the garden. The number seven is symbolic of wholeness or completeness. In this case, it is probably a symbol of the whole number of the nations of the earth who will be included in the new creation. The community of the people of God is a sign of this future unity of the peoples of mankind.

41.19. I will set: The same word is used for the mission of the Servant to 'establish justice' in the earth (42.4). Again, the author was suggesting a link between the work of God in 41.19 and the work of the Servant in 42.4.

41.21. Your proofs: The Hebrew word means literally 'your strong ones'. It probably refers to the gods of nations. The intention of the author is to show that the nations must bring out the gods. The gods cannot act on their own.

41.22. The former things: This means world-events of the past which reveal God's purpose and show continuity of results into the present. The author was probably referring to events like creation, the new beginning with Noah after the flood, the call of Abraham, the Exodus, the establishment and downfall of the kingdom, and including the Exile.

41.25. From the north . . . from the rising of the sun: Ecbatana, the Median capital conquered by Cyrus in 550 BC, lay north of Susa and north-east of Babylon.

He shall call on my name: It is not clear whether the author expected Cyrus to be one of the future sons of Zion, or whether another meaning is intended here.

42.1. Parts of this verse appear in the words from heaven at the time of Jesus's baptism (Matt. 3.17). 'Behold' is equivalent to 'this is'; 'in whom my soul delights' is equivalent to 'with whom I am well pleased'; 'my chosen' is something like 'my beloved'. The intention in using this verse was to show that Jesus was fulfilling the mission described in 42.1–4.

42.4. Wait for: Although the Hebrew word is not the same as the word 'wait' in 40.31, it seems that some relationship is intended. The distant coastlands will learn to 'renew their strength' (41.1) when they wait expectantly (42.4) for the teaching of the people who have renewed their strength by 'waiting for the Lord' (40.31) – the Lord who has created the ends of the earth (40.28).

Law: See Glossary: *Law.*

STUDY SUGGESTIONS

REVIEW OF CONTENT

1. Why were the people of Babylonia worried about the future?
2. What are the two pictures of Cyrus in 41.2–3?
3. Why did the nations make idols at that time?
4. What were the three tests of whether the god of any nation could be considered a true God?
5. Why could the defeated nations not explain the coming of Cyrus?
6. What are the two chief characteristics of the Servant community?
7. In the picture of the harvester at work, what does the Servant community do?
8. What is meant by the 'former things' in 41.22?

APPLICATION, DISCUSSION, RESEARCH

9. Look at the three occurrences of the word 'coastlands' in this poem. Write down what is said about them in each case. What does this tell you about the mission of the Servant community?
10. On page 25 there is a list of reasons why people are afraid of the future today. What reasons for fearing the future do you observe among people in your country?
11. Give an example of an 'idol', in the sense in which this word is used in 41.5–6 and on pp. 20, 28, in your Church, or home town.
12. Each of the following believes there is some way to control the future. Tell how each one differs from the way in which God controls the future.
    (a) an engineer (b) a political leader (c) a Marxist (d) a person who uses scientific methods to make artificial rain (e) a practitioner of magic.
13. Give your reasons for believing *either* (a) or (b) below:
    (a) 'God has been acting in the life of my people from the very beginning.'
    (b) 'God had nothing to do with my people's history until missionaries brought the Christian religion, and the knowledge of God, through Jesus Christ.'
14. Evangelism and planting new Churches are often called 'gathering the

harvest' (from Matt. 9.37–38). Does the picture of the harvest in Isa. 41.14–16 mean the same thing as the picture in Matthew? Could Isa. 41.17–20 be interpreted as 'planting' the new 'seed' for the new Churches? Give reasons for your answer.

15. Compare John 7.37–38 and 15.1–11 with Isa. 41.17–20 and 42.1–4. What are the similarities and differences between these passages?

42.5–17
Birth-Pangs of the New World
541 BC

BACKGROUND AND OUTLINE

In the years 542–541 BC, Cyrus was busy among the desert tribes of Arabia, where Nabonidus had lived for ten years. Cyrus made a series of friendship treaties, to protect the southern and western flanks of his army before attacking Babylonia. There is evidence that the desert tribes welcomed him because he helped them break free from Babylonian control.

Perhaps the 'villages of Kedar' in Isaiah 42.11 is an actual historical reference to one of these tribes. 'The inhabitants of Sela' may refer to the Edomite city of Petra. If so, this means that the prophet used historical events as a part of his prophetic poem about the new work of the Creator. He had told his hearers that the gods of the defeated nations were powerless (41.29). In this poem he told them what the Lord of the nations was doing, and what their part would be in it. He was saying to them, 'As things get worse and worse, remember that a new world is being born, and that you must prepare yourselves for it!'

Main theme: The Birth-Pangs of the New World

Introduction: The creating God (42.5)

Part 1: Call and appointment of Israel for service in the new world (42.6–9)

Vv. 6–7: A new ordination.

V. 8: To God be the glory.

V. 9: God's announcement of His intention to create a new world.

Part 2: A new song for the new world (42.10–13)

Vv. 10, 11: From the distant places:

V. 12: To God be the glory.

V. 13: The warrior's battle fury.

Part 3: The birth of the new world (42.14–17)
V. 14: The pain of birth.
V. 15: The death of the old order.
V. 16: A new way for the survivors.
V. 17: Defeat for idol-worshippers.

READING SUGGESTIONS

Find the *place-names*: Tema, Kedar, and Sela (the Hebrew name for Petra) on a map.

Read the Glossary notes on 'people', 'glory', 'create', 'mountains', 'righteousness'.

Look for the words used *twice*: 'people', 'blind', and 'glory', and *three times*: 'praise', in this passage. Why did the author want to emphasize these words?

Note the verbs describing *God's action* in vv. 5, 6, 16, and contrast them with the verbs in vv. 13–15.

Look for the *key verse* of this poem. When you have worked through this chapter, decide whether you agree with the view expressed in this Guide (see Interpretation).

INTERPRETATION

THE NEW CREATION

The key verse in this poem is v. 8. It is a solemn announcement to the newly-ordained Servant community, telling them that they were living in the period between the 'former things' (see Glossary) of the past, and the 'new things' of the future. This poem told how God would begin His 'new things', according to v. 16: 'These are the things that I will do'. The function of religion in many societies is to conserve the past. The prophet told his people that their God was creating the future.

THE COST OF NEW CREATION

In v. 5 we see a picture of the design of creation (Glossary: *Justice*). God is continually:

1. Creating *living space* (stretching out the heavens; Glossary: *Heaven and earth*);

2. Extending the area of *living place* ('spreading out the earth', not only for humans but for all other living creatures and the whole of nature – 'what comes from it');

3. Giving *life force* ('breath') to those who live ('walk') on the earth as a family of nations (Glossary: *People*). The duty of the inhabitants of the earth is to maintain it as a garden of life.

'As things get worse and worse, remember that a new world is being born . . . God Himself shares in the pain of new creation' (p. 34).

After an earthquake in Venezuela, townspeople begin the painful task of clearing the ruins. Then they will start to rebuild their city.

Can 'new creation' ever be achieved *without* pain?

In vv. 13–16 we see four word-pictures which show how God struggles to restore the earth to His design of creation.

1. In the first picture (v. 13) the prophet said that God was like a *warrior* preparing to use all His great power to defeat His enemies. These enemies are the forces which break the design of creation, and destroy the living space and living place of people on earth. In the time of the prophet, the chief enemy was the Babylonian empire.

2. In the second picture (v. 14), the prophet said that God was like a *woman in labour pains*, giving birth to a child. He wanted to emphasize that the time of greatest pain is also the time of greatest hope. By using this picture he meant that God Himself shares in the pain and struggle for new creation.

3. In the third picture (v. 15), he said that God's presence in the world was like a *hot desert wind*, (a) destroying the vegetation growing on 'mountains and hills' (Glossary: *Mountains*), and (b) drying up the rivers. The mountains probably symbolized the foundations of the old disordered world. The prophet meant his hearers to see a reference to the Babylonian Empire, which another writer had called a 'destroying mountain' (Jer. 51.25). By 'rivers' he probably meant the Euphrates and Tigris, which were the source of water for irrigation, and life for the people (Jer. 51.13).

4. In the fourth picture (v. 16) he said that God was like *an anxious person* searching among the ruins for survivors, and leading them out to freedom.

These four pictures tell us the prophet's idea of how God is present in the world: like a warrior, a woman in labour, a killing wind, and an anxious friend. Each of these pictures tells us that God himself is ready to pay the cost of new creation.

Perhaps this can help us understand the meaning of the Incarnation and the Cross. When 'the Word became flesh and lived among us', it meant that God was willing to pay the cost of the new creation. Jesus was like the anxious friend who 'came to seek and to save the lost' (Luke 19.10).

Paul expressed this same idea when he wrote that 'the whole creation has been groaning in travail until now' (Rom. 8.22), and that God, through the Holy Spirit and Jesus Christ, shared the pain of this new creation (Rom. 8.26, 32). Paul applied this idea to himself when he said to the Galatians, 'I am in travail until Christ be formed in you!' (Gal. 4.19).

When Jesus wanted to explain His struggle to get people out of the control of evil power, He said, 'No one can enter a strong man's house and plunder his goods, unless he first binds the strong man; then indeed may he plunder his house' (Mark 3.27). Paul echoed this idea of struggle when he wrote, 'We are not contending with flesh and blood, but against principalities, against the powers, against the spiritual hosts of wickedness in heavenly places' (Eph. 6.12).

So today, too, any new creation is costly to God and to those who share

His pain (Col. 1.24). A counsellor must be ready to share the suffering of a person in trouble. A pastor must be ready to pay the cost of building a congregation which is truly responsive to God's will. A person who wants to help his country must be ready to share in the pain of necessary change.

THE OLD AND THE NEW 'NATIONS'

In vv. 15 and 17 we see the prophet's picture of the end of the most powerful nation of that time. Because of Babylon's great power, her people thought that she was also the most important nation. But Babylon was not the place of the new creation. It was the place of death and defeat.

In vv. 10–12 the prophet showed the exiles a picture of peoples far distant from the centre of the old dying order (Glossary: *End of the earth*; *Coastlands*; *Desert*). They were on the mountains (Glossary: *Mountains*) of the new creation singing praise to God, and showing forth His glory (Glossary: *Glory*).

If we translate these words of 'distance' into everyday language, they mean all people who are oppressed or underprivileged, the victims of the strong, those who are exploited. Paul used this idea when he wrote, 'God chose what is weak in the world to shame the strong' (1 Cor. 1.27). God's strength comes to those who are weary and exhausted (Isa. 40.30–31; 2 Cor. 11.30; 12.9).

THE CONSEQUENCES OF SERVICE

In vv. 6–7, the prophet pictures a new 'ordination' of the people of God for the new age. The first 'ordination' at Mount Sinai made them 'a kingdom of priests and a holy nation' (Exod. 19.6). That was one of the 'former things' (Isa. 42.8). The new ordination meant that Israel had come to a new stage of her mission in the last days of Babylon. It was a very different world from that of the thirteenth century BC. There were two tasks for the Servant people:

1. *A covenant of the people* (Glossary: *People*). This first task was to restore a lost unity to the divided nations of the earth. The Servant community was to be a *sign* of God's intention to gather the divided 'nations' into a new family called a 'people', according to the design of creation (42.5). But this community was also to send out an *invitation* to all to become a part of this covenant community, as the first beginning of the new 'people'.

2. *A light to the nations* (Glossary: *Nations*). This was a further explanation of the mission already described in 42.1–4. Here the prophet referred especially to those among the 'nations' who were in 'darkness', in 'dungeon', who were 'blind', and 'prisoners'. Probably the author was using symbolic words to describe suffering people. He may have been thinking of the words in Deuteronomy 28.28–29, where there was

38

'madness and blindness and confusion of mind', where people would 'grope at noonday as the blind grope in darkness', and where people were 'oppressed and robbed continually', with 'no one to help'. The 'light' for such people would be the help they needed.

These two missions, of covenant and of light, are also important for the Servant community of today. The first is a ministry of reconciliation, to overcome the divisions which destroy the living space and living place of people, and to recall people in their 'nations' to the unity intended by God in His design of creation. The second is a ministry of help to individuals in need, or to disordered institutions like families, or schools, or tribes when they are suffering, or are failing to live according to God's purpose for them.

In contrast to this picture of the newly-ordained Servant community, perhaps feeling full of energy for the task, the prophet gave his hearers a picture in v. 16 of the survivors of the coming disaster. They were 'blind' and in 'darkness'. They did not know the way out of the ruins of the old order. Perhaps the prophet was telling his hearers that their ordination did not protect them from the blindness and darkness of their age. Only when God gave them 'eyes' could they be a light to the blind. Only when God turned their 'darkness to light' could they be a help to those in darkness. In Isaiah 50.10 the prophet said that the Servant had to 'walk in darkness with no light'. He meant that the Servant community had no light of their own. They were entirely dependent on the light of God's glory on them.

NOTES

42.5. Created, stretched, spread out, gives: These are all present participles in Hebrew. In this form they emphasize God's originating and continuous activity.

42.6. I have called you: In this Guide we assume the unity of the poems of Isaiah 40—55. On this assumption we can say that the 'you' (singular pronoun) in this verse refers to the Servant community of 41.8–16, where it is also referred to with the singular pronoun 'you'. In 42.1–4 the prophet used 'he' for the Servant community, because he pictured God speaking to the nations about His Servant. In 42.8 the prophet used the plural pronoun 'you' to indicate that he was referring to the Servant as a community of people.

42.9. New things: Since the verb 'spring up' is used, the new creation is seen as vegetation. For other references to the new creation as vegetation, see 41.16–20; 43.19; 44.3, 23; 45.8; 51.3. Also remember the new seed from the threshing (41.14–16).

42.10. Sing to the Lord a new song: The author was referring to the ways of worship that had been customary in Jerusalem, as we can see from a comparison with Psalms 96—98. Perhaps the exiled Israelites used these psalms in their worship.

42.11. Kedar: The name of an Arabian tribe living to the east of Damascus. Its importance is seen by other references: Isa. 21.16; 60.7; Ps. 120.5; Jer. 2.10; 49.28–29.

42.15. Rivers: For rivers as symbols of Babylon and Egypt, see Jer. 2.18 and Isa. 19.5–10. The river of Babylon was also described as the chaos monster or the 'sea' in Jer. 51.36, 37, 55; Isa. 44. 27; 50.2.

42.16. A way . . . rough places into level ground: These are recurrences of the theme of the new Exodus, first mentioned in 40.3–4.

The things I will do: 'The things' is a translation of a Hebrew word meaning both words and events. Perhaps a translation like this would give a better idea of the meaning: 'These are the *commanded events* that I will accomplish'.

STUDY SUGGESTIONS

REVIEW OF CONTENT

1. What events in the region of Kedar and Petra (Sela) made the prophet think of them when he wrote this poem?
2. What is the difference between the ordinary function of religion in many societies, and the action of God as described by the prophet?
3. What four pictures in this poem help us to understand how God is present in a changing world?
4. In what sorts of places were the people living, who welcomed the new creation with hymns of praise?
5. What is meant by the 'two ordinations' of Israel?
6. What are the two duties of the Servant community as 'covenant of the people'?
7. To what sorts of places, and to what people, would the Servant community have to go, as 'a light to the nations'?
8. What sorts of experiences of the people of the world did the Servant community have to share?

APPLICATION, DISCUSSION, RESEARCH

9. Read the following verses and tell what each says about the meaning of 'light':
   Prov. 4.18; Ps. 119.130; Isa. 9.2; Matt. 5.16; Luke 2.32; Eph. 5.8.
10. Read Rev. 7.9–10; 21.24–25; and 22.2. In what way do these verses help you to understand the task of being a 'covenant of the people', or a 'light to the nations'?
11. Read again Isa. 42.8. It deals with the relationship between the past and the future. Choose one of the following statements and say why you agree or disagree with it.

(a) The new should have no relationship to the past. It should be completely new.

(b) We should recognize the value of the past because it teaches us lessons, and helps us to avoid mistakes. But we should press on to find new solutions.

(c) The new should be a fulfilment of the best of the past, with as much continuity as possible.

12. Of the four pictures of how God is present in the world, (see p. 37), which, if any, fits your own idea of God? Which ones do you find the most difficult to understand, and why?

13. Read 2 Cor. 6.4–10. What does this tell you about the cost of working with God in the new creation?

14. Suggest two specific ways in which a congregation could: (a) be a sign of God's intention to reunite all 'nations' into a family; (b) carry an invitation to 'nations' to join in a fellowship which would anticipate the future.

15. Many organizations, including government agencies, take care of unfortunate, or underprivileged, or handicapped people. Hospitals and schools and other institutions which were formerly sponsored by the Church are now operated by others. Why is this so? Which if any of these activities are (a) part of the proper function of government or society according to the 'design of creation' (see discussion of Isa. 40.15), and which are (b) really the function of the Servant community as 'light to the nations'? By whom are these activities undertaken in your country?

Special Note A
Historical Background to Isaiah 40—66

Isaiah 40—66 consists of a series of urgent messages from God to the Israelites in Babylon before 538 BC (chapters 40—55), and in Jerusalem after that year (chapters 56—66). In order to hear God's message for today in these prophetic poems, we must first try to find out as much as possible about the time and circumstances of those who first heard the messages.

First of all we must remember why the Israelites were in Babylon. They, or their parents, had been deported as prisoners either in 597 BC, when King Nebuchadnezzar of Babylon had conquered Judah, or when he destroyed Jerusalem in 587 BC. The death of Nebuchadnezzar in 562 BC divides the period between the fall of Jerusalem to the Babylonians and the fall of Babylon itself to the Persians, into two parts of about 25 years each. In the first period some of the Israelites were able to build their own houses, plant gardens, own cattle, and to work as craftsmen, traders, and bankers. There is a hint of this in Jeremiah 29.6, 7. They lived in such places as Tel-abib (Ezek. 3.15), Tel-Melah, Tel Harsha, Cherub, Addan, and Immer (Ezra 2.59). Here they carried on their worship, read their Scriptures, and remembered their God. People who lived in such circumstances were probably either slaves of wealthy individuals, or stateless refugees. Other less fortunate ones may have been temple slaves or slaves on royal labour projects. Perhaps there were old slaves (Isa. 47.6) as well as young ones (Lam. 5.5, 13).

After the death of Nebuchadnezzar, a time of troubles began for the exiles, which grew worse until the fall of Babylon. The next two kings, one the son and the other the son-in-law of Nebuchadnezzar, ruled only three years each. During their reigns fierce tribes under the leadership of Media invaded Babylonia from the north.

Besides these attacks from outside, there was conflict within Babylon itself. The last king of Babylon was Nabonidus of Haran in north-west Mesopotamia. He worshipped the moon god, Nannar-Sin. His mother and daughter were both priestesses of this god, one in Haran and the other in Ur. The priests of Marduk, the chief god of Babylon, were angry about the favour which King Nabonidus showed to the moon god. According to an inscription by Nabonidus discovered in Haran, the priests of Marduk stirred the people of many cities of lower Mesopotamia to revolt against Nabonidus while he was away fighting enemies in the west.

Nabonidus did not wish to fight against the Marduk priests or the people. He moved his royal capital from Babylon to the Arabian desert city of Tema for a period of ten years (552–542 BC), and left his son Belshazzar to manage affairs in Babylon. According to Babylonian court records, there was no New Year ceremony during those years. The purpose of the ceremony was to ask Marduk and the other gods to give rain, fertility, prosperity, and peace for the coming year. But, without the king there could be no ceremony. The canals which brought water to the fields went untended and filled up with silt. Crops dried up. There was famine in the land. According to an inscription from 545 BC, when Nabonidus was still in Tema, the famine was so severe that a widow sold her two sons as temple slaves, hoping that they would find food there.

Nabonidus returned to Babylon in 542 BC, but he failed to bring back order and prosperity to the nation, even though he did participate in the New Year ceremonies of 541, 540, and 539 BC. By October 539 BC, according to an inscription, the people were fighting each other 'like dogs'.

There can be no doubt that the slaves or refugees in Babylonia not only shared the chaos and suffering, but as foreigners without rights or privileges they were probably worse off than the rest of the people, and were victims of oppression. Many references in Isaiah 40—55 refer to their sufferings (41.11–13; 42.22; 49.26; 51.14).

However, there were also signs of hope after the death of Nebuchadnezzar. Avil-Marduk released King Jehoiakin from prison in 562 BC. Northern invasions stirred hopes that God's time of deliverance might be at hand. Many scholars think that Isaiah 13; 21.1–10; and Jeremiah 50 and 51 express this hope.

God's time came with the rise of Cyrus, king of Persia. He conquered Media in 550 BC, and marched west in March–April 547 BC to conquer the kingdom of Lydia in Asia Minor in December. In 546 BC he completed the conquest of Asia Minor, and turned east as far as India and south to the Arabian tribes. In 539 BC he marched down the Tigris River to attack Babylon. The battle of Opis in October was a complete victory for Cyrus. He executed Nabonidus on 13 October, and marched into Babylon as conqueror and liberator on 29 October, 539 BC. In 538 BC Cyrus issued a proclamation permitting the Israelite exiles to return to Jerusalem and rebuild their temple (2 Chron. 36.22–23; Ezra 1.1–4).

It seems probable that the prophetic poems of Isaiah 40—55 were written during the New Year celebrations of 541, 540, and 539 BC, and later in 539 BC. The themes and content seem to fit this time. However, it is not possible to *prove* that they were written at these times.

42.18—43.7
Hear, You Deaf! Look, You Blind
541–540 BC

BACKGROUND AND OUTLINE

In this prophetic poem and the next three, the prophet turned his attention away from the creation of the world, the distant lands, and the coming struggle against Babylon, towards the group of exiles. The newly ordained Servant community had important lessons to learn, before they would be ready for their mission.

There is little in this poem to suggest the date of its composition. The mention of Egypt, Ethiopia, and Seba in North Africa (43.3) may reflect the prophet's expectation that Cyrus would attack these lands before turning to Babylon. In fact, Egypt fell to Cyrus's son Cambyses in 525 BC.

Main theme: Hear you deaf! Look you blind!

Part 1: The meaning of the past and present (42.18–25)
Vv. 18–21: Blind to God's purpose.
Vv. 22–23: Ears for the time to come.
Vv. 24–25: Confession and insight.

Part 2: Assuring words for the future (43.1–7)
Vv. 1–3b: I am your saviour.
Vv. 3b–4: You are precious in my sight.
Vv. 5–7: Bring my sons and daughters.

READING SUGGESTIONS

Look for two words in 42.6 which are *repeated* in 42.18, 19 and 22. The author's purpose was (a) to connect the two poems together, and (b) to teach the Servant people a lesson. What do you think that lesson was?

Look for two new words in addition to 'servant' in 42.19 which describe the *people of God*. What additional information do they give about the question 'who are we?'

Look for the words related to *seeing* and *hearing* and *understanding* in 42.18–25. They will help you find the main theme.

Look in 42.22 for the words describing the Israelite *exiles' suffering*. Compare this with 41.11, 12.

Look for a word in 42.25 which is repeated in 43.2. What did the author want to tell his people about past and present?

Look for the phrases which tell about *God's relationship with Israel* in 43.1, 4, 7. How many are there? Which words are repeated for emphasis? What did the author mean by each one?

Try to find the *key verses* (or climaxes). You will find some indirect help in the Interpretation section below.

Glossary words for this poem: 'servant', 'purpose', 'law', 'righteousness', 'offspring', 'sons'.

INTERPRETATION

THE BLIND AND DEAF SERVANT (42.18–20)

One of the serious problems in Churches is that those people who should be closest to God, and who have received the most from Him, often cannot understand what He is doing, or they do not recognize the signs of God's activity in the world around them. Not only that, they do not obey His commands. They live in a small world of 'Churchly affairs'.

Jesus called the Pharisees 'blind guides' because they emphasized detailed regulations of the law, but did not practise 'justice, mercy, and

44

faith'. They were blind to the real meaning of God's law (Matt. 23.23–24). The Pharisees were the religious leaders of the people, who were meant to be 'a guide to the blind, a light to those in darkness, a corrector of the foolish, a teacher of children, having in the law the embodiment of knowledge and truth . . .' (Rom. 2.19, 20). But Paul said: 'You who boast in the law, do you dishonour God by breaking the law?' (Rom. 2.21).

But Jesus also called His own disciples whom He had personally selected and trained, 'blind and deaf'. Probably He was quoting from Isaiah 42.19 when He said to them, 'Having eyes do you not see, and having ears do you not hear . . . do you not understand?' (Mark 8.18, 21).

'Blindness' was the prophet's way of describing his people's lack of understanding. 'Deafness' meant their lack of obedience.

BLINDNESS TO GOD'S PURPOSE (42.21)

The Israelite exiles did not understand their part in God's long-range purpose. They could only understand: (1) that God had allowed Jerusalem to be destroyed so that they had no home (42.25), and (2) that they were having a very difficult time in Babylonia (42.22). They thought God's law was only for Israel, to show how the people of God were different from the other nations.

The prophet said to them, 'Look, you blind!' He wanted them to see that God's 'law' was really His 'teaching' for the whole earth (Glossary: *Law*). He wanted them to understand that God gave them this 'teaching' so that they could carry it to all nations (42.4).

DEAFNESS TO GOD'S CALL (42.23)

In Hebrew the same word may be translated in English as 'hear', 'listen', and 'obey'. At the time when God first 'ordained' Israel to service, He said 'If you will obey (hear) my voice and keep my covenant . . .' (Exod. 19.5). In Jesus's parable of the sower, 'those that were sown on the good soil are the ones who hear the word, accept it, and *bear fruit*' (Mark 4.20).

Verse 23 suggests that no one among the exiles heard the prophet's call to service among the nations in his third prophetic poem (42.1–4). Their primary concern was to be delivered from their troubles. They were not interested in being God's messenger, sent by Him with His 'revealed teaching' for the nations (42.19).

The prophet said to them, 'Hear, you deaf!' He wanted them to prepare for 'the time to come' when God would send them to the nations.

CONFESSION AND INSIGHT (42.24–25)

The prophet told His people that they must look honestly at their past, in order to find understanding for the present, and be obedient for the future. He invited them to join him in a confession of past sins: 'Our fathers did

45

'The prophet's call to service . . . he wanted them to prepare for the time to come' (p. 45).

A team of British Scouts and Rangers live up to their motto, 'Be prepared'. They are receiving instructions before taking part in a community service project.

What do you consider the most important part of a Christian's 'preparation for service'?

not obey God's teaching; they did not learn the lesson of the destruction of Jerusalem.' He thought that unless the exiles joined in that confession, they could not understand God's purpose in sending them into exile. They would only complain that God had forgotten them (40.27).

There is a deep spiritual insight here. The prodigal son in Jesus's parable had to recognize his own sin before he could find a new life (Luke 15.21). A Hebrew poet said,

> When I declared not my sin,
> my body wasted away . . .
> my strength was dried up . . .
> I said, 'I will confess my transgressions to the Lord';
> then thou didst forgive the guilt of my sin.
>
> (Ps. 32.3, 5)

NEW EYES AND EARS (43.1–4)

After confession comes the assurance of God's grace. The prophet saw that the main question of the unhappy people was this: 'Does God love us?' This was more important to them at that time than the question, 'Who created the universe?' It was more personal. It was a question of the heart (Isa. 40.1).

The prophet said to them, ', 'Look, you blind – see what I am showing you!

Did God *create* the ends of the earth (40.28)? He also *created* you! (Glossary: *Create*).

Did God's hands *form* the earth and the mountains (45.18)? His hands also *formed* you! (43.1; 43.21; 44.2, 21, 24).

Did God *call* Cyrus (41.2, 25) ? He has also *called* you by your name!

Does God plant the nations, and watch over them (40.22)? You belong to Him, you are His own people! You are so precious in His sight that He would give the whole world for your redemption!

The sum of it all is: 'God loves you!'

The prophet also said to them, 'Hear, you deaf!' Listen to what I am telling you! God himself will go with you, when you pass through the disaster of the destruction of Babylon. But you must go with Him! Neither fire nor flood will be able to stop you if you are obedient.'

GOD'S NEW SONS AND DAUGHTERS (43.5–7)

With new eyes and ears, the people were now ready for a final word from the prophet. He told them two things:

1. Out there among the nations, in the four directions of the compass, are your descendants (Glossary: *Offspring*). Do not forget them. *They* are a part of *you*, the restored Israel (look at the word 'restore' in 42.22 and in 49.6). When I gather *them*, I am gathering *you*. I will use *you* to gather *them* (49.6).

2. In addition to gathering your own descendants I want you to bring my new sons and daughters (Glossary: *Sons*) from among the nations. I have also *created* and *formed* them, and called them by my name, to be a revelation of my glory (Glossary: *Glory)*.

NOTES

42.19. My dedicated one: The translation is not certain. A possible alternative would be 'my covenanted one'.

49.21. The Lord was pleased: (see Glossary: *Purpose*)
His righteousness' sake: (see Glossary)
His law: (see Glossary)

42.25. The might of battle . . . on fire round about: The reference is to the fall of Jerusalem in 587 BC.

43.1. Redeemed you: (see Glossary: *Redeem*)

43.3–4. Ransom: The prophet said that God would give three nations – Egypt, Ethiopia, and Seba as 'ransom' for His people. This did not mean that God had to pay a ransom price to anyone to redeem His people from slavery. He was probably using an idea that was part of the tradition of the Exodus. According to Exodus 13.15, God took the first-born of Egypt in place of His own first-born, which was Israel (Exod. 4.22). So, in this new 'Exodus', God would allow Cyrus to take these three nations in exchange for the freedom of His people.

In verse 4, the 'exchange' is all of mankind ('men' is 'adam' as in Genesis 1.27), and all of the peoples of the world. The meaning could be (a) God's way of saying 'You mean more than all the world to me', that is, a way of showing how great His love was for them. Or it could be (b) a way of saying that His Servant people were to be the beginning of a new mankind, and a new family of nations.

43.6–7. Sons and daughters: Most scholars believe that this is a reference to Israelite exiles in other lands. But there are several reasons for believing that the author intended to refer also to the peoples of the other nations themselves. For some of these reasons, see Glossary: *Sons*. In this verse there are two pieces of evidence. First, the author repeated the two key words 'created', and 'formed' from 42.1, as though to point to a new creation. Second, he used the words: 'afar' and 'end of the earth' which are used elsewhere in relation to other peoples. 'Afar' is used in 49.1 in parallel with 'coastlands', and 'peoples from afar' certainly means those belonging to other nations than Israel. The 'end of the earth' (see Glossary) was the distant place from which the new song would be raised by the peoples (42.10), and was also the goal of the mission of the Servant people (49.6). For these reasons, it is probable that the author wanted his hearers to think of their mission to the peoples of other nations.

STUDY SUGGESTIONS

REVIEW OF CONTENT

1. In what ways were the following people 'blind'?
   (a) the Pharisees; (b) the disciples of Jesus; (c) the Israelite exiles in Babylonia.
2. What was God's purpose in giving Israel the 'law',
   (a) in the mind of the exiles?
   (b) in the mind of the prophet?
3. What does 42.23 tell us about the exiles' response to God's call through His prophet to service among the nations?
4. For what reason did the prophet ask the exiles to 'think honestly about their past'?
5. What was the most important question in the mind of the exiles at that time? What was the prophet's answer to it?
6. What was God's double plan for the Israelite exiles in Babylonia?

APPLICATION, DISCUSSION, RESEARCH

7. According to 42.25, the 'fire' at the time of the destruction of Jerusalem 'burnt' a disobedient Israel. According to 43.2, the fire of affliction will not 'burn' the obedient Servant. Discuss the following two possible explanations of this difference:
   (a) If God's people are disobedient, they will meet destructive trouble, but if they are obedient, then no harm will come to them.
   (b) A disobedient people have many things which need to be changed, reformed, or destroyed in their lives in a time of change, but when they learn to be obedient, they will see that nothing important can be destroyed.
8. What is the difference between 'messenger', 'servant' and 'dedicated one' (42.19)? Prepare an outline of a talk for Christians on the subject: 'Who are we?', based on each of these three words, and using some of the ideas from this poem.
9. Many of the laws in the Old Testament do not seem relevant or important today, such as laws against eating pork, or any meat with the blood in it; laws commanding circumcision; those concerning certain garments for the priests; and tests for diseases, etc. Are these what the author of Isa. 42.21 meant when he spoke of the 'law' of God? Discuss the following alternative ways of looking at these laws and their meaning:
   (a) These laws are all a part of God's revealed teaching for mankind. A true servant of God will obey them all.
   (b) There are two levels of meaning in the laws: (i) the regulations, and (ii) God's purpose behind the regulations. We should concentrate on God's purpose and pay no attention to the regulations.

(c) Jesus Christ brought all those laws to an end. We should pay no attention to them.

(d) Mixed in with the regulations are various kinds of laws or standards of behaviour which are valid for all mankind, such as (i) the Ten Commandments, (ii) the command to love God with our whole heart, (iii) the command to love our neighbour. We should concentrate on these and pay no attention to the other regulations.

Some Christian groups have a particular point of view with regard to the laws of the Old Testament. Find out the point of view of the Seventh Day Adventists, and one of the Pentecostal groups.

10. Give one or two examples from your experience, or even from your own life, of how unconfessed sin (not being honest about the past) has blinded a Church, or an individual, so that the group or person could neither understand the present, nor obey God's will for the future.

11. Explain how the question 'Does God love me?', or 'Does God love our Christian fellowship?' can be (a) a selfish question, or (b) a question of personal identity. How does the prophet's answer to this question help us to avoid the problem of selfishness?

43.8–13
Witnesses of the True God
541–540 BC

BACKGROUND AND OUTLINE

God's Servant people are His way of showing the people of the world who He is, and what He does. They are His witnesses. This is the message of this short poem for those who serve God today. It was the prophet's second lesson for the Israelite exiles in Babylonia, after their ordination as 'a covenant of the people and a light to the nations' (42.6). He was preparing them for their task in the world of nations after the fall of Babylon.

There is no indication of the historical background of this poem. It follows closely on the previous poem with its theme of the blind and deaf people who have the possibility of seeing and hearing, and the theme of the saviour God.

Main theme: Witnesses of the True God

Vv. 8–9: The context of the witness.
V. 10: The witnesses.
Vv. 11–13: The God of the witnesses.

READING SUGGESTIONS

Look for *connections* between this poem and previous poems through words of seeing and hearing, 'servant', 'saviour', and others.

There are fifteen first-person-singular pronouns referring to *God*. Find them and think of the meaning in each case.

The word '*witnesses*' appears three times; look for the different contexts.

There are two sets of three verbs – one related to Israel, the other related to God. They will help you find what the author said that Israel must do, and what God does.

INTERPRETATION

In the previous poem the prophet had told his people that they were God's 'messenger' (42.19), to take His 'revealed teaching' or 'law' to the nations (42.21) 'in the time to come' (42.23). They would have to go through fire and water to distant places in order to gather God's new 'sons and daughters' (43.1–7). In this poem he led them to think more carefully about where they would go, what they should do, and who God was.

THE CONTEXT OF THE WITNESS (vv. 8–9)

The prophet told them, through the picture of a second debate between God and the nations (see 41.1—42.4 for the first debate), that they must bear their witness among the nations. God's purpose was that the nations might see how God acts, hear what God wills, and say 'it is true!' (v. 9). The spoken and lived word of the witnesses must be in the sight and hearing of these nations. This would make it possible for them to understand, turn, and believe in the one true God.

The prophet said that these nations had their own witnesses (v. 9). Today we would say that these 'witnesses' should include all of a nation's institutions – its arts, its agriculture, its trade and industry, the army, the schools, the government, the newspapers, radio and TV – all the people's work and leisure activities. These are all good and important in themselves. When these 'institutions' are working properly, they are a part of God's design of creation. When they are not, they become 'idols'. But they cannot *fully* witness to God, because they are limited by the understanding of the particular people or nation. Only a people who know God, believe in Him, and understand His ways, can be witnesses to Him among the nations.

This was one of the results of the coming of Jesus: the narrow boundaries of the Israelite nation were broken down, and God could have His witnesses in every tribe, people, village, and city of mankind.

THE WITNESSES (vv. 8, 10)

At the beginning of the poem the prophet introduced the Servant community as a 'people who are blind yet have eyes, who are deaf, yet have ears'. He meant that they did not yet fully understand the ways of God, and had not arrived at a perfect faith in God, but that they had the *possibility of growing* in understanding and faith.

In verse 10 he said that the growth would come through the experience of bearing witness by the spoken and lived word: 'You are my witnesses, that you may know and believe me, and understand that I am he.'

When we first read this it seems contradictory. How could a person speak before he knew what to say? How could he obey unless he already had faith? In fact, the prophet was expressing something that every good teacher knows: learning comes by practice. He was saying that the best way to get to know God is to begin introducing Him to others and helping them to know Him. The best way to grow in faith is to be faithful in the matters at hand, so that others can observe the meaning of faith. The best way to gain more understanding of the way God works is to try to make what you do know clear to others. Being a witness requires skill which comes only from experience.

What is it that the witnesses communicate? The challenge to the witnesses in v. 9 is to 'declare this', and 'show the former things'. The prophet did not make the exact meaning clear. Perhaps he could not foretell what the situation of the witnesses among the nations would be, and which of the saving acts of God they should declare in the particular situation.

For the prophet, the meaning of 'this' was the coming defeat of Babylon by Cyrus, and the liberation of the Israelite exiles, as the redeemed people of God, going among the nations to gather the sons and daughters of God. Some years ago, a Christian leader spoke of a 'great new fact of our time', meaning the planting of the Christian Church in the lands of Asia and Africa in the nineteenth and twentieth centuries. More recently, in most parts of the world the end of colonialism is one of the important facts of our time. God's witnesses might see God's hand in that. Others would wish to point to a new openness to the Gospel of Christ in the lands of Asia, as an example of what God is doing today – or some new event in a particular village, or city, or nation. The witnessing people will help others to see the hand of God (v. 13) at work in their own time and place.

The witnessing people will also make the acts of God visible by their obedience ('hearing'). The prophet spoke of the way of life of the Servant people in 42.1–4. He said that they would endure suffering patiently, and keep going in spite of fatigue and discouragement. In our day, some people make their witness to God by going to prison, or by working for the freedom of the victims of discrimination. Some Churches try to work for reconciliation between two sides in a conflict situation, or build unity between divided groups such as rich and poor, employers and employed, or even between differing political parties.

The witnessing community must speak words which will help people to know what God is doing. They must also show by their actions that God is at work in them. The word of witness must be lived as well as spoken.

THE GOD OF THE WITNESSES (vv. 11–13)

How will the witnesses know God? The word 'know' is best understood from the family relationship between a father and son, or between a husband and wife. *Knowing* God means having a relationship of covenant love and promises with Him. But we must also know *about* God, if we are to know Him. The prophet told his people that God introduces *Himself* to His people. Inspired by God, the prophet used the pronoun 'I' six times in these three verses, to emphasize that God is His own witness to Himself. These statements help us to know God *and* to know about Him. From our side, we might try reading these verses as though we were speaking with God. In that case we would change the 'I' to 'you', and the 'you' to 'us', for example:

> You, you are the Lord,
>   and beside you there is no saviour.
> You declared and saved and proclaimed,
>   when there was no strange god among us;
>   and we are your witnesses.
> You are God, and also from henceforth you are He.
>   There is none who can deliver from your hand;
>   You work and who can hinder it?

The witnessing people must carefully consider these words from God through the prophet, and try to understand them in the context of the 'nations'.

I am the Lord (Yahweh). This is the name of the God who met Moses, who delivered the slaves from Egypt, who gave them a covenant and laws at Mount Sinai, and who guided them in the desert. He is 'the Holy One of Israel, your Saviour' (43.3). The witnesses would say among the nations: This is the Saviour. He saved us. He can save you. Turn to Him (45.22).

I am God (El). This is the general title for 'the everlasting God, Creator of the ends of the earth' (40.48), who is always protecting the earth from chaos by making living space, ('stretching out the heavens' 40.22), extending the area of garden living place ('spreading out the earth' 42.5), giving strength to all the inhabitants of the earth ('breath' 42.5), and governing the nations of the earth (40.23–24). The witnesses would say among the nations: This God has always been at work all over the world. He is the source of your strength, the protector of a just society, the judge

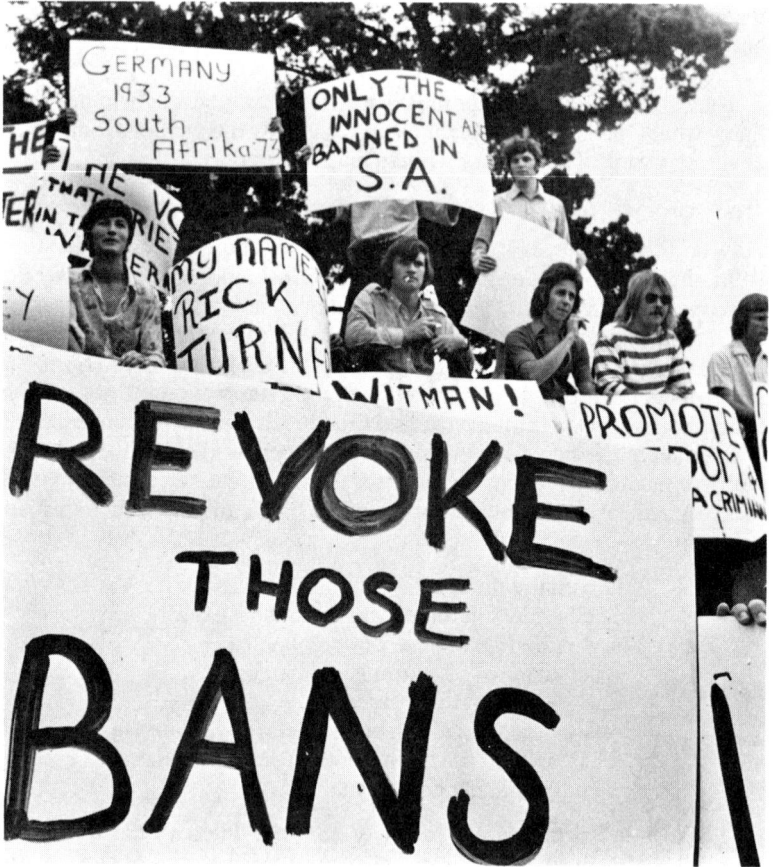

'What it means to be God's witnesses in our own time and place' (p. 55).

Students in South Africa witness to their belief that their government's policies are wrong. This means they risk being 'banned' themselves.

What, if any, are the risks of witnessing as Christians in your country?

of injustice. He is the hidden power between and behind every aspect of life. Put your faith in Him.

I am He. This statement is twice repeated for emphasis. It does not mean that God is masculine. The Hebrew pronoun He can also mean 'that one'. It means that God is 'number one', and there is no other 'number one' in the whole universe. The Saviour and Creator are the same God, and the work of creation and salvation are from the same hand. The witnesses would say among the nations: God is one, not many. Power and love are united in Him. He wills all nations of the earth to be a unity in diversity. He is the one all people seek.

In the New Testament, we see that Jesus fulfilled this role of being witness to God (Rev. 1.5), and that the community of Christians must be witness to the true God as far as 'the end of the earth' (Acts 1.8). This poem helps us to understand what it means to be God's witnesses in our own time and place.

NOTES

43.9. Former things: See notes on 42.9 and 41.22.
Justify them: That is, prove their case. See note on 43.23.
43.10. Know me: This means the sort of close, living, and personal knowledge with which a son knows his father, or man and wife know each other. In Jeremiah 31.34, knowing God is a relationship within the new covenant.
Believe me: The Hebrew verb means to take a firm stand upon. This sort of trust in God can come only by practice and by the discovery that God is faithful and reliable.
Before me . . . after me, no god was formed: According to the mythologies of Babylon, gods were created or came into being at different times.

STUDY SUGGESTIONS

REVIEW OF CONTENT

1. Who were the ones to hear and see the witnesses?
2. What are some examples of the 'witnesses' of the 'nations'?
3. For what reason can the witnesses of the 'nations' not be 'witnesses' to God?
4. What was one result of the coming of Jesus?
5. How did the prophet apply the educational principle that 'learning comes through practice', to the task of bearing witness?
6. For what reason did the prophet leave the matter of the exact words of the witnesses open?
7. What must the witnesses do in addition to speaking?

8. What is the difference between the following three statements?
'I am the Lord.'
'I am God.'
'I am He.'
9. Who are the 'witnesses' to the true God, according to the New Testament?

APPLICATION, DISCUSSION, RESEARCH

10. What is the difference between a 'messenger' and a 'witness'? What are the similarities between them?
11. Look up the meanings of the words 'know', 'believe' and 'understand' in a word-book of the Bible. How do they describe our relationship with God?
12. (a) Do you agree that dialogue with people who do not believe in God is a good way to grow in our own knowledge, faith, and understanding of God?
(b) Must we be absolutely certain of our own faith and knowledge of God *before* we enter into dialogue with people of other faiths and ideologies?
Give reasons for your answers.
13. (a) What are some of the events in your own situation which could be the result of 'God's hand' at work?
(b) Some people say that Christians are blind to what God is doing in our own time. What is your opinion?
14. (a) 'The conflicts within and between Churches make the word of witness they speak of no value.' Comment on this statement.
(b) What acts done by Christian groups or individuals in your own situation would help people to know more about God?
15. How does evangelistic work as you know it conform, or not conform, with the work of the 'witnesses' in this passage?
16. Paul said 'We preach Christ crucified . . . the power of God and the wisdom of God' (1 Cor. 1.23–24). Does the message of the cross emphasize one particular side of God's activity as described in Isa. 42.11–13, or all sides of it? Explain your answer.

43.14—44.5
From Past Failures to new Possibilities
March–April, 540 BC

BACKGROUND AND OUTLINE

How can we deal with the guilt and glory of the past? On the one hand, the failures of past generations affect the present generation and restrict people's freedom to act. Wrong teaching or the bad example of parents can ruin the life of their children. When nation-building requires that two tribes live together in peace, a long history of conflict, revenge, murder, and brutality between those tribes may seem to make peace impossible. The heritage of the past is often a burden and a curse to those who must face new situations in the future.

On the other hand, the solid achievements of the past may mislead us into dreaming about past glory. Some people spend all their efforts to bring back former glory to their own country, or tribe, or family.

This was the problem which the prophet faced as he began to prepare the exiled Israelites for their work as servants of the true God among the nations after the expected fall of Jerusalem. He had to deal with two sorts of attitude toward the past:

1. One group believed that their most important and urgent task was to restore Jerusalem. They hoped that a descendant of David would once again sit on David's throne in a restored city, and lead the people to worship in a restored temple. They believed that if they achieved this, God would bless them with prosperity and peace. *Then* would be the time for bearing witness to the nations about the power and goodness of the true God (see Notes).

This group seems to have thought that God had not given them their due rights as covenant partners (40.27). They saw God's support of Cyrus against Babylon as His way of righting the wrong done to His 'chosen people'. When the prophet asked them to take an honest look at their past (42.24), they would have responded that he was giving too much emphasis to the dark side. The thought of past glory was like a chain binding them to the past. To use a picture from the prophet's first poem, this group lived on 'hard-heart mountain'.

2. A second group among the Israelites were burdened with the guilt of past failures, and felt completely hopeless about the future. They asked: 'Can the prey be taken from the mighty, or the captive of a tyrant rescued?' (49.22). They thought of themselves as 'a prey with none to rescue' (42.22), and said that God 'had no power to deliver' (50.2).

57

When they thought of the past, they remembered the words of the Deuteronomy scroll which they had with them in Babylon, about the punishment they had brought upon themselves by breaking their covenant with God: 'All these curses shall come upon you and overtake you' (Deut. 28.15). They looked at their condition: 'robbed and plundered, trapped in holes, hidden in prisons' (42.22), and felt that God's curse was heavy on them. When the prophet told them the words of God, 'I am He! There is none who can *deliver* from my hand' (43.13), they thought that God's 'hand' of punishment (Glossary: *Hand of God*) was so strong that He would not let Cyrus set them free from the curse of the broken covenant. When the prophet told them to take an honest look at their past (42.24), it put them in a deep depression. We could say that these people lived in a 'valley of despair'.

The reference to the 'shouting of the Chaldeans' and other parts of the Babylonian New Year ceremonies (see note on v. 14) suggests that this poem may have been composed during the month of Nisanu (March–April) in the year 540 BC. At that time Cyrus had not yet completed his preparations for his attack on Babylonia.

Main theme: From past failures to new possibilities

Vv. 14–15: God will bring Babylon down *for your sake*!

Vv. 16–18: You should forget past failures.

Vv. 19–21: Open your eyes to recognize the first signs of the new creation!

Vv. 22–28: God has forgotten your past failures *for His sake*!

44.1–5: A new garden in the wilderness.

READING SUGGESTIONS

This poem is connected with the following verses from previous poems: 41.17–20; 42.9; 42.16; 42.24; 43.13. Try to discover what the *connection* is, by looking for key words or phrases repeated from one poem to another. Ask yourself what the author had in mind.

Use a concordance to find two previous uses of the phrase 'the former things'. In each case there is a different emphasis due to the context. Ask yourself what that emphasis was.

Look for the following words which occur *three times*, ask yourself why these words were important to the prophet: 'waters', 'sin', 'weary', 'chosen'. Do the same for the following words which are repeated *twice*: 'transgression', 'burned', 'servant', 'remember', 'way', 'now', 'rivers', 'streams', 'for my (or your) sake', 'the Lord's'.

Notice that both 'Israel' and 'Jacob' are *repeated* five times, usually in the same verse. Why did the prophet emphasize these names so strongly in this particular poem?

INTERPRETATION

In this poem the prophet was trying to help his people overcome the guilt and curse of past failures, and turn to God's new possibilities.

FOR YOUR SAKE (43.14–15)

The prophet first told the 'broken hearted' group – the people who felt that because of their past failures God was either unable or unwilling to save them – that God's chief interest was in *them*, not in their past. The coming defeat of Babylon was 'for your sake'. He selected names of God which emphasized the personal relationship of love, protection, and support, not only in a glorious past, but in the discouraging present. He told them:

God is your *Redeemer* (Glossary: *Redeem*): Don't only dream about the miraculous crossing of the sea at the time of the Exodus from Egypt. Your Redeemer has given His covenant promise to liberate you *now*. He will do it!

God is your *Holy One* (Glossary: *Holy One of Israel*). Don't only dream of the past holiness of the temple and priesthood. All the power, purity, and purpose of His holiness is turned to you *now*!

God is *the One Creating you* (Glossary: *Create*). This process of creation has reached a critical moment. He is creating you *now*!

God is your *King* (Glossary: *King*). Do not be despondent about the end of the Davidic dynasty. Your true king has always been God, and *now* you can see it more clearly than ever.

This prophet had not yet seen the revelation of God in Jesus Christ. But his message of God's love in spite of past failures was very close to the New Testament message. 'In this is Love, not that we loved God, but that He loved us' (1 John 4.10), and 'God shows His love for us in that while we were yet sinners Christ died for us' (Rom. 5.8).

LET US ARGUE TOGETHER (43.22–28)

In his second sharp criticism of the exiles (for the first, see 42.24, and for the third and fourth, see 46.8–11 and 48.1–8), the prophet told them that what they imagined to be past glory was in fact past guilt. These verses are in the form of a debate between God and the exiled community. We must assume that the first speech in the debate by the 'hard-hearted' group gave their version of the past: 'Our blessed ancestors, our glorious temple, our faithful prophets and priests all show what a wonderful people we were and how God blessed us.'

God's reply as interpreted by the prophet was very pointed: 'Your ancestors (especially Jacob) rebelled against me! Your temple worship was not a true calling on me, but corrupted by injustice and idolatry! Your prophets and priests were self-seeking leaders who did not know me. Your past failures are the very reason why you are here in Babylon!'

The prophet was calling for an honest look at both the failures and the achievements of the past. We can adapt his words to express this truth: 'Cease to dwell on the glories of days gone, by, and brood over the failures of past history' (43.18, NEB adapted). The lesson for us today is that we can use past experience as a firm basis in the present, while we seek for new solutions to new problems.

FOR MY OWN SAKE I WIPE OUT YOUR TRANSGRESSIONS! (43.25)

The prophet used the words 'I am He!' in verse 25 from the previous poem to tell the Israelites that the only true God (43.10) whose 'hand' was more powerful than any other power (43.13), was also the one who (1) will not allow past failures to block new possibilities, and (2) has a plan for the forgiven sinner.

Forgiveness of sin, as interpreted by this prophet, does not mean escape from the *consequences* of past failures. The destruction of Jerusalem and the exile in Babylon were very painful consequences of the past failures of the people of Israel (42.25; 43.28). Forgiveness means that God accepts us to be His chosen servant again, with no *burden* of past failures, no more *guilt*, no more *curse* of the past to hinder our service. The prophet emphasized this by using the words 'my servant', 'my chosen' twice in 44.1–2, *after* the announcement of forgiveness. Forgiveness means the possibility of a new start *in His service, for His sake*.

BEHOLD, I AM DOING A NEW THING. NOW IT SPRINGS UP! DO YOU NOT RECOGNIZE IT? (43.19a)

The new possibility to which the prophet wanted the exiles to turn was God's own work. He first announced it at the time of Israel's ordination as 'covenant of the people' and 'light to the nations' (42.9). The prophet wanted to say that the work of the Servant and God's work of new creation go together. So also in this poem, forgiveness is 'for my sake', that is, for God's work of new creation.

In 43.19b–21 we find a picture of the new creation. In 44.1–5 the prophet explained some parts of the picture. There is, first, a picture of 'the way in the wilderness'. On this way God's chosen people walk, singing His praise (v. 21). It is like the way in the wilderness at the time of the Exodus from Egypt, because there are rivers of water there from which the people can drink freely. It is also like the Garden of Eden, because the animals will honour their Creator, and live in peace with human beings.

When the prophet said that the new garden plants were already visible before their eyes (43.19a), perhaps he was referring to fellow slaves from other countries who worked alongside the Israelites, and were ready to become believers in Yahweh, and take the name of 'Israel'. His question 'Do you not recognize it?' showed that the exiles were not yet ready to accept these believers as signs of God's new creation from the 'nations'.

'The work of the Servant and God's work of new creation go together' (p. 60).

A Thai farmer ploughs up his ricefield, and his daughters follow, planting out the rice seedlings from which the new crop will come.

Think of some other ways in which human beings collaborate with God in the work of 'new creation'.

The climax of the poem unites its key subjects. 'For your sake' (v. 14) means that God will liberate the Israelites so that they may grow into this new community. 'For my sake' (v. 25) shows that this new community is the purpose behind God's forgiveness of the sins of Israel. This community of the future is the reason why Israel must not dwell on past failures, but turn to new possibilities.

NOTES

43.14. I will send: A reference to Cyrus.

The shouting of the Chaldeans will be turned to lament: The Chaldeans were Babylonians from south-east Mesopotamia. In the Old Testament the word means the same as the Babylonians. The Hebrew of this passage is not clear. Some scholars suggest that it should be translated: 'The Chaldeans in their masted ships'. If this is correct, it would refer to the New Year procession of the gods by ceremonial ship to the pavilion specially built for the occasion along the Euphrates river north of Babylon.

43.20. The wild beasts, the jackals, and the ostriches were a part of God's creation, as in Genesis 1.24–26 and 2.7, 9. In the new creation as seen in Isaiah 11.6–9, the animals would no longer be enemies of each other or of humans. The new creation will mean a new relationship between human beings and animals.

43.21. Declare my praise: Note that in 42.8 God does not allow the praise which is due to Him to be given to idols; and that in 42.10 and 12 the distant peoples sing His praise. So in 43.21 it is made clear that Israel's true praises of her creator, as in 42.8, became the example and witness for the nations at the end of the earth, so that they too may sing His praises (42.10, 12).

43.22. Call upon: This is a technical term for worship. The meaning seems to be that in the ceremonies of temple worship, or even in non-sacrificial worship in Babylon, the Israelites were not 'calling on' God in spirit and in truth, but were only presenting Him with their sins and self-glorification, or with deep despair.

43.26. Proved right: The Hebrew word here is the same as that translated 'justify' in 43.9. The meaning is that Israel was imitating the nations, by trying to prove herself to be in the right. This was her sin.

43.27. Your first father: a reference to Jacob (see Gen. 32. 22–30; Hos. 12.3–5).

Your mediator: The meaning of the Hebrew word is not clear. The NEB translation is 'your spokesmen'. It may refer to the false prophets or the priests. See Jeremiah 2.8 for the three sorts of leaders who rebelled against God.

43.28. The princes of your sanctuaries: The word 'princes' may mean 'officers' as in 1. Chronicles 24.5 ('officers of the sanctuary'). If so, these would be the priests.

44.2. Jeshurun is a poetic name for Israel which appears only here and in Deuteronomy 32.5; 33.5, 26.

44.3. My blessing: This is a word used by writers of the old Testament to mean power of life. It meant that a person with 'blessing' would have fertility of crops and herds, numerous descendants, and material prosperity. The meaning also included overall well-being, and a life-giving relationship with God, the source of life. When a person was 'blessed', he prospered, and no one could succeed in opposing him. To 'bless' a person who had blessing meant to acknowledge the power of life within him. He in turn would communicate strength to the one who 'blessed' him. A good description of blessing is in Deuteronomy 28.1–14. The rest of that chapter tells what it means to have the blessing changed to curse. Isaiah 44.3 seems to be a reference to the blessing which God promised to Abraham (Isa. 51.2), and through Abraham to all the families of the earth (Gen. 12. 1–3). It was the reversal of the curse which came because of disobedience. The immediate result is seen in 44.5.

44.4. Grass amid waters is a strange expression. Another possible translation is 'like the green ben tree'. The ben tree is something like the willow. It seems natural to expect that the growth in God's garden would be trees, as in 41.9, instead of grass as in 40.6–7.

44.5. Write on his hand 'the Lord's': In ancient Babylon slaves had the name of their owner tattooed on the hand or wrist. Temple slaves were marked with the star of Ishtar (Venus).

Surname himself: This means to give oneself an honorary name or title. It shows clearly that the people referred to here were not Israelites by birth.

STUDY SUGGESTIONS

REVIEW OF CONTENT

1. What two problems did this prophet meet concerning the understanding of the past?
2. What sort of names for God did the prophet select when he wanted to speak to the discouraged exiles?
3. What wrong thoughts about the past become like a chain to prevent people from facing present problems with new solutions?
4. What was God's reason for forgiving the sin of his people?
5. In what way is the picture of the new creation in 43.19–21
   (a) like the Garden of Eden?
   (b) like the wandering in the time of the Exodus?
6. What was wrong about the worship of the Israelites, according to this prophet?
7. What is the meaning of 'Jeshurun' in 44.2?
8. To what ancient custom was the prophet referring when he spoke of writing the name of Yahweh on one's hand (45.5)?

9. What is the reason for thinking that this poem may have been composed at the time of the Babylonian New Year ceremonies?

APPLICATION, DISCUSSION, RESEARCH

10. The following sentences show attitudes similar to those of (i) the backward-looking exiles, or (ii) the discouraged exiles. Write either (i) or (ii) beside each one, and say what you would reply to it.
    (a) He tries to keep everything in the Church just as it was.
    (b) Our Church is caught in a trap of rising costs and falling income.
    (c) Why change? It won't do any good.
    (d) Don't change! What has been is best.
    (e) Our Church has very few young people. What can we do?
    (f) Our Church worship should be in the language we have always used. Why change because a few young people haven't yet learned to understand it?

11. Compare each of the following texts in the New Testament with Isa. 43.14, and say how each is (i) the same, (ii) different:
    (a) Matt. 12.29; (b) Col. 2.13–15; (c) 1 John 4.10; (d) Rom. 5.8.

12. The first line of Isa. 43.22 is about the heart of true worship. See the comment and the note which relate this verse to John 4.23.
    (a) What can a congregation do to make the worship of its members a true 'calling on God'?
    (b) What worship traditions in your Church or denomination (i) help or (ii) hinder true worship as 'calling on God'?

13. Consider these statements and explain whether they are in agreement with (i) the teaching of the author of Isa. 40—55 and (ii) the teaching found in the New Testament.
    (a) God's forgiveness is unconditional. He forgets the past.
    (b) God's forgiveness is conditional. He requires service.
    (c) God forgives because it is His *nature* to forgive (an ancient prayer says that it is His 'property always to forgive').
    (d) God forgives because of His purpose for the whole earth.

14. The prophet gives several pictures of God's new creation. His purpose was to show how it could become visible here and now. Choose two of the following figures, and (i) explain the meaning so that your friend could understand it, (ii) express the same meaning in a new picture of your own.
    (a) The new creation is like a way in the wilderness.
    (b) The new creation is like rivers in the desert.
    (c) The new creation is like a garden.
    (d) The new creation is like people coming to write God's name on their hands.

15. The word 'praise' is used in a special way by the author of Isa. 40—55. Look at the following verses in their context, using the

Glossary where necessary to get the meaning of important words. Then write a short paragraph on this question: 'Who will "declare" God's praise?' 43.21; 42.8, 10, 12; 48.9.

44.6–23
From Empty Idols to Your Redeemer
March–April, 540 BC

BACKGROUND AND OUTLINE

The second commandment is a strict prohibition against the use of any sort of image to represent God: 'You shall not make a carved image for yourself, or any likeness of anything in the heavens above, or in the earth below, or in the water under the earth. You shall not bow down to them or worship them; for I the Lord your God am a jealous God' (Exod. 20.4–5).

The Israelites lived among peoples, from Egypt to Canaan to Mesopotamia, who used images in their worship. Many Israelites were attracted by the customs of their neighbours. So the prophets warned them that worshipping images was against the laws of God's covenant, and would bring destruction to the nation.

The images of the great Babylonian gods must have impressed the Israelite exiles. Ezekiel reported that some of the exiles wished to 'be like the nations, to worship wood and stone' (Ezek. 20.32). Another prophetic voice said that Babylonian culture was like poisoned wine, which tasted very good, but which drove mad those who drank it (Jer. 51.7). Perhaps some of the Israelites had tasted this 'wine'. The prophet's plea to them to 'return to God' may be a hint of this, especially as it follows a long passage on idol worship.

Today, the 'idols' which 'nations' worship are not all visible ones, and not all 'idols' of today are used in religious ceremonies or related to formal religion at all. That is why the words of the prophet are of value to us. They help us to understand the reality behind the 'idol'.

Some scholars have suggested that this prophet must have observed idol manufacture at first hand. If so, he may have been working in the labour force of a temple. He probably composed this prophetic poem during the New Year ceremonies of 540 BC. (See note on p. 66 on the unity and authorship of the poem.)

Main theme: From Empty Idols to Your Redeemer

Part 1: Israel's Redeemer (vv. 6–8)

Part 2: The empty idols (vv. 9–20)
Vv. 9–11: The failure of the idol makers.
Vv. 12–17: How the workman makes a 'god'.
Vv. 18–20: The blinding effect of idol worship.
Part 3: Return to your Redeemer! (vv. 21–22)
Part 4: A hymn of redemption, by the whole cosmos (v. 23)

Note: Some scholars believe that a single author composed the whole of 44.6–23. Others believe that vv. 6–8 and 21–23 are a poem by the same author as the other parts of Isaiah 40—55, but that vv. 9–20 were composed by another author, and were inserted at a later time between vv. 8 and 21. Some scholars also believe that the author of vv. 9–20 did not intend them as poetry. That is why they are printed in prose form instead of poetry in modern translations like the RSV, NEB, TEV, and the Jerusalem Bible. Others believe that vv. 9–20 are poetry, or prose-poetry. In this Guide we accept the whole of 44.6–23 as a single prophetic poem, and vv. 9–20 as a passage of prose poetry within it.

READING SUGGESTIONS

THE THEME OF REDEMPTION

Find the three words of redemption, and two verses with the word 'deliver'. How did the prophet show the difference between the idols and the God of Israel?

Use a concordance to find where else the prophet has used the phrases 'I am the first and the last', 'the things to come', and 'witnesses', and the question 'who is like me?' All of them show that the prophet wanted to point out a relationship between those poems and this one. What was it?

THE THEME OF THE IDOL MAKERS

Find the six verses where the word 'god' appears. Compare them and try to find the prophet's message.

The expression 'put to shame' means to suffer dishonour, failure, defeat. Find three occurrences of this verb in the poem, and discover *who* will be defeated. Now look in 41.11; 42.17; 45.16, 24 and find out *who* will be defeated. Finally, look in 45.17; 49.23; 50.7; 54.4 and find out who will *not* be defeated.

Find the verbs related to idol manufacture in 44.12–17. Use a concordance to find how many of these same verbs are used by the author of Isaiah 40—55 to describe God's creative activity. What do you think the prophet was trying to say?

Read 44.18, and compare it with 43.10 and 41.20. Now look at 42.6–7: how will blinded idol worshippers be able to see the truth about God?

INTERPRETATION

This poem, like 43.8–13, is about the two kinds of 'witnesses'. The idols were 'witnesses' of the nations, and the servant community of Israelites in Babylon were 'witnesses' of the true God among the 'nations'. The prophet wanted his people to understand the inner meaning of the idols which were carried in the New Year procession, *and* the greatness of God, their Lord, who was *Redeemer, King, Lord of Hosts,* and *Rock,* for them and the 'nations'.

THE MEANING OF THE IDOLS IN BABYLON

Isaiah 44.9–20 is the longest passage by this prophet explaining the meaning of idols. There are many other shorter passages. As we look at them, we must keep the following points in mind:

1. The prophet was living in Babylonia in the sixth century BC. He did not know about the great religions of India and China, nor the tribal religions of many other parts of the world. In fact, several great religious leaders were living and working in other parts of the world at the same time. In India there were the founders of Buddhism and Jainism. In China there were the founders of Taoism and Confucianism. But this prophet did not know them, and was not reacting to their thought.

2. This prophet was trying to help his people to understand the meaning of the idols. He was not talking about religion in general, nor about various ideas of supernatural power, nor about ancestor worship.

If we remember this, we can be ready to listen to what the prophet had to say, and learn from his words.

The real idol-makers are the 'nations' (41.5–7; 44.9). When the prophet talked about the craftsmen, he had in mind the intention of those who employed them.

The idols are 'witnesses' of the 'nations'. By this he meant that the idols were visible symbols which a tribe, people, clan, or nation had constructed to represent their particular history, customs, ideas, and way of living. This is what the prophet meant by the words 'He shapes it into the figure of a man', that is, an image of the 'nation' itself.

The idols serve the purpose of those who construct and handle them. The religious leaders call the idol '*my* god' (44.17) because they want to use the idol to keep the people in order, and to strengthen the power and policy of the government. That is why the idols were 'carried about' in procession (45.20; 46.7), 'set up' (40.20) in a shrine (44.13), and 'fastened with nails' (41.7) so that they could not be moved out of the control of those who used them for their own purposes (40.20; 41.7; 46.7).

The idols symbolize the need of all human beings for deliverance. The 'nations' construct a 'god' (44.10, 15, 17) in order to ask it for help in their trouble (44.17; 46.7).

The idols deceive those who construct, use, and ask them for deliverance. The prophet put great emphasis on the 'blinding' effect of idol worship. 'They know not, nor do they discern, he has shut their eyes so that they cannot see, and their minds so that they cannot understand (44.18). 'No one considers, nor is there knowledge or discernment' (44.19). 'A deluded mind has led them astray' (44.20). The idol worshippers were like sleep-walkers, or drugged persons, unable to see the truth.

The idols symbolize whatever corrupts the design of creation (Glossary: *Justice*). The prophet called them 'nothing' (44.9), or 'empty wind' (41.29), and used the same Hebrew word to describe the nations who constructed the idols ('emptiness' 40.17), and the rulers who used them for their own power ('nothing' 40.23). They were of no use (no 'profit', 44.9–10) in the design of creation. That is why the Creator would not allow the idols to share His glory (Glossary: *Glory*) (42.8), and why those who worshipped idols would not succeed (42.17; 44.9–11; 45.16).

The idols are contrary to God's design of creation because through them the 'nations' try to get control of 'the Creator's power and wisdom' (see pp. 18, 19), without 'waiting on the Lord' (40.31). People of the ancient world believed that the gods controlled the powers of nature – the sun, moon, stars, wind, rain, rivers, earth, etc. They thought that by making idols of these gods, they would be able to influence the powers of nature and use them for their own purposes.

The idols thus symbolize the pride of 'nations', which causes the divisions between them and opposes God's design of creation, that all 'nations' should live together in peace as one 'people'.

YOUR REDEEMER

The prophet used this as his key idea in this poem, by placing the name 'Redeemer' at the beginning (v. 6) and the word 'redeemed' at the end (vv. 22, 23). He showed his great interest in the idea of redemption by using the noun 'redeemer' or the verb 'redeem' fifteen times in Isaiah 40—55. His ideas on the subject are important for us to study, because redemption is one of the key themes of the New Testament. It was to be the heart of the message of the witnesses among the nations (48.20).

'Redemption' is the act of the faithful covenant Lord who delivers His Servant from trouble (Glossary: *Redeemer*).

1. *The Redeemer has promised to deliver His servant.* His Servant people can have complete confidence in Him (44.21). There is no doubt about His willingness to save them.

2. *The Servant people must accept the fact of redemption by faith.* The prophet told them that God had *already* redeemed them, while they were still in Babylon. Even before they experienced deliverance, they should 'return' to their Redeemer in faith (44.22).

3. *The act of redemption is a process.* It begins with (a) the *decision* of

'The idols symbolize the pride of nations, which causes the divisions between them' (p. 68).

The 'pride' of many nations is symbolized by military power. As in Babylon, this 'idol' is displayed to the people on national festivals like the May Day parade in Moscow.

What other 'idols' symbolize national pride today?

the Redeemer to deliver His people from the oppressor (43.14; 49.26). It continues with (b) the Redeemer's *acceptance* of the Servant in spite of past failures (43.25; 44.22; 48.9–11). The Redeemer offers (c) *repeated deliverance* through fire and water (43.1–2), through the sea (51.11), and along the way (48.17). The process of redemption comes to (d) a *fulfilment* with the restoration of the whole cosmos to the design of creation (44.23).

All nature rejoices when God makes the decision to redeem Israel, because it means the end of the corruption of nature by idolatry and the exploitation of nature by human beings. The redemption of Israel is a sign that the proper relationship between God, human beings, and the other parts of nature is being restored. Redemption begins with Israel, but it continues until it includes all nations and the entire cosmos.

This picture of redemption is strikingly similar to that which we find in Ephesians 1.7–10: 'In him we have *redemption* in his blood (a fact to be accepted by faith), the *forgiveness* of our trespasses (acceptance by the Redeemer), according to the riches of his *grace* (continual guidance and deliverance) which he lavished upon us. For he has made known to us in all wisdom and insight the mystery of his will according to his purpose set forth in Christ, as a plan for the *fullness of time* (fulfilment), to unite all things in him, things in heaven and on earth' (restoration of the cosmos to God's design for creation).

KING OF ISRAEL

By repeating this title for God from the previous poem (43.15), the prophet was telling the Israelites that their King (God) was also Lord of all history from beginning to end. Israel's king was not king of Israel only. On the contrary, Israel was witness among the nations because her King was Lord of all nations.

LORD OF HOSTS

'Hosts' originally meant the armies of Israel. As the commander of these armies, the Lord was called 'Lord of hosts'. The prophet thought of 'hosts' as being the powers of nature under God's command. A similar idea is in Psalm 103.21, where 'all His hosts' are God's 'ministers who do his will'. The prophet thought of all the powers of the natural world as servants of God, and part of the design of creation. When he used this name for God, he wanted the witnesses to remember that no power in nature or among human beings is able to be 'God'.

ROCK

The witnesses among the nations would testify to God as the only solid 'rock' in the midst of change. This was in contrast (a) to the idols, which were made by men and could be destroyed by them, and (b) to the 'gods' of nature and of the 'nations', who were not dependable.

STUDY SUGGESTIONS

REVIEW OF CONTENT

1. Why was the second Commandment important for the Israelite exiles in Babylon?
2. What evidence is there that the prophet may have been working in a temple labour force?
3. What religious leaders in China and India lived at the same time as this prophet?
4. Who or what were the 'witnesses' of the nations?
5. What was the value of the idols to those who constructed them?
6. What need in the hearts of all human beings makes them want to construct idols?
7. What is the effect of idol worship on God's 'design of creation'?
8. What was the responsibility of the 'Redeemer' within the covenant relationship?
9. What are the four steps in the process of redemption?
10. What was (a) the original meaning, and (b) the meaning in the mind of the prophet, of the word 'hosts'?

APPLICATION, DISCUSSION, RESEARCH

11. Read the following verses and explain what sort of object or attitude is described as an 'idol' in each:
(a) Phil. 3.19 (b) 2 Tim. 3.4 (c) Rom. 8.5 (d) Col. 3.5 (e) 1 Cor. 10.20.
12. Review the reading suggestions under the subject of idolatry. Why did the prophet say that those who worship idols will always end up in defeat, and that Israel will not end up in defeat? What is your opinion?
13. Which of the following do you think could *become* an 'idol' according to the meaning of this prophet?
a national flag,
a sacred tree,
an atomic power plant,
a government leader,
a worship centre.
14. The 'idols' symbolize anything that corrupts the design of creation (p. 19). Is a *nation* idolatrous? Is the *use of commerce* to gain national power idolatrous? Give reasons for your answer.
15. Read the following passages and say how, in each case, the worship of idols 'corrupted the design of creation':
(a) Ps. 106.35–39 (b) Hos. 4.17–18 (c) 1 Kings 21.1–26.
Give examples of other actions or values that have similar effect.

16. From the following passages in the New Testament, we can see what sort of people idol-worshippers were.
    (a) Would this description fit any people in your country today?
    (b) Was this true only for Roman society?
    (c) Do those who lead that sort of life in your society also worship idols?
    1 Cor. 5.11; 6.9; Gal. 5.20; Rev. 21.8; 22.15.
17. Imagine you are trying to explain 'redemption' to a new Christian. How would you interpret the 'process of redemption'?
18. What does 'Lord of Hosts' mean for people who practise black magic, demon worship, and sorcery?

44.24—45.13
Cyrus, Man of God's Purpose
March–April 539 BC

BACKGROUND AND OUTLINE

During the Babylonian New Year festivities in 539 BC, Cyrus was beginning his march on Babylon. The prophet wrote this poem in order to help the Israelite exiles to see what God was doing at that moment in history. Behind the poem lies the question of how God acts in history. Does God use for His purposes people or movements not related to the history of the people of the covenant? Previous prophets had told them that God used Assyria to punish Israel (Isa. 10.5). But could God use leaders and nations outside the covenant with Israel to accomplish His purpose of making a new creation? No previous prophet had faced this question, or spoken about it with such clarity as this prophet. Perhaps most of the Israelites in Babylon disagreed with him. Yet his words are of great value to Christians today as we try to think of how God is working in our world.

This poem begins a third series of four, in which the prophet turns from the internal problems of the community of exiles, to the broader scope of God's purpose in relation to the coming victory of Cyrus. There is no direct evidence to show when he composed this poem. However, the next three poems do contain such evidence, which makes it probable that this poem too was composed in March–April 539 BC.

Main theme: Cyrus, Man of God's Purpose
Part 1: God's dynamic activity (44.24–28)
V. 24: Redeemer and Creator.
Vv. 25–28: Lord of history.

CYRUS, MAN OF GOD'S PURPOSE

Part 2: God's action through Cyrus (45.1–7)
Vv. 1–2: God's promised support.
Vv. 3–6: For the sake of Israel, Cyrus, and all mankind.
V. 7: The creator of *shalom* and adversity.

Part 3: A hymn of the new creation (45.8)

Part 4: God's ultimate purpose (45.9–13)
Vv. 9–11: God's answer to Israel's complaint.
Vv. 12–13: The city of God.

READING SUGGESTIONS

44.24–28

Look at the word 'redeem' or 'redeemer' in the two previous poems, and then at the beginning of this poem. The prophet's characteristic teaching method is to begin with an idea which the Israelites can accept, and then lead them to a new and wider idea. Try to see this process in the way he uses the words for 'redeem' in these three poems.

The structure of verses 24–28 shows a series of clauses describing God's continuing work. Each clause begins with 'who . . .'. Find twelve such clauses, and look for the verbs. What sort of action do they describe?

45.1–7

Look for the verbs in verses 1, 4, and 5 which describe God's personal support for Cyrus. Now read 41.13; 42.6; 43.1. According to these verses, who receives God's support? What was the prophet's purpose in using these particular words here?

Look for the three statements beginning 'I will . . .' describing what God will do for Cyrus, and His three purposes in calling Cyrus. These are introduced by 'that . . .', 'for the sake of . . .', 'that . . .', with the climax on the third. Can you see the prophet's teaching method? (See 44.24–28 above.)

45.8

Note the picture-language here: 'rain from heaven', and 'a new growth on the earth'. What is the 'rain', and what is the 'new growth'? Notice the word 'created', and compare it with 41.20 and 45.12 where the word 'created' is used.

45.11–12

This is the climax of the entire poem and the use of words shows important ideas.

1. Consider the connection between 'Maker' in v. 11, 'made' in v. 12, and 'made' in 44.24. Here is the meaning: The one who makes Israel also

made the earth (living place), and makes 'all things'. If you connect 'earth' in v. 12 with 'earth' in v. 8, you can see the prophet's idea that God is making a new 'earth'.

2. In the same way, connect 'my hands' in v. 12 with 'grasped' (an action of the hand) in 45.1. Consider the meaning of this as in the previous example.

3. Consider the connection between 'righteousness' in v. 13 and this word as it is used twice in 45.8. Read the Glossary note on *Righteousness*, and write down your interpretation of the meaning in this poem.

This whole poem is especially rich in names of God. 'Lord' occurs ten times, and the statement 'I am the Lord' five times. It will help if you remember these, and the pronoun 'I', 'my' and 'me', all as referring to God.

INTERPRETATION

GOD'S PURPOSE (44.24–28)

At the climax of this section are the key words: 'He (i.e. Cyrus) shall fulfil all my purpose'. In this poem the prophet showed how the work of Cyrus was related to God's purpose (Glossary: *Purpose*) of restoring the design of creation. God's action in accomplishing this purpose is His 'righteous resolve', or 'righteousness' (Glossary, *Righteousness*), which occurs three times in this poem. God's righteous resolve supported Cyrus (45.18) as it has supported God's servant people Israel (42.6). This righteous resolve continues to be at work in the world and as a result communities grow up in obedience to it (45.8). Thus Cyrus and God's Servant people both had a part in the accomplishment of God's purpose at that moment in history. We could say that God's plan for the restoration of the earth requires both the group of people who know Him, and the leaders of the 'nations' who do not know Him.

GOD'S DYNAMIC ACTIVITY (44.24–28; 45.7, 12)

In the first part of this poem (see note on v. 28), the prophet told the Israelite exiles about God's dynamic activity, which helps us to understand the work of Cyrus.

1. *Your Redeemer.* God, who was using Cyrus for His purpose, was also the one who 'formed' His people in the 'womb' of the 'nations', and who was 'redeeming' them from oppression in Babylon. What the prophet was going to tell them about Cyrus did not cancel out what he had said about God's chosen Servant people (45.4). God was still the 'Holy One of Israel, the Maker of his people' (45.11).

2. *Creator.* The prophet then reminded his people that God was the Creator of the whole universe, with all its natural forces ('host', 45.12; 'all things', 44.24). The Creator God is the one who protects *living space* by

God's plan for the restoration of the earth requires both the people who know Him and the leaders of the nations who do not know Him' (p. 74).

Two great 'leaders of nations' of today exchanged greetings when President Nyerere of Tanzania visited Chairman Mao Tse-tung in China.

In what ways, if any, do you think that God has used these leaders (and their peoples) 'for the restoration of the earth'?

'stretching out the heavens', and who extends *living space* by 'spreading out the earth' (44.24; 45.12). He also created mankind on the earth (45.12). In 44.24, the prophet describes the continuing creative work of God. He wanted to stress that the victories of Cyrus would be a part of God's continuing creative work: new living space, new living place, for a new mankind.

3. *Bringing Babylon down.* Following this, the prophet turned to Babylon. He said that God was at work through Cyrus, proving that the magical incantations and predictions of the astrologers were good for nothing (44.25), while the predictions of the prophet would come true. The Babylonian empire was like the great deep (44.27; Glossary: *World-view*), or like a great mountain (45.2, Glossary: *Mountains*). These pictures meant that the Babylonians were the chief enemies of the Creator God, because they brought disorder into the design of creation. Cyrus would be God's agent in bringing the forces of disorder under control, so that the design of creation could be restored.

4. *Rebuilding 'Jerusalem'.* God then told the Israelites that He was commanding the rebuilding of 'Jerusalem and the cities of Judah' (44.28, Glossary: *Jerusalem, Cities of Judah*). By relating these places to the victories of Cyrus and to the work of the Creator as a whole, the prophet was suggesting in an indirect way that the Israelites' plans for restoring Judah must be broadened to include the whole of the earth.

5. *Creating Shalom.* In 45.7 the prophet added the important word that the Creator was at work creating shalom ('weal', i.e., peace, prosperity, well-being) in the world, but that this would mean adversity ('woe') for those who were preventing *shalom*. *Shalom* is the result of God's blessing (44.3), and means wholeness, harmony, and welfare for all. It is part of God's design of creation.

GOD'S SUPPORT FOR CYRUS (45.1–7)

1. *Personal Support.* The prophet described God's support for Cyrus in words which he had previously used only for God's support for Israel: 'grasp the right hand' (45.1; 41.13; 42.6), 'call you by name' (45.3, 4; 43.1). 'I surname you' (45.4) meant that God adopted Cyrus as a member of his 'family'. The prophet used the same word in 44.5 to show how people from the 'nations' would be adopted into the family of the 'offspring of Israel'. These words are very important for our understanding of the prophet's boldness of thought. He emphasized God's support for a world leader who did not know the God of Israel. This support was the same kind of support which God gave to Israel.

2. *Anointed king.* The prophet used two titles to show God's support for Cyrus: 'my shepherd' (44.28), and 'my anointed' (45.1). These titles also show the prophet's boldness of thought. The Israelites had used them to describe their own kings. They called David 'the shepherd of God's people'

76

(2 Sam. 5.2), and 'the anointed of the God of Jacob' (2 Sam. 23.1). Many thought that an Israelite king would rule the nations. But no one had ever said that God would appoint a world leader of the 'nations' as his 'shepherd' or 'anointed king'.

Probably the prophet wanted to tell the Israelites that the old political order of the monarchy was finished. God was now their 'king' (41.21; 43.15; 44.6) and 'shepherd' (40.11), but He was using a man from outside Israel to rule the nations. Many of the Israelites probably disliked this idea, and disagreed with the prophet.

3. *Opening doors.* The prophet described God's support for Cyrus to show that the political and social changes brought by Cyrus's victories would open up new possibilities for the world. (a) Existing political systems ('nations', 'kings') would lose their power (45.1). (b) Doors which were formerly barred shut between nations and cultures would be forced open (45.1–2). (c) New forms of wealth and knowledge would be uncovered (45.3). The prophet was telling the Israelites to keep their eyes open for signs of God's new creation among the nations, and to stimulate such growth.

4. *For whose sake?* The prophet urged his people to think about the importance of Cyrus's victories not only for themselves, but for the whole world. When he told them that Cyrus's victories were *for the sake of Israel* (45.4; 43.14) it did not surprise them. They thought immediately of their return to their ruined home land. But then he went on to tell them that God wanted *Cyrus* to know the true God (45.3) and to 'call on God's name' in worship (41.25), even though at that time Cyrus did not know the God of Israel.

We do not know what the prophet meant by these words. Here are two suggestions: (a) He thought that Cyrus would actually come to believe in the God of Israel, although as far as we know, this did not happen. (b) He saw Cyrus as a symbol of the leaders of the earth who would in the future come to know God as a result of Israel's witness. There may be a suggestion of this idea in 49.7.

Finally, the prophet told the Israelites that Cyrus's victories were *for the sake of all mankind*, so that all should know the one true God. He did not mean that Cyrus would tell them about the one true God. That would be the work of God's chosen Servant people.

THE HYMN OF THE NEW CREATION (45.8)

By putting this hymn in the centre of this poem about Cyrus, the prophet was telling the Israelites that Cyrus was God's agent in the new creation. In the previous hymn of redemption (44.23), he had focused on Israel. In this hymn he focused on communities of human beings in which the fruits of salvation (Glossary: *Salvation*) would become visible, and life would be ordered in accordance with God's righteous resolve. This would be the result of God's own work in those communities (Glossary: *Righteousness*). These communities were a part of God's new creation, and Cyrus's victories would make this new growth *possible*.

GOD'S ANSWER TO ISRAEL'S COMPLAINT (45.9–11)

In these verses the prophet criticized the Israelites sharply for the third time (see 42.24 and 43.22–28). This was the only time he used the strong word 'woe', which had been so often used by prophets before the exile (see for example Isa. 5.11–23). Previously he had criticized them for not looking honestly at their past. This time, he criticized them for being too narrowly nationalistic about their future.

From these verses, we can see that many of the Israelites in Babylon were not happy with the prophet's teaching. They did not like the idea that other 'nations' would be included as new members of the family of God's people. They thought that the prophet was giving them a wrong picture of God's intention. They liked to think that God was concerned only about His chosen people.

The prophet gave his answer in three pictures:

1. A craftsman is free to make anything he likes according to his purpose. How can something made by the craftsman criticize his new work?

2. A potter is free to make a pot, or a jug, or a jar, according to any pattern that he chooses. How can a jar criticize the potter for making a jug?

3. A parent is free to plan for new children in the family. How can a child tell his parents that he or she does not want any more brothers or sisters?

The prophet's message was this: If God chooses to enlarge His family by adding new children (45.11) from the nations, the 'first born son' (Exod. 4.22) should not be jealous, but should rejoice (41.16). If the communities of the children of God in other nations have a different cultural pattern from that of the Israelites, is this not the will of the 'potter'?

The prophet had already hinted that Cyrus might be preparing 'clay' for the 'potter' by his victories over the nations (41.25). When Jesus Himself spoke of 'other sheep that are not in this fold', i.e. Christians who would belong to other nations (John 10.16), perhaps He was using the ideas of this prophet from Isaiah 43.7; 44.5; or 45.11.

GOD'S CITY (45.12–13)

This is the climax of the whole poem. By speaking for the second time about God's activity in creating, the prophet was suggesting that God was at that moment in history making a new creation, including the new communities mentioned in the hymn of creation (45.8).

When he said that Cyrus would build God's city, without referring to

'Jerusalem and the cities of Judah' as he had in 44.26, he was telling the Israelites in Babylon that God's intention in supporting Cyrus was to build a new society that would restore the design of creation.

Finally, when the prophet said that Cyrus would 'send forth' (this is the meaning of the Hebrew word translated 'set free') God's exiles, he meant that Cyrus's victories would make it possible for the exiles to go forth to the ends of the earth with God's 'revealed teaching' ('law' as in 41.21; 42.4, 21). They were to bear witness among the 'nations' to the one true God (43.10–12; 44.8), and to prepare them for living in God's city.

NOTES

44.24. From the womb (see also 44.2; 46.3; 48.8; 49.1, 5, 15): What was the 'womb' from which Israel was born? We may find a clue in 41.9 where it is said that God took Israel 'from the ends of the earth', meaning the whole community of nations. Haran, Egypt, Canaan come to mind. The new sons of Israel would be born from the womb of their own culture.

44.25. Omens of liars: Many records of oracles addressed to the Babylonian and Assyrian kings have been found by archaeologists. Not one has ever been found which proclaimed a complete and final fall of the empire. They always foretold salvation for the empire. The fall of Assyria and Babylon proved these oracles futile.

44.28. Saying of Jerusalem . . . the temple: Most biblical scholars think that this line was added by a scribe who wished to emphasize the geographical Jerusalem and the temple. The style is different from the rest of this part of the poem.

45.11. Command me: This word showed the hard pride of some Israelite exiles who were not pleased with what God seemed to be doing. Compare Jonah 4.

My sons: Israel was God's *first-born* son (Exod. 4.22). There would be other 'sons' too. This idea is found in other parts of the Bible. Jeremiah speaks of God's 'sons', of which Israel was one (Jer. 3.19). God has 'made' all the nations (Ps. 96.9) and so they all belong to Him (Ps. 82.8). In the New Testament, Jesus is called 'the first born among many brethren' (Rom. 8.29), who would 'bring many sons to glory' (Heb. 2.10), so that they might be 'adopted as sons' (Gal. 4.5; John 1.12–13). In Isaiah 45.11, the word 'sons' meant whole peoples.

45.13. Exiles: The word means anyone forcibly removed from his own land. It was commonly used by writers of the Bible to refer to people conquered and exiled from Israel or Judah, as in Jeremiah 24.5. However, it could also apply to exiles from Syria (1 Kings 16.9; Amos 1.5), slaves sold by the Philistines (Amos 1.6), Egyptians, and Ethiopians (Isa. 20.4). The prophet may have been thinking that exiles from the 'nations' might join the Israelites as they journeyed to the ends of the earth.

STUDY SUGGESTIONS

REVIEW OF CONTENT

1. What two groups of people does God use for restoring the earth?
2. What five sorts of God's activity did the prophet tell his people about?
3. Give three expressions which the prophet used to describe God's support for both Cyrus and Israel.
4. What two titles usually reserved for Israelite kings did the prophet give to Cyrus?
5. What three changes brought by Cyrus opened up possibilities for a new social order?
6. For whose sake did God support Cyrus?
7. What were the farthest points north, south, east, and west in the world known to the Israelites?
8. (a) Why did some Israelites in Babylon complain to the prophet?
   (b) What three 'pictures' did the prophet use in his reply?
9. What did the prophet mean by the 'city of God'?

APPLICATION, DISCUSSION, RESEARCH

10. Choose *three* of the following leaders, and say in what ways you think that each is
    (a) like, or (b) unlike, Cyrus.

Mao Tse-tung	Ferdinand Marcos	Lee Kwan-yew
John F. Kennedy	Kenneth Kaunda	Julius Nyerere

11. (a) Give examples of people in your country who are being used by God in His new creation although they hold another faith than Christianity, or do not believe in any religion.
    (b) Give examples of Christians in your country whom God is using in His new creation.
12. Following are some suggestions of human activity which reflects God's creative acts. Give at least one other example of each kind of activity:
    (a) *Protecting living space.* Example: giving an orphan a home.
    (b) *Extending living place.* Example: reclaiming desert land for human habitation.
    (c) *Bringing Babylon down.* Example: working for legislation to control greedy money lenders.
    (d) *Rebuilding Jerusalem.* Example: building new towns to house the victims of war.
    (e) *Creating shalom.* Example: working for better relations between racial groups.
13. This prophet showed his boldness by stating that God gave the same kind of support to Cyrus as he did to His own people. Consider the following statements and give your own opinion on each subject.

(a) Political life is dirty. God could have nothing to do with it.

(b) God works in society through the Church and Church people. He supports them in their jobs because they believe in Him.

(c) God supports good political leaders whether they are Christian or not.

14. Which of the following questions should Christians ask about a proposed government policy? (Perhaps you would like to ask more than one, or all of them. In each case, say why.)

(a) How will it affect Christians? For example, in regard to freedom of worship, exemption from taxes, etc.

(b) How will it affect groups in our country, such as the rich, or the poor, minority groups, etc.?

(c) How will it affect the countries around us, i.e. will it make us better neighbours or worse neighbours?

(d) How will it affect the whole world?

15. What do you think is the main message from this poem about Cyrus for your Church today?

45.14–25
The Saviour of the Nations
March–April, 539 BC

BACKGROUND AND OUTLINE

According to the historical records at the Babylonian court, the last New Year celebrated by the Babylonian King Nabonidus was in 539 BC. The records contain evidence of the external troubles of the decaying empire, by referring to attacks by Arabian tribes from the south-eastern border. They do not refer to Babylon's internal problems, nor to the fact that King Cyrus of Persia had begun his march along the Tigris river toward the city. Within seven months Nabonidus would be dead and Babylon in the hands of Cyrus.

When the prophet spoke ironically in this poem about 'those who carry about wooden idols, and keep on praying to a god that cannot save', and challenged the gods of Babylon to 'declare . . . and take counsel together' about what will happen (45.20–21), he probably had the New Year ceremonies in mind. At the time when Babylon, the tyrant of the nations, was about to collapse, the prophet told his people about the Saviour of the nations.

The theme of this poem is salvation. This is perhaps the most important theme in the New Testament, and has been the heart of the preaching of the Christian Church over the centuries. Our understanding of salvation cannot be complete until we consider what this prophet said about the saving work of God. His thoughts on the subject are collected in this poem, which deeply influenced the writers of the New Testament.

Main theme: The Saviour of the Nations

Part 1: The 'nations' confess their faith in the God of Israel as their saviour (14–17)
V. 14a: They will come over to Israel.
V.14b: They will confess their faith to Israel.
V. 15: They will confess their faith to the God of Israel.
Vv. 16–17: They will confess their faith to Israel.

Part 2: The Saviour speaks to His people (18–19)
V. 18: A message in a time of social breakdown.
V. 19: The Word of truth.

Part 3: The Saviour speaks to all the 'nations' (20–25)
Vv. 20–21: God's debate with the 'nations': Who is the true Saviour?
V. 22: God offers salvation to all the nations.
V. 23: God's sworn word about the nations.
Vv. 24–25: The transforming effect of salvation.

READING SUGGESTIONS

THE MAIN THEME: SALVATION

Look carefully at the speeches by the 'nations' and God, in which the words related to salvation ('Saviour', 'save', 'salvation') occur. What do you find in v. 17 about what will *not* happen to those who are 'saved by the Lord'?

MAJOR THEME: THE IDOLS

Look at vv. 16, 17, 20. Where do you find a word connecting this section with the major theme? Go back to the passage on idols in 44.9–20 and find words there which are also in these verses. One hint: 'knowledge' in v. 20, and 44.19. Note also the relationship of idols with chaos (see Glossary).

MAJOR THEME: THE 'OFFSPRING' (i.e. CHILDREN, DESCENDANTS) OF ISRAEL

Find the two occurrences at the climax of Part 2 and Part 3. Note that in Part 2 the people receive a revelation about the design of creation, and in Part 3 they 'all' celebrate their salvation. Re-read vv. 16, 17 and find words there that are repeated in v. 24. Why did the author repeat them? Now read v. 22. Whom did the author say would be included in the 'offspring'?

MAJOR THEME: THE LORD

Consider the connection between the words 'Lord', 'God', 'Saviour', and all pronouns referring to God (I, myself, me, thou, him). Note the verbs in each case. For example 'a God who hidest thyself' (v. 15). This will help you find what the author was saying about God.

INTERPRETATION

Instead of following the prophet's order, we will first look at Part 2, containing God's word to His people. Then we return to Part 1, which describes the conversion of some caravan merchants, and belief in Israel's God. Finally we study Part 3, which contains God's direct revelation to all nations of the earth.

SALVATION: FROM DEATH TO LIFE (vv. 18, 19)

God did not create the earth a chaos, he formed it *to be inhabited* (v. 18). 'Chaos' (see Glossary) is the prophet's word for breakdown, confusion, death. Chaos destroys life. It results from past failures (sin) and dependence on false gods (idolatry). In other words, it happens when people or nations behave in ways that conflict with the design of creation. It is the power of death. Babylonian society in 539 BC was a vivid example of chaos at work, with no power to stop it.

'Salvation' is God's action to overcome the destructive power of chaos and to put in its place the power of life (blessing). This action of God creates freedom (breathing space), security (firm foundations), and wholeness (a garden for life). It results from God's victorious will ('truth', v. 19).

The prophet told his people that the disorder which they saw around them was not a part of God's design, and that God was beginning His new creation in their community even before the power of Babylon was ended. He said to them: 'Do not let outward breakdown (chaos) break us down. Our Saviour (43.3) has promised to be with us (43.2), and this time of darkness can be the starting point of His salvation.

SALVATION IS FOR OTHERS (vv. 14–17)

See additional note on interpretation, below. *God is with you!* (v. 14). Paul quoted this verse to show the Corinthian Christians how important their worship life was. Even a chance visitor attending their worship services would be convinced by what he found, and would 'bow down and worship God, confessing "Truly God is here with you!"' (1 Cor. 14.25). Paul understood what this prophet was trying to say, i.e., the only way in which the 'nations' can learn about the Saviour is from those who show in their lives that they have been saved by Him.

The prophet used picture language to express this message: Some caravan merchants from South Arabia, Egypt, and Ethiopia (see note) might be visiting some of the Israelite exiles, and observe their worship and life in the midst of the disorder of the time. The strangers would be so convinced by this Israelite group, 'saved by the Lord with an everlasting salvation' (v. 17), that they would bow low and say 'Today, through you, we have found the only true God!' And then they would speak directly to the hidden God, and call Him 'Saviour!'

We do not know whether the prophet was referring here to a real incident. Probably it was something like a parable, to emphasize that salvation is not to be kept for oneself. It is for others.

ACCEPTING SALVATION

They shall come over to you and be yours (v. 14). *Turn to me and be saved* (v. 22). *Repent and believe!* (Mark 1.15).

Salvation is a gift from God. It must be accepted. The prophet said that the caravan merchants were convinced that the society of their time based its belief on 'confusion' and false gods (v. 16). The 'survivors of the nations' too would come to know that their gods could not 'save'. By this he meant that there must be *a turning away* from the forces that destroy life and make for chaos, a turning away from past failures, past guilt (see pp. 57, 58), from false gods (see p. 67), and from all that conflicts with the design of creation (see p. 68).

At the same time there must be *a turning towards* the Saviour of the nations, an acceptance of His gifts of freedom, security, and wholeness.

The prophet also made it clear that God's saving action takes place within the nations themselves. The individuals mentioned in Isaiah 44.5, the group of merchants in 45.14, the 'survivors' in 45.20, were all representatives of their own 'nations'. The prophet did *not* say that in order to be saved they would have to reject their 'nationality' and accept Jewish customs like circumcision, or particular food laws. He probably assumed that they would keep many of their own customs, much of their culture and their own languages. Even those parts of their national religions which were supporting freedom, security, and wholeness, were part of the saving work of God.

THE PROCESS OF SALVATION

Turn to me and be saved! (Isa. 45.22) *To those of us who are being saved, (the cross) is the power of God* (1 Cor. 1.18).

Like Paul, this prophet understood salvation as a *process*. It begins as something a person says for the first time: 'I am the Lord's' (44.5), and prays for the first time: 'You are my Saviour' (45.14). And it continues until he arrives at the New Jerusalem (52.10; Glossary, *Jerusalem*). In this process the culture, customs, political and social life of each person and each nation will be transformed as suggested in vv. 23–25.

1. *New loyalties.* All other loyalties, whether to family, clan, party, tribe, racial group, or nation, will be under the supreme loyalty to the Creator and Saviour (see note on v. 23, 'bow the knee').

2. *New wholeness.* Words and actions will be united in truth, justice, and uprightness (see note on v. 23, 'swear').

3. *New and continuing struggles* will be waged against all forces of chaos, and *victories* will be won for freedom, security, and wholeness in co-operation with the Saviour's righteous will (see note on v. 24, 'righteousness).

4. *New and continuing strength* for participation in the new creation will come from waiting on the Lord in prayer and faith (40.31).

5. *New and continuing self-examination* will be needed, to overcome the enmity to God found in the heart of every 'nation' (see note on v. 24, 'all who are incensed against him').

6. *New and continuing rejoicing* will celebrate victories of the Lord and His gift of salvation (see note on v. 25).

SALVATION FOR ALL NATIONS

Turn to me and be saved, all the ends of the earth! (Isa. 45.22). *Go make disciples of all nations.* (Matt. 28.19). *Our God desires all men to be saved, and come to a knowledge of the truth.* (1 Tim. 2.4). *All nations are fellow heirs, members of the same body.* (Eph. 3.6).

The leaders of Judaism disagreed strongly with the idea which was expressed by New Testament writers, that all nations should come to share in God's salvation. But it is firmly based on teaching found in the Old Testament, and was most clearly stated by this prophet more than five hundred years before Christ. One New Testament writer spoke of it as a 'mystery kept secret for long ages, *but now* disclosed through the prophetic writings' (Rom. 16.25–26). This seems to mean that the prophet's world-wide vision was not correctly understood until the time of Christ. And it shows how bold his faith was, as a prophet ahead of his time.

He presented the offer of salvation to all nations on an equal basis as God's sworn word, to mark a turning point in the history of His dealing with all mankind (see note on v. 23). So we see that even before the coming of Jesus, God entrusted His people with a mission to carry the message of His salvation to all the world's people from that day to the present. Vv. 22 and 23 form the climax of the prophet's teaching, and the key to understanding the rest of his poems.

Here are four themes which the prophet clarified in 45.22–23:

1. The work of Cyrus in building the city of God (45.13) and shepherding the nations (44.28) is a part of God's saving work of creating freedom, security, and wholeness for them.

2. The work of Cyrus in sending forth God's exiles is to make possible the mission of God's Servant (42.1–4), who is His messenger (42.18, 21)

and His witness (43.8–13) among the nations, to carry His invitation to them and to teach them how to turn and accept His salvation.

3. The new growth of God's garden in the wilderness (41.17–20; 42.9; 43.19; 44.1–5; 45.8) is to demonstrate to the 'nations' the wholeness of salvation.

4. The growth of the 'offspring of Israel' (see Glossary) comes to a climax in this poem, where 'all the offspring of Israel' will one day include all the nations, not as Jews, but as members of the peaceful family of nations, a 'people' under God.

ADDITIONAL NOTE ON THE INTEPRETATION OF 45.15–25

Some scholars believe that this passage is a collection of shorter pieces put together by an editor, and that the various sections were originally separate. In this guide we agree with scholars who see the whole passage as a single poem, because there are certain themes which seem to bind it together; e.g: *salvation* (vv. 15, 17, 20, 21, 22); 'no other God' (vv. 14, 18, 21); the idol makers (vv. 16, 20).

Secondly, some scholars believe that verse 14 is a picture of the 'nations' as captives of Israel, because it describes them as being 'in chains', and bowing down to Israel. Others see it as a picture of Cyrus, conqueror of the nations. In this guide we follow those scholars who see the verse as a picture of the conversion of the nations to Israel's God. Here are some reasons for this view:

(a) The word translated 'come over' is never used in the Old Testament to describe the defeat of an enemy. In Deuteronomy 29.2 it means 'to enter the covenant'. The author of Isaiah 40—55 used it twice to mean 'pass through' waters of suffering (Isa. 43.2; 51.10). Here it probably means that the nations 'come over' in faith to Israel.

(b) The phrase 'be yours' is the same Hebrew idiom as in Isaiah 44.5, where the nations confess that they are 'the Lord's'. It could mean the same here. If we accept the unity of the poem, this would mean that these 'nations' were joining the new community of the 'offspring' of Israel (v. 25, see Glossary, *Offspring*).

(c) Alternative meanings of the other words are possible, e.g.: enslavement (see 49.7); 'make supplication' could be translated 'make confession'.

(d) The words spoken by the 'nations' are not words of submission, but of faith.

Many scholars see the speech of the nations as ending with v. 15, and in most modern translations, quotation marks are placed at the end of v. 15. These scholars think that vv. 16, 17 do not have any relationship to vv. 14, 15. In this Guide we agree with those scholars who believe that vv. 16, 17 are also a part of the speech of the nations.

Some scholars believe that the phrases 'survivors of the nations' (v. 20) and 'all the ends of the earth' (v. 22) refer only to the Israelite exiles scattered among the nations. They think the prophet believed that God offered salvation only to His own chosen people. In this Guide we agree with most scholars, who believe that the prophet was referrring to the 'nations' of the whole earth, to whom the message of salvation was addressed. In 52.10 'the ends of the earth' mean 'all the nations', as we can see from the previous line.

NOTES

45.14. Wealth of Egypt . . . merchandise of Ethiopia . . . Sabeans: The author was chiefly interested in the merchants, rather than their merchandise. He described them in this poem as representatives of the 'nations'. He repeated their names from 43.3, saying that the nations whom God gave to Cyrus as 'ransom' for the freedom of his people would later 'come over' as new members of the community of the 'offspring of Israel' (45.25).

To you . . . be yours . . . follow you: The pronouns in Hebrew are all in the second person singular feminine, showing that they refer to Israel, and not to Cyrus.

Come over: This is not the act of submission by a conquered enemy, but an act of faith. The Hebrew word is never used in the Old Testament to describe defeat. It often describes passing through waters, as in Isaiah 43.2; 51.10; Exodus 15.16; Ps. 66.6; and Joshua 1.2, 3. It may be an act of religious pilgrimage, as in Amos 5.5, or an act of entering the covenant, as in Deuteronomy 29.12. Here the word means that the merchants have crossed over from their former way of life and former loyalties to accept the covenant way of life.

Be yours: i.e., belong to the covenant federation of the 'offspring of Israel' (v. 25).

Follow you: i.e. follow Israel's example.

Come over in chains: This is probably a marginal note to explain the words 'come over' as a defeat. It changes the original meaning.

Bow down to you: This phrase comes from earlier writings about the Israelite kings, as in Psalm 72.11: 'May all kings fall down before him.' In view of the meaning of the word 'come over' and 'follow', it cannot be understood in the sense of Psalm 72.11. As we see in v. 15, the merchants were really bowing down to God, while paying deep respect to Israel.

With you: The Hebrew for 'with' can be translated in various ways. Perhaps 'in' or 'within' would be preferable.

Only: The Hebrew word may be translated 'surely' and this would be a better translation. The author is not meaning to limit the scope of God's activity, even in the testimony of the nations.

45.15. A God who hidest thyself: God does not 'sign His name' when He acts or speaks. It is difficult to see or hear Him. He works in mysterious ways. But it is possible to get clues to the way in which He acts by looking at Israel. Such a revelation is intended in the picture-language of Isaiah 41.20.

45.18. To be inhabited: This states God's purpose in creating the earth as a fruitful living place. According to 40.22, He created the heavens to give broad living space for people to live in.

45.19. In secret: This may be a reference to the secret formulas of the magicians or spirit doctors.

Speak the truth: The word which is translated 'truth' in this passage is also translated as 'righteousness' in other passages (see note 42.21). Here it means that God speaks words which come true in events, according to His righteous will.

45.20. Survivors of the nations: In Isaiah 4.2–3, we read of the 'survivors of Israel'. Here the word is broadened to include the survivors from each nation who will be able to form a new group of the 'sons' of the nation. There is a picture of the survivors of the nations in Ezekiel 27.35. Now they can turn their anguished faces to their Saviour.

45.23. By myself have I sworn: Oaths were normally taken in the name of someone greater than the person taking the oath. God could swear only by Himself, since there was none greater than He (Heb. 6.13–17). Such oaths taken by God are of the greatest importance. We find other oaths by which He promised land to Israel in Genesis 22.16; Exodus 32.13; Deuteronomy 9.5. In Psalm 89.35, God promises a continuing dynasty to David. The prophets spoke of oaths to punish Israel for her sins (Amos 4.2; 6.8; Jer. 22.5). This is a new oath of God for the new age, and it remains valid down to the present time, 'a word that shall not return'.

Every tongue shall swear: Taking an oath was a serious act of social responsibility, made before God in a shrine. The covenant way of life in Israel was to 'fear the Lord, serve him, and swear by his name' (Deut. 6.13; 10.20). In a time of corruption, people would swear falsely in God's name (see Hos. 4.15), or by other gods (see Amos 8.14; Zeph. 1.5; Jer. 5.7). The prophets told the Israelites that they should go back to the custom of oaths in God's name only, 'in righteousness, justice, and truth', so that the nations would see and be blessed (Jer. 4.2). The nations would then learn the ways of God's people, how to swear in God's name. When they swear in God's name in truth, righteousness, and justice, there will be a renewal of integrity and trustworthiness in human relations.

45.24. Righteousness: The Hebrew is plural, as in Judges 5.11, where it means God's triumphs and the triumphs of His people. In Micah 6.5 the word is translated 'saving acts'. Here the word refers to the continuing victories of the saved people.

Strength: See 40.28–31.

Incensed against him: This is not a reference to burning incense, but to the strong (burning) feelings of those who refused to believe in the God of Israel. A study of the words 'be ashamed' will show that the author thought of these people as idol-worshippers.

45.5. All the offspring of Israel: These now include those of the 'nations' over the entire earth who have turned to the Lord and accepted His teaching.

Triumph: The Hebrew word comes from the same root as the word translated 'righteousness'. It means to participate actively in God's righteous resolve.

Glory: The Hebrew word used here means to 'boast' in God, or to be joyful because of complete confidence in His victories. In this verse, it is the 'nations' as 'offspring of Israel' who express joy in their confidence in God, in fulfilment of Jeremiah 4.2.

STUDY SUGGESTIONS

REVIEW OF CONTENT

1. What two enemies were attacking or preparing to attack Babylonia in March—April, 539 BC?
2. What words of this prophet pointed out how helpless Babylon was to avoid destruction?
3. What is the main theme of this poem?
4. (a) Give a definition of the words (i) 'chaos', and (ii) 'salvation'.
   (b) According to the prophet, what could happen in the 'darkness' of chaos?
5. Why did Paul quote from Isaiah 45.14?
6. Who were the visitors in the worship service of the exiles, according to the prophet's parable?
7. (a) When the 'nations' accept salvation, *from what* must they turn, and *to whom* should they turn?
   (b) What parts of their customs, culture, and religion should the 'nations' who accept salvation from God keep, according to this prophet?
8. When does the process of salvation (a) begin, and (b) end?
9. What are the six sorts of transformation that will happen in a society that is being saved?
10. Give three New Testament verses which are based on Isaiah 45.22.
11. Why did people call the idea of the salvation of the nations a 'mystery'?
12. Isaiah 45.22, 23 are the key verses which help us understand other ideas of this prophet. Give four of these ideas.

APPLICATION, DISCUSSION, RESEARCH

13. Read John 5.25; Isaiah 45.18–19, and the explanation on page 83 of this Guide entitled 'From death to life'.
   (a) In what ways are these passages similar? (b) In what ways are they different? (c) How does the one help you to understand the other?

14. (a) Give two examples of social disorder ('chaos').
   (b) What actions can you suggest for bringing 'freedom, security, and wholeness' to the people caught up in that kind of disorder?
   (c) How would such actions be related to God's saving action?

15. Read the parable of the visitors attending the worship meeting of the exiles (Isa. 45.14–17), and Paul's application of the words of the parable to another situation. Now write a parable of your own, using the same ideas but applied to a different situation. Remember that a parable should have a message.

16. Discuss the following alternatives and give your opinion about them: A person who accepts salvation in Christ should:
   (a) Turn his back on his past, as the old which has gone;
   (b) Change as little as possible so as to keep his identity;
   (c) Give up his bad habits, but keep whatever is good in his past:
   (d) Allow God's saving power in Christ to transform his relationship to his culture and customs;
   (e) Work with God in bringing freedom, security, and wholeness to others.

17. Choose one of the 'newnesses' listed on page 85.
   (a) Explain why you think it should transform the life of a Christian community or the general community you know;
   (b) Give an example of the way the saving power of God might use Christians to bring this transformation about.

18. Think about the words of Isaiah 45.22. What do they mean for:
   (a) Our attitude toward different groups from our own, for example, racial, cultural, national, or religious groups?
   (b) The mission of the Christian Church where you live?
   (c) Our view of God's will for the future?

46.1-13
Strong Words for Stubborn Doubters
March–April, 539 BC

BACKGROUND AND OUTLINE

On the 11th day of the month of Nisanu, 539 BC, the prophet was probably watching the images of the gods as they were carried from the New Year pavilions, loaded onto barges, lifted onto processional carts, and finally carried back to their shrines (see p. 7).

He used this picture to compose two satirical parables about the helpless gods of Babylon, unable to save. His real message, however, was not about the gods, but about the power of Israel's God to accomplish His purpose. The Israelites in exile probably did not accept what the prophet told them about God's will for the nations, or God's power to accomplish His will. The tiny, helpless group of exiles in Babylon probably felt that the prophet was being unrealistic. Because of this doubt, the prophet called them 'transgressors' and 'stubborn of heart', and composed this poem to change their doubt to faith.

Main theme: Strong Words for Stubborn Doubters

Part 1: A parable: the helpless idols (vv. 1–2)

Part 2: The first word: I will carry you (vv. 3, 4)

Part 3: A parable: the deluded idol-worshippers (vv. 5–7).

Part 4: The second word: I will accomplish all my purpose (vv. 8–11)

Part 5: The third word: My deliverance is near (vv. 12, 13)

READING SUGGESTIONS

Notice the great emphasis which the prophet places on God's purpose, plans, and actions. He does this by using the first personal pronoun more than in any other poem. Count the number of times he uses 'I', 'my', and 'me'. This is the prophet's answer to the doubts of the exiles.

Notice the contrast between the idols and the God of Israel. The prophet shows this by using the words 'carry', 'bear', 'loaded', 'borne', 'lift', and 'save'. Find out *who* carries *what*.

There are many *connections* with previous poems, especially 45.14–25. Look up the following and find out the prophet's purpose.

(a) 'Bow' used twice in vv. 1, 2 is related to 45.23.

91

'Salvation . . . from death to life' (p. 83).

The man on the stretcher was injured and nearly drowned in floods in Brazil, but a rescue team were able to save him and carry him to safety.

What is the most important difference between this sort of 'salvation' and the salvation of which the prophet was speaking to the Israelite exiles?

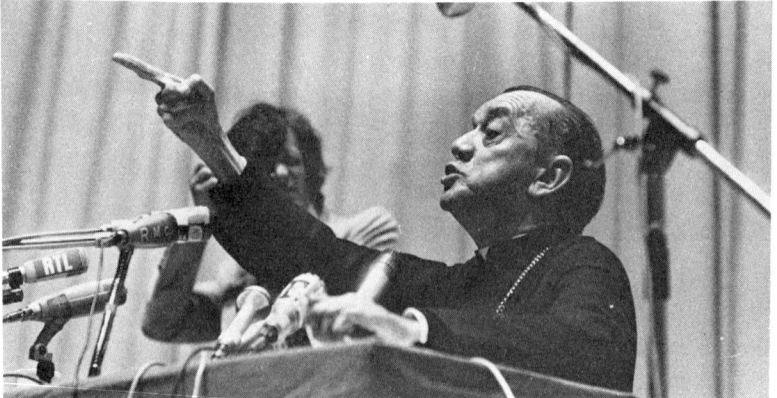

'Be careful that you do not hinder God's purpose' (p. 94).

Bishop Helder Camara broadcasts 'strong words' against the injustice and oppression which have hindered God's purpose for the people of Brazil.

What are some ways in which Christians themselves may be 'hindering' God's purpose for the world today?

(b) 'Counsel', 'no other God', 'spoken', 'salvation', 'deliverance' (same Hebrew word as 'righteousness').

(c) Look for references to the New Year procession in each poem. Find the relationship between:

(d) 46.7; 40.20; and 41.7;

(e) 46.8; 43.25; and 44.22.

(f) 'I am He' is a theme which last appeared in 43.10, 13, 25.

INTERPRETATION

I WILL CARRY YOU (vv. 3–4)

1. *You are a part of God's plan, announced long ago.* When the prophet told the exiles of his dream for a future community of 'nations' called 'all the offspring of Israel' (45.25), many of them began to have doubts, (a) about the future status of the Israelites as God's 'first-born son', (b) about whether God's will was really as broad as that, and (c) whether such a dream could ever come true.

The prophet reminded them that they were a part of God's plan, announced long ago, by calling them 'all the remnant' of Israel. He was referrring to prophecies by Isaiah of Jerusalem more than 150 years earlier that 'a remnant of survivors' would go out of Jerusalem (Isa. 37.32). He told them: 'As you are a part of God's plan, leave the future to Him!'

2. *God has carried you through every crisis of the past and will continue to carry you in the future.* The prophet told the Israelites not to concentrate their thoughts on past failures ('remember not the former things' 43.18), but on God's help to them ('victorious right hand', 41.10), at every stage of their national life. Perhaps he was remembering some verses from Hosea when he spoke of the birth and growth of Israel as God's 'son'. In Hosea 11.1–4 we read of the Exodus as the time of their 'birth', the period of the Judges as their 'youth', and the period of the monarchy as their mature years. When the prophet spoke of the time of 'old age', he probably meant the time of exile, because it was a time of weakness. By comparing Isaiah 40.31 with Psalm 105.5 we can find a suggestion that the Prophet was thinking of a renewal of Israel's youth, as a part of God's 'new thing' (42.9; 43.19). He said to them: 'This is not the end of "Israel", but a new beginning!'

The meaning of the first parable was this: 'The true God "carries" His people. He does not depend on his people to carry him, as the idols do.'

I WILL ACCOMPLISH ALL MY PURPOSE (vv. 8–11)

1. *Do not try to lead God in procession!* The prophet called his people 'transgressors' because they did not yet understand God's purpose. In this poem, the only name for God is 'I am He' (46.4). In 43.10, the prophet told

them that they would only understand 'I am He', the God who is always active (43.13), after they began to bear witness to Him in life and word among the nations.

Then, in 43:25, the prophet said the God known as 'I am He' forgave past 'transgressions' for the sake of His own purpose. But until they understood and accepted this purpose, they were still 'transgressors'. This was not because of their past failures, but because of their present blindness. In other words they wanted God to act according to *their* purpose. The meaning of the second parable was this: 'You are a part of *God's* procession. *He* determines where you should go!'

2. *Put your trust in God's plans and His power to make them work.* The prophet told the people that God was like a king, who first fixed His aims ('the end'), and published them ('announced them'). Then He worked out a series of steps ('all my purpose') and a definite plan for fulfilling them ('counsel'). His long-range aim was the one stated in 45.22, 23, that all nations should turn to Him and be joined together as a peaceful family of nations. Part of His purpose was to have Cyrus defeat Babylon and begin the formation of a new society (God's city), and to send out the exiles to the 'nations'. There was more to God's purpose, but this was enough for the Israelites to understand at the present. The prophet said to the exiles: 'Be careful that you do not try to hinder God's purpose!'

MY DELIVERANCE IS NEAR! (vv. 12, 13)

1. *Your hearts are not yet ready.* The prophet told them that their hearts were proud and stubborn, not yet prepared for the coming victory of God's righteous will ('deliverance'; Glossary, *Righteousness*). Paul may have used this verse as the basis for Romans 10.3: 'Being ignorant of the righteousness that comes from God, and seeking to establish their own, they did not submit to God's righteousness.' The prophet said, 'Soften your hearts, and hear what God is doing!'

2. *The good news.* The prophet told his people that God's victory was a double one: (a) victory over Babylon through Cyrus, (b) victory over the stubbornness of their hearts. He said that God was ready to give a free gift of 'salvation' to His stubborn people as a lovely ornament for all the nations to see. This, too, was part of the fulfilment of 'all God's purpose'! His message was this: 'Open your hearts to receive God's free gift!'

NOTES

46.1, 2. According to the Babylonian court chronicle, the images of the gods in the cities along the Tigris River were moved to Babylon shortly after the New Year, 539 BC. Some scholars believe that the prophet was thinking of this event when he composed 46.1, 2. The reference to a procession in v. 7, and the evidence of a New Year setting for 45.14–25 and chapter 47 make it probable that the barge and cart journey of the gods on the 11th day of Nisanu was the actual background.

Some scholars believe that several unconnnected passages were put together by an editor to compose this longer passage. In this Guide we assume that it was a single poem composed by the same author as the other poems.

46.1. Bel was originally god of the city of Nippur, which was near to Babylon. The people of Nippur worshipped this god as the father of the gods, and god of heaven. When Babylon grew strong and dominated Nippur, the priests took Bel as their god. They used his name for their own god Marduk in order to add his ancient prestige to Babylon's god.

In fact, the god Marduk had a history too. The god of the ancient city of Babylon was originally named Asaru. This was the minor god of a sacred spring or stream. When Babylon became a great power in the first dynasty the priests wanted to have a more important god than the water god Asaru, so they gave him the name of a sun god and war god called Marduk. Then Babylon could be proud of its god, for he was 'king of all gods', since Babylon was the strongest nation.

Nebo. See p. 7.

Bows down. This word probably refers to the awkward swaying of the images as they were carried, loaded, and unloaded. It could also present a picture of defeat, like that of Sisera in Judges 5.27, where the same word is used three times (translated 'he fell'). Read also Psalm 20.8. The same word appears in the great oath of God: 'to me every knee shall *bow*'. The prophet used it in 45.23 and 46.1–2, to suggest that even the great Marduk (and his city Babylon) will bow!

On beasts and cattle. The preposition 'on' in Hebrew would be better translated 'belong to'. The idea is that the weary priests who strained to carry the heavy images entrusted them to the oxen. This gives a vivid contrast to v. 13. God gives salvation *to* (same preposition) Israel, but the priests give the images over to the oxen.

Burden. The root of this word means to 'lift up', or to 'carry'. A literal translation could be 'a lifted thing'. The same root is in the expression 'these things you carry'. The word 'carry' comes three times in vv. 3, 4, and clearly shows the contrast between the true Saviour who lifts up and carries His people, and the powerless gods who are burdens which their followers have to carry. Even the animals are made to help carry the burden of the images.

Loaded. The same word is used in v. 3, translated 'have been borne'. Again the contrast is between the images which must be 'loaded', and the Saviour who bears up His people. There is a beautiful expression of this in Psalm 68.19:

46.1–13

Blessed be the Lord,
who daily bears us up.
God is our salvation!

46.3. All the remnant. The exiles in Babylon were the 'survivors' from the destruction of Jerusalem in 587 BC. Note the following references to the remnant and survivors: Amos 5.5; Micah 2.12; Isaiah 10.20–22.

46.10. My counsel, means God's plan (see 40.13; 41.28; 44.26; and especially 45.21). While King Nabonidus was presiding at the ceremony of fixing the fate of the nation for the coming year, God's plan would make liars of the priests, as in 44.25.

My purpose: See Glossary.

46.11. Bird of prey: This means Cyrus. The emblem of the Persian army was a golden eagle.

46.12. Stubborn of heart. This meant they were unwilling to believe what God had promised, and unwilling to co-operate with His new plans for the new age.

Deliverance. The root of this word is usually translated 'righteousness' (see note on 42.6). Here and in v. 13 the author means the fulfilment of God's righteous will, which in turn means deliverance for Israel.

Salvation. See the discussion of this subject in chapter 10, and in the Glossary. 'Deliverance' places emphasis on God's act. 'Salvation' emphasizes what happens in Israel.

Put might be better translated as 'give' or 'grant'.

46.13. My glory. See Glossary. The word means 'beauty', as in 'the beauty of a human being' (44.13). The meaning is clearly shown in Jeremiah 33.9: 'This city (Jerusalem) shall be to me a name of joy, a praise and a *glory* before all the nations of the earth, who shall hear of the good that I shall do for them; they shall fear and tremble because of all the good and the prosperity (*shalom*) that I provide for it.'

STUDY SUGGESTIONS

1. What is the probable historical fact behind the prophet's words in 46.1–2? What is an alternative suggestion made by some scholars?
2. What words, spoken 150 years earlier, helped the Israelites to understand why they were in Babylon?
3. What three doubts did the Israelites have about the message of the prophet in 45.14–25 which lay behind Isaiah 46?
4. What events in Israel's history may be called their birth, youth, maturity, and old age?
5. (a) What was the message of the prophet's first parable?

(b) What was the message of the prophet's second parable?
6. How did the prophet explain God's work on earth?
7. What were God's two messages to the stubborn people, in vv. 12, 13?
8. Of what city in Mesopotamia was Bel the chief god before the Babylonian priests adopted him?
9. What was the 'history' of the rise of Marduk?
10. What is the meaning of 'counsel' and 'bird of prey' in 46.11?

APPLICATION, DISCUSSION, RESEARCH

11. In many countries, Christians form a very small part of the population, in some cases less than 1 per cent. Which of the following statements would help you to explain to them their part in God's plan for the whole world? Give reasons for your choice.
(a) They are elected by God for salvation after death, and should invite as many as possible to accept salvation.
(b) God has chosen them to pray for the welfare of the whole country.
(c) God has chosen them to be a sign to the people of that country that He is at work in all parts of the life of the nation.
(d) God has chosen them to be a sign of the future salvation of the whole nation, as a member of God's family of nations.
12. (a) Which periods in the history of the Church in your country might be called its birth, youth, maturity, and old age, as far as they are applicable?
(b) Make an outline of a sermon on the text: 'I have made, I will carry, I will save' (46.4).
13. The prophet's application of the parable about the carried images was that the true God carries His people (see p. 93 and 46.3–4).
(a) Does this mean that God does everything, and the people remain passive?
(b) What is the place of human effort in this picture?
(c) Is there a change in the amount of 'carrying' that is needed as a Church moves from childhood through youth and maturity to old age?
(d) How does God's 'carrying help' actually come to His people?
14. How can we be sure that we are not trying to dictate to God where we should go, instead of joining *His* procession? In what ways do the following help or hinder us from joining God's procession?
(a) tradition, (b) Bible study, (c) worship, (d) preaching, (e) organizations within the Church, (f) government regulations, (g) the power or prestige of the Church in a village, city, or nation, (h) political organizations, (i) voluntary organizations for the welfare of the people, (j) international organizations like Councils of Churches.
15. Read the Glossary note on *Righteousness*, and then compare Isaiah 46.12 with Romans 10.3. In what ways are the passages (a) similar, (b) different?

16. Read the Glossary note on *Salvation* and the discussion of salvation on pp. 83–85. Choose one of the following passages from the New Testament about salvation, and compare it with Isaiah 45.17, and 46.13. In what ways are the passages (a) similar, and (b) different? Rom. 1.16; 13.11; 2 Cor. 7.10; Eph. 1.13; Phil. 2.12; 1 Thess. 5.8; Heb. 5.9; 1 Pet. 1.9; 2.2.

47.1–15
The Destructive Pride of
a Powerful Nation
March–April, 539 BC

BACKGROUND AND OUTLINE

The prophet wanted his people to understand the meaning of the coming fall of Babylon. In their future mission, as he saw it, they would be living among the nations, and would be witnesses to the one true God. The lessons of the fall of Babylon would be a part of the message they were to carry: 'Turn to me and be saved, all the ends of the earth.'

This poem was composed during the New Year ceremonies when the images of the gods were in their pavilions on the bank of the Euphrates river outside Babylon. This was the time when Babylon was without her gods.

In our day of super-powers, of revolutions, of old and new imperialisms, and the rise of new nations, the lessons of the fall of Babylon are also important as a part of the Christian message to the nations.

Main theme: The Destructive Pride of a Powerful Nation: Lessons from the Coming Fall of Babylon

Part 1: God's Lament over Babylon's failure (vv. 1–7)
Vv. 1–4: The death of an empire.
Vv. 5–7: Babylon's irresponsible use of power.

Part 2: The false security of power (vv. 8–13)
Vv. 8–9: Self-indulgent luxury.
Vv. 10–11: Technological power.
Vv. 12–13: A Religion of success.

Part 3: God's judgement on irresponsible power (vv. 14–15)

READING SUGGESTIONS

Look at vv. 6–8, 10, and note the prophet's statements about *Babylon's Pride*, where he uses the pronoun 'you'.

Read vv. 1–3, 5, 9, 11, 14 and note the word-pictures describing the *fall of Babylon*.

Find the connections between this poem and other poems in Isaiah 40—55. Use a concordance to compare the way the following words and phrases are used in this and other poems: 'Rivers' (v. 3), 'darkness' (v. 5), 'I am and there is none beside me' (vv. 8, 10), 'Knowledge' (v. 10), 'stubble', 'fire', 'flame' (v. 14), 'save', 'deliver' (vv. 14, 15).

INTERPRETATION

In this poem, the prophet used Babylon to represent every powerful and wealthy nation. He chose a day when there were no images of the gods in Babylon, in order to make it clear that he was speaking directly about the nation itself. This nation did not know the God of Israel, and yet the prophet said that its people were responsible to the God who created all the universe and even 'planted' the nations (40.24). The servants of the God of Israel had a message for all nations because their God was the Creator of the nations also.

GOD'S LAMENT (vv. 1–7)

1. *The failure of a strong wealthy nation makes God sad.* The first part of the poem is a lament about a beautiful, powerful queen who became a slave. In the poet's imagination God was speaking the words of this lament because He was sorry about Babylon's failure. Amos also used this sort of song to show God's sadness over the failure of Israel (Amos 5.1–2). And Jeremiah described God's grief over the destruction of Moab (Jer. 48. 32, 36). This prophet was even bolder than Jeremiah, in using this sort of song about the mighty tyrant, Babylon. He did not agree with other writers of the Old Testament (Ps. 137.8–9; Jer. 51.48–9; Nah. 3.19) who said that those who are opppressed should rejoice when the oppressor is defeated. The prophet said God was sad for two reasons. First, God had 'planted' Babylon and knew that Babylon was a nation which could make a good contribution to the family of nations. Second, the people of Babylon would have to suffer.

2. *There is no place for human vengeance on a fallen oppressor* (v. 3). This prophet agreed with the writers of Psalm 94.1 and Deuteronomy 32.35, who declared that God alone must be judge between nations. Human revenge only creates more hatred. Those who turn to God for salvation must leave it to God to set things right. They must not take revenge into their own hands. Paul gave the early Christians the same advice (Rom. 12.19–21).

3. *Powerful nations must remember the limitations of their power* (vv. 5–7). When the prophet said that God gave His people into the control of Babylon, he meant that God would use Babylon's power for His own purpose. God would use Babylon to punish His people for their rebellion (40.2), to purify them from their evil ways (48.10), and to prepare them for their mission to the nations (42.1–4, 21). But the Babylonians went beyond God's purpose, and put oppressive burdens on the captive Israelite slaves, in order to support their own imperial power. In the New Testament, we see that Paul understood God's purpose for rulers (Rom. 13.1–7). The author of Revelation, also, saw how Rome had exceeded the limits of God's purpose by misusing her power (Rev. 13.1–10; 18.2–3).

Some present-day Christians say that God gave many nations and peoples into the control of colonial powers in past years for His own purpose. If this is true, we must ask whether those nations, or the powerful nations of today, are not exceeding the mandate given them by God.

4. *Great wealth must serve justice and mercy* (vv. 6–7). 'On the aged you made your yoke exceedingly heavy.' The Babylonians mercilessly exploited the slaves in order to increase the wealth of their empire. Their official policy was aimed only at gaining more wealth. They had no concern for those poorer than themselves. The lesson for the nations was clear: great wealth without mercy and justice cannot endure. Consider Babylon!

FALSE SECURITY (vv. 8–13)

5. *Self-indulgent luxury with oppression of the weak is against God's will* (vv. 8–9). The prophet called Babylon a 'lover of luxuries', as the prophets of former times had spoken of the ruling classes of Israel (Amos. 4.1; 6, 4, 7; Isa. 3.16, 18–23). Today wealthy people can live in beautiful homes, eat rich food, ride in expensive automobiles, send their children to good schools, and take their vacation in distant lands. Many do not trouble themselves about justice and mercy for the weak and aged. It is too easy for them to shut their eyes to the sufferings of the poor. The people of the rich nations may be unwilling to look honestly at the inequality between the peoples of the world, and to accept that they may have to give up some of their luxuries to save others from starvation.

6. *Technology used for wicked ends is against God's will* (vv. 10–11). The prophet used the words 'wisdom and knowledge'. We may interpret them to mean the skills we now call industrial, electronic, nuclear, and financial technology. These skills add greatly to the power and wealth of nations. They also help to increase the inequality between the rich nations and poor nations. The prophet was saying that technology must serve the benefit of *all* the world's people. If it is used for selfish purposes, it will lead to destruction.

7. *A religion of national success is against God's will* (vv. 12–13). By 'enchantments and sorceries' the prophet meant the practices of

'The people of Babylon would have to suffer': they had 'aimed only at getting wealth . . . had no concern for those poorer than themselves' (pp. 99 and 100).

Rich tourists on holiday in Puerto Rico sit up far into the night at the gambling tables, hoping to gain still greater wealth.

In what ways, if any, are they likely to suffer, or cause others to suffer, as a result of their riches? In what ways are wealthy nations likely to suffer if they misuse their power and exploit those poorer than themselves?

Babylonian religion, including the study of the movements of the stars and planets (v. 12). All of these practices were intended to make Babylon 'succeed' (v. 12), i.e. to maintain itself as the most powerful and wealthy nation in the whole known world. The prophet was saying that this is the wrong idea of what religion should be. Religion should not be used merely to increase a nation's power. It should be a way for a nation to live according to the purposes of God, and within the limits set by His will.

GOD'S JUDGEMENT (vv. 14, 15)

8. *Nations cannot be God.* Two themes dominate this poem: the pride of Babylon, and the judgement of God. 'Babylon without her gods' showed that Babylon herself was trying to act like God: 'I shall be a mistress forever . . . I am and there is none beside me . . . no one sees me' (vv. 7, 8, 10). These boasts show the inner nature of powerful and wealthy nations or groups of people. This is the message of the story of the Tower of Babel (Gen. 9.1–11). For this reason, the Servant people must help all nations to develop in ways that are based on justice, and which reflect God's design and purpose for all His creation (42.1–4).

NOTES

47.1. Virgin daughter of Babylon: This is a symbolic way of saying that Babylon had not yet been humbled by an enemy. The same picture-language is used to describe Egypt (Jer. 46.11) and Israel (Amos. 5.2).
Sit (also in v. 5) can also mean 'dwell'. It thus means a kind of existence in dust and darkness.
Dust is symbolic of a death-like existence, as in 1 Sam. 2.8; Psalm 22.15, 29; Isa. 29.4; Lam. 3.29. It emphasizes the frailty and weakness of human existence, as in Ps. 103.14 and 104.29.
47.2. Grind meal: This was the job of women in ancient West Asia, as in Exodus 11.5; Job 31.10; and Matthew 24.41. Babylon, once a mighty queen, will be reduced to the level of a female salve.
Pass through rivers: This refers to the experience of captivity and exile. For Israel, however, it would be the experience of the missionary journey, as in 43.2.
47.4. Lord of Hosts: See note on 44.6. This title is important here because of the reference to astrologers. See note on 40.26.
47.8. I am, and there is none beside me: This had been the proud boast of Assyria which was now in ruins (Zeph. 2.15). It was very similar to the message of the Servant witnesses about God (43.11; 45.22), and shows that Assyria was claiming that her god, Asshur, was supreme.
A widow: The 'virgin' of v. 1 is called a 'widow' in this verse. This also is symbolic language, meaning the loss of security, and oppression by the powerful.

The loss of children: Children are the hope for future continuation across the generations. Loss of children would mean no hope for the future. An ancient description of a defeated Israel on the stele of the Pharaoh Merneptah reads 'Israel is ravaged and has no offspring.' If we understand 'children' as dependent cities (see note on 40.9), the word could also mean loss of territory and of financial support.

47.9. Sorceries: In using this sort of magic the Israelites were influenced by Baalism (2 Kings 9.22). It was widely practised in Israel (2 Chron. 33.6). Covenant law (Exod. 22.18; Deut. 18.10–11) and prophetic teaching (Mic. 5.12; Mal. 3.5) were aimed at driving out these practices.

Enchantments: From the root word in Hebrew, it is possible to see this as a sort of magic performed by tying knots as charms.

47.10. You said in your heart: Notice that there is no reference to Marduk or Nebo or any of the gods. By these words the prophet was saying that these were gods which the nation had created for itself.

47.11. Cannot atone: This is probably a reference to a magical rite intended to stop the activities of an evil demon.

Expiate means to cover over sins by a sacrifice, and so to avoid punishment for sin.

You know nothing: Compare 'your knowledge' in v. 10.

47.12. Laboured from your youth: This describes the enormous amount of effort, and thought, which had been used to develop a system of magic and enchantments from the beginning of Babylonian power.

47.13. Counsels: See notes on 41.28; 45.21; 46.10, 11.

Who predict: Literally, 'those causing (you) to know'. Compare with vv. 10 and 11, where knowledge is mentioned.

47.14. Stubble means the short dry stalks of grass or grain left after the cutting or the harvest. In 40.24 and 41.2, stubble is a symbol for kings, rulers, and princes who are destroyed by enemies. Here the magicians and astrologers are fuel for the fire, as in Exodus 15.7; Joel 2.5; Nahum 1.10.

Fire – like the fire which destroyed Jerusalem (42.25). In Isaiah 10.17, the Holy One of Israel is described as a flame. See also 30.30; 33.14; 65.15–16.

No coal for warming oneself: A reference to 44.15, 16, 19.

47.15. Each one in his own direction: A description of religious chaos, giving no help to the people in the disaster which engulfs them.

To save you: See note on 43.3. Also 44.17, 20; 45.15, 17, 21, 22, 46.2, 4, 7.

STUDY SUGGESTIONS

REVIEW OF CONTENT

1. The author of Isa. 40—55 spoke of the fall of Babylon at a time when Babylon was without her gods. What time was this?

2. For what reason did the prophet speak to the exiles about the fall of Babylon?
3. What is the form of vv. 1–7? What does this tell us about God's attitude toward Babylon?
4. What is the probable effect of human revenge?
5. What was God's purpose in giving His people into the control of Babylon?
6. How did the Babylonians treat the aged Israelite captives?
7. What are the responsibilities of those who are wealthy?
8. What was the aim of Babylonian religion?
9. What are the two themes of this poem?

APPLICATION, DISCUSSION, RESEARCH

10. What historical event, if any, has there been in your country or region which might be compared with the fall of Babylon in 539 BC? Which of the eight lessons from Isa. 47 are relevant to that event?
11. Read Psalm 137.8–9, Jeremiah 51.48–9, Nahum 3.19. In what way do these passages differ from Isa. 47.1–7 in the attitude toward a fallen oppressor which they express? Which passage is closest to the ideas expressed in the New Testament? Give an example from the teachings of Jesus, or of Paul.
12. List five activities which are possible for wealthy people, but not possible for the poor?
13. (a) Read Rom. 12.19–21, and compare this passage with Isa. 47.3. Give one example, from history or from your own experience, of the destructive effects of human revenge.
    (b) What is the difference between punishment and revenge?
14. Think of a country or a people (perhaps your own) which has been a colony in the past.
    (a) List the possible purposes of God in giving that people or country into the control of the colonial power.
    (b) In what ways do you think the colonial power helped or hindered the purposes of God?
15. The attitude of a people towards its weak and powerless members is shown by its laws. In what way do the laws of society in your country today, and the way those laws are enforced, (a) show mercy, (b) show *no* mercy, to the weak and powerless?
16. Compare Isa. 47.8–9 with James 5.1–6. How are they (a) alike, (b) different, (c) relevant to society today?
17. The gap between rich and poor seems to be growing wider in the world today. Suggest two ways in which Christians can act to close that gap.
18. Technological advance depends on research, education, investment of funds, and national policy.
    (a) For what purposes should nations use technological skills?

   (b) Does God want all nations to possess advanced technology?
   (c) Is technology always of benefit to a nation?
   (d) Can a nation survive in today's society without modern technology?
   Give reasons for your answers.
19. Discuss the following possible reasons for the failure of Babylon:
   (a) The people worshipped idols;
   (b) They practised injustice;
   (c) They imagined that their power and wealth were eternal;
   (d) They did not know God;
   (e) Their religion was aimed at national prosperity;
   (f) They oppressed the weak and poor.

48.1–22
The Redeemed Rebel
After April, 539 BC

BACKGROUND AND OUTLINE

As New Year 539 passed, and the time of liberation from Babylonian oppression came nearer, the prophet turned again to the inner problems of the community of exiles. This poem is the last in which he mentioned Cyrus, probably because he came to see that his most important task from that point on was to train his people for their future mission.

As we have seen from his earlier poems, this prophet who proclaimed salvation was also a man of conflict. Many of his people refused to accept his message, and their opposition seems to have upset him. Two men who *did* accept his message, were also men of conflict. Jesus of Nazareth came into sharp conflict with the religious leaders of his day, and died by crucifixion. Paul of Tarsus also suffered much because of the opposition of his fellow Jews, as well as that of some of the Jewish Christians.

In all his poems dealing with the failures of his people, the prophet also spoke of God's forgiving and redeeming power. Through this power, God would overcome their hard hearts, in order to claim them as His servants for accomplishing His purpose in the world. The two themes of rebellion and redemption give this poem its structure and message.

Main theme: The Redeemed Rebel

Part 1. The rebellion of Jacob (1–8)
Vv. 1–2: Insincere religion.

105

Vv. 3–5: Treating God as an idol.
Vv. 6–8: Betraying God.
Part 2. The Redemption of Jacob (9–21)
Vv. 9–11: Forgiveness of sins.
Vv. 12–17: The New Thing: Completing the garden (12–13); Cyrus's victory (14–15); God's people on the way (16–17).
Vv. 18,19: The fulfilment of redemption.
Vv. 20, 21: The mission of the redeemed.
Postscript (v. 22)

READING SUGGESTIONS

Read through the whole chapter with the outline for a guide. Some verses may not be clear. Do not be worried about them on your first reading.

Words for hearing are much used in this poem. Find them. For what reason did the prophet use them so often?

Look for *words which are repeated several times*, and think what the prophet meant by them, e.g: 'name', 'call', 'declare', 'proclaim', 'Redeemer' and 'redeem', 'for the sake of'.

Look for *themes repeated from other poems*: 'former things' (this is the seventh time!), 'new thing' (the third time), 'God of Israel', 'forgiveness of sins' (third reference), 'redemption', 'descendants of Israel', 'peace' (*shalom*), 'the end of the earth'.

INTERPRETATION

REBEL, YET REDEEMED

Before we consider the first part of this poem in detail, it will be helpful to summarize what the prophet had said in previous poems about the sins of the Israelites:

1. They were *blind to God's purpose* and *deaf to God's call* for service in the time to come (42.19, 21, 23; see p. 45);

2. The previous generations before the destruction of Jerusalem *had not obeyed God's law* (revealed teaching, 42.24; see pp. 45, 47);

3. In their temple worship and religious leadership they were *not faithful to God* (42.22, 27, 28, see pp. 45, 47).

4. Some of them were *dreaming of restoring past glories* in Jerusalem, while others were *despondent about past failures* (43.18; see p. 57);

5. They were *narrowly nationalistic*, and unwilling to accept the prophet's teaching that God wanted to include the 'nations' in the covenant fellowship (45.9–11; see p. 78);

6. They were *trying to make God into an 'idol'* which they could control, by expecting Him to follow their wishes (46.8–11; see pp. 93, 94).

The prophet's purpose in making these sharp criticisms was constructive in each case. He wanted to help the Israelites (a) to see God's purpose and hear His call, (b) to accept God's teaching in their hearts, (c) to confess their past failures and stop dreaming of restoring the past, (d) to enlarge their vision of God's will towards the 'nations', and (e) to be willing to follow God's guidance. He emphasized that God had forgiven them already, and was waiting for them to turn to Him and make a new beginning.

In this poem, the prophet repeated many of these themes at greater length and with new emphases. His teaching that Israel was a redeemed rebel is very close to ideas expressed by the New Testament writers.

THREE ANCESTORS, THREE ASPECTS OF GOD'S PEOPLE

The prophet began his message by recalling the Israelites' ancestors who symbolized the true nature of God's people. He had already reminded the exiles (41.8) that they shared the mission which God gave to *Abraham*, of being a blessing to the nations, and gathering all nations into a covenant family (see p. 30). Now he mentioned Jacob (Israel) and Judah.

1. *Jacob the rebel.* The prophet had already referred to Jacob as their 'first father', who sinned against God (43.27–28). According to tradition, Jacob wrestled with God (Gen. 32.28), and Hosea interpreted this to mean that Jacob rebelled against God (Hos. 12.2–4). This was the 'Jacob-aspect' of the people of God: blind to God's purpose, deaf to God's call, 'a rebel from birth' (48.8).

2. *Israel the redeemed.* According to tradition, God gave the rebellious Jacob a new name, and blessed him, and gave him a promise that 'a company of nations shall spring from you' (Gen. 32.28, 29; 35.10–11). This was the 'Israel-aspect' of the people of God: chosen, forgiven, redeemed.

3. *Judah, ancestor of David.* According to tradition, Judah was to be the ancestor of a king who would rule the nations (Gen. 49.10). The Israelites believed that King David and his descendants were the fulfilment of this prophecy. In fact no Davidic king ever ruled the 'nations', but many Israelites hoped that one day a descendant of David would actually be king. At the time of the exile, many of the Israelites in Babylon were hoping that a son or grandson of King Jehoiakin would be the anointed king chosen by God. When the prophet called the exiles descendants of the tribe of Judah, he was emphasizing their 'Judah-aspect': they were to be the heirs of the mission of the family of David, not to 'rule' the 'nations' but to lead them to God (Glossary, *King of Israel*).

The prophet's message was this: 'Remember that these three ancestors all live on in you. God needs the strength of "Jacob", the loyalty of "Israel", and the winsomeness of "Judah" or "David"'.

THE 'STIFF NECK OF JACOB'

In v. 4 the prophet used a picture of a man with a neck as stiff as iron, and a forehead as hard as brass. By 'stiff neck' he meant a person who would not bow to accept God's will. A 'brass forehead' meant one who was 'headstrong', and insisted on having his own way. Both Jeremiah and Ezekiel used the same picture to describe God's stubborn people (Jer. 7.26; Ezek. 3.7).

In vv. 1–8 the prophet explained what he meant by this picture:

1. *Insincere religion* (vv. 1, 2). Following his remarks in a previous poem about religion in Jerusalem (see p. 59), the prophet now criticized the people's religious attitudes and practices in Babylon:

(a) *Insincere speech:* They would promise in God's name to do something, and then not do it. Perhaps the prophet was thinking of words they would say at a worship service, and then after the service they would fail to do what they had promised. This was what he meant when he said that they 'swear by the name of the Lord', but 'not in truth'.

(b) *Insincere worship:* The prophet said that they would 'confess the God of Israel', i.e., they would remember God and meditate on His wonderful works. Psalm 77.11–12 describes this kind of religious practice. But the prophet said it was 'not in truth'. It was honouring God with the lips, while the heart was far away (Isa. 29.13; Matt. 15.8–9).

(c) *Insincere holiness:* He said they boasted that they were the holy people of Jerusalem, God's holy city. Probably they were dreaming of restoring Jerusalem just as it had been before (see p. 57). They were not concerned about 'the Holy One of Israel'.

(d) *Insincere prayer:* According to Israelite belief, worshippers should depend on God for help – 'stay themselves on', 'lean on' Him (see Ps. 71.6). The prophet accused the people of saying the words of the prayers without accepting any responsibility or trying to discover God's will. They wanted to have 'strength' without obedience (Isa. 40.21).

All of these practices and attitudes were good in themselves. But the prophets said that they were 'not in truth or right', i.e., the people were not sincere, and were not obeying God's righteous will.

2. *Treating God like an idol.* According to v. 5 the Israelite exiles had some object called 'my idol'. The prophet may not have meant that they had an actual physical object in their hands. He may have been saying, as in a previous poem (see p. 91), that they were trying to influence God and persuade Him to give them what they wanted (see p. 94).

God had rescued the Israelites from Egypt, and brought them victories over their enemies. If they claimed that God acted in these ways because of their demands, that would be treating Him like an 'idol'. But God prevented them from doing this. He announced in advance what He was going to do. This showed them that it was *His* plan and purpose, *not theirs*.

'The prophet . . . criticized the people's religious attitudes and practices' – even those which were 'good in themselves' (p. 108).

Christians often criticize each other. Some, like the members of a revivalist group in the USA (above), may be criticized for paying too much attention to their own holiness. Others may be accused of thinking that the number of services they attend on Sunday – as here in an English parish (below) – is more important than how they live during the week.

What attitudes and practices do you think a modern 'prophet' would chiefly find to criticize among members of your own congregation? How could such criticism be overcome?

3. *Betraying God.* In v. 8, the prophet said that when trouble came the Israelite exiles turned against God. They were like traitors who betray their country in a time of war. They were like a son or daughter who turns against parents, or a man or woman who breaks marriage vows. God had a very important work for the Israelites to do, and He was counting on them to do it. But they couldn't be trusted.

To summarize: The exiles in Babylon were not ready to accept a mission to the ends of the earth; they wanted to return to Jerusalem. They were not willing to be a 'light to the nations'; they wanted to keep God's 'light' for themselves and so build up a strong nation. They did not want to carry God's invitation to all 'nations' to join the covenant fellowship; they wanted to keep the covenant relationship for themselves. They did not want to be God's witness to the 'nations'; they wanted to have God's protection from the 'nations'.

THE REDEMPTION OF JACOB-ISRAEL (vv. 9–21)

The prophet reminded the exiles that God was not content to leave them in their rebellion. The Redeemer would not forget His covenant people, but was at work transforming their inner hearts and their outer situation, so that they would be ready to proclaim the message to the end of the earth: 'The Lord has redeemed Jacob!' (v. 20).

1. *The forgiveness of sins.* (vv. 9–11) This is a vital step in the process of redemption (see pp. 68, 70). The statement in vv. 9–11 is the last of the three declarations of the forgiveness of sins (43.25; 44.22), and is the most detailed and forceful. The prophet used the phrase 'for the sake of . . .' four times to emphasize:

(a) that God's forgiven people should *praise* their Redeemer among the 'nations', and teach the 'nations' to join in this *praise* (see 43.21 and 42.10–12).

(b) that God's forgiven people should show His true *glory* to the 'nations' (Glossary, *Glory*), so that they would not try to find true *glory* in powerless gods or idols.

(c) that God's forgiven people should introduce the 'nations' to God's *name*, which also describes His character: 'I am He', 'first and last', 'Lord of Hosts', 'Redeemer'. Then the nations also would say, 'I am the Lord's (44.5), and be called by His *name* (43.7).

The prophet was telling them for the third time that forgiven sinners have a part to play in God's plan for all the nations. God forgives His people so as to make it possible for them to serve Him.

2. *God's new thing.* (vv. 12–16) In v. 6 the prophet made his last reference to the 'new thing' of God. Vv. 12–17 are his summary of what he meant.

(a) *The completion of the garden* (vv. 12, 13). In 42.9, the prophet suggested that the 'new thing' was like seed planted in the earth, but not yet visible. In 43.19 he said that the new growth was already visible. In 44.3–5, the growth had begun, and in 45.8 it was bearing goood fruit of 'salvation' and 'righteousness'. In 48.12–13 he repeated some ideas from 40.12, 23, 26. With the new garden bearing fruit, God gave permanence and *security* by laying the foundations (Glossary, *Mountains*). He gave *freedom* by stretching out a tent, (Glossory, *World-view*). Then He commanded all nature to work together to make the garden a pleasant place for human beings to live in.

(b) *The victory of Cyrus over Babylon* (vv. 14, 15). In this last reference to Cyrus as God's agent in the new creation, the prophet emphasized God's support for this world leader. He did this to show God's people that their redemption was a part of the historical events of that time.

(c) *God's people on the way* (vv. 16, 17). This is the 'way of the Lord' in the wilderness of the world after the fall of Babylon (40.3; 42.16; 43.19–21). The prophet told the exiles about their part in God's plan. It was so important, that their Redeemer would Himself *teach them* how to work effectively ('to profit'), and would *clear the way* ahead of them as their guide. Perhaps v. 21 belongs here, with the familiar theme of rivers bringing life to the waste places of the earth.

3. *The fulfilment of Redemption* (vv. 18, 19). As they appear here, these words refer to the past. But the Hebrew tenses can also refer to the future, and this seems to be more appropriate. The poem gives a picture of the fulfilment of Israel's redemption, with three aspects: (a) The *shalom* (wholeness) of Israel will be like a river of life for the whole world; (b) Their righteous deeds in response to God's righteous purpose will cover the earth, 'as the waters cover the sea' (Isa. 11.9); (c) The descendants of Israel will be numberless in fulfilment of God's promise to Abraham, that he would be the father of many nations (Gen. 17.5), and in fulfilment of Israel's mission as 'covenant of the people'. We notice the yearning in the words of the Redeemer of the rebel: 'If only you would hearken to my commands . . .'.

4. *The mission of the redeemed* (v. 20). At the climax of the poem, God commands His people to begin the life of obedience:

> Go out from Babylon, go free!
> Shout the news gladly; make it known everywhere:
> 'The Lord has redeemed his servant Israel!'
> (TEV adapted)

Once again, the prophet was offering the people God's call to them to accept His redemption, and to take the message of redemption to all 'nations'.

ADDITIONAL NOTE ON THE INTERPRETATION OF CHAPTER 48

This chapter presents several difficult problems. For example, most scholars agree that v. 22 is an addition by a later editor, but no scholar has yet found a satisfactory interpretation of the second part of v. 16.

There are also problems of unity. Some scholars believe: (1) that an editor arranged this chapter in its present form in the period after the exile; (2) that he put several shorter poems of this prophet together, but perhaps not in the order in which the author composed them; (3) that he added some verses about the sinfulness of the Israelites, the 'holy city', and the 'name' of the Lord in order to make the poems more useful for teaching the Jerusalem community after 538 BC.

In this Guide we agree with other scholars who, in spite of the difficulties, believe that this is a single poem composed by the prophet in the period before the fall of Babylon. The themes of the 'redeemed rebel', the new creation, and others give the poem its unity.

NOTES

48.3. Declared is a form of the verb 'To be clear'. It means to *make* clear or visible. This form shows what happens to the other person. Thus it implies real communication to produce understanding and insight. In vv. 3 and 5, God makes 'the former things' clear. In v. 14 it is 'the new things'. In vv. 6 and 20, Israel as God's messenger must make the new things plain to the nations.

Made them known is a similar form of a verb whose meaning is to 'hear'. It can also be translated 'announce' (v. 5), 'make you hear' (v. 6), and 'proclaim' (v. 20). Emphasis is on the 'hearing' of the spoken word by the listeners. What God made Israel hear (vv. 3, 5, 6), Israel must make the nations hear (v. 20).

48.6. From this time forth is in contrast to 'of old' (vv. 3, 5 and 7). Note the emphasis on the present time in the words 'now' in vv. 7 and 16, and 'today' in v. 7. The author was emphasizing the urgency of the present moment, as in Ps. 95.7 and Heb. 3.13.

48.9. Not cut you off: The penalty for consciously committed sin was to be excluded from the people (Num. 15.30). This decision of God was like the word from Proverbs 23.18: 'Surely there is a future, and your hope will not be cut off.'

48.10. Not like silver: This phrase probably means that pure silver had not yet come out from the refining process (see Is. 1.22).

48.16. Sent me and his spirit: This line does not seem to make sense as it stands. No single interpretation or explanation has been generally accepted.

THE REDEEMED REBEL

48.17. To profit also appears in 44.9, 10 and 47.12. It does not mean personal benefits, but the effective result of action based on truth.

Leads you. The Hebrew word means 'to make a path'. This would mean that God goes ahead of his people to tread down a pathway.

48.19. Your offspring . . . Your descendants. See Glossary.

Like the sand. The ancient promise to Abraham (Gen. 22.17) is repeated for Israel in Jer. 33.22. The historian who wrote 1 Kings 4.20 thought that the promise had come true in the days of Solomon.

48.21. This verse may be (a) a memory of the past, or (b) a hope for the future. In Hebrew, the verb tenses are flexible.

Deserts. The Hebrew word should be translated as 'waste places' here as in 49.19; 51.3; and 52.9. In 44.26 it is translated as 'ruins'. It does not mean the wilderness of the first Exodus, but the countries which had been ruined by war.

48.22. This verse is identical with 57.21. It does not seem to make sense here. It may have been added by a scribe.

STUDY SUGGESTIONS

REVIEW OF CONTENT

1. What are the two chief themes of this poem?
2. What were the six sins of the Israelites which the prophet had pointed out in previous poems?
3. What was the meaning of 'Jacob', 'Israel', and 'Judah' for the prophet?
4. What did the prophet mean by the 'iron neck' and 'brass forehead'?
5. What were the four 'insincerities' in the religion of the Israelite exiles?
6. What did the prophet mean by 'treating God like an idol'?
7. In what way were the Israelite exiles 'traitors' to God?
8. In what three passages did the prophet tell the Isarelites that God had forgiven their sins?
9. What three things did God want his forgiven people to do?
10. In what way did God complete his new garden?
11. In what two ways would God help his people in their work?
12. What three things would happen when the redemption of God's people was complete?
13. Where should the exiles go *from*, and where should they announce the news of redemption?

APPLICATION, DISCUSSION, RESEARCH

14. How does the theme of the 'redeemed rebel' appear in the following New Testament passages? Gal. 4.4, 5; Col. 1.13, 14.
15. In what way do 'Jacob', 'Israel', and 'Judah' represent three aspects of the life of an individual, and of the Church?

16. In what way can 'truth' and 'right' (God's righteous will, see Glossary, *Righteousness*) be standards for judging the insincerity of: (a) our speech, (b) our worship, (c) our holiness and (d) our prayer?
17. If I pray regularly, read the Bible, and go to Church, God will
    (a) always do what I ask;
    (b) help me to serve Him and my fellow human beings more effectively;
    (c) assign me a small part in His plan for all mankind;
    (d) give me success in whatever I do.
    Which of these statements treats God like an 'idol'? Which do you think represent the right attitude toward God? Give reasons for your answers.
18. In what ways does a self-centred Church or individual 'betray' God?
19. Suggest some activities which would show others: (a) the praise, (b) the glory, (c) the name, of God. (Examples: A public procession of Catholic and Protestant Christians to show unity; a project to help people of another religious faith; support for a person who has been unjustly imprisoned.)
20. In the prophet's thought, 'garden' is a society or group, large or small, where there is love, justice, and peace. But these 'gardens' tend to be temporary. How can we help them to become more permanent, and yet preserve their freedom?
21. God's will is that His people should 'work effectively' (Isa. 48.17).
    (a) What obstacles are there to the effective working of the Church?
    (b) How do we measure effectiveness?
    (c) How does God help us to be more effective?
22. God goes ahead of us to prepare the way (v. 17). How did God prepare the way in your country before the coming of Christianity?
23. Read 1 Peter 1.4–5.
    (a) Do the 'hope', 'inheritance kept in heaven', and 'salvation' mentioned there, have any relationship with the picture of the fulfilment of redemption in Isa. 48.18, 19? *Should* there be a relationship?
    (b) Now find similarities in Rev. 7.9; 21.24; 22.2 to the picture in Isa. 48.18, 19.
24. Where in your country should the 'message of redemption' be proclaimed? How would you go about planning for this?

Special Note B
Who wrote the Book of Isaiah?

Questions about authorship and about the date when a book was written are modern questions. People in the ancient world did not ask such questions. We need to keep this in mind when we read the New Testament and find in it quotations from the Old Testament. The writers usually introduced a quotation from the Psalms with the words, 'as David says . . .' (Mark 12.35–37). If he wished to quote from the first five books of the Old Testament, the writer would not mention the name of a particular book like Genesis or Numbers, but simply say 'Moses said . . .' (Mark 10.3). People today would be likely to ask 'Who wrote this passage?' and 'When did he write it?' A present-day reader who is completely respectful of the authority of the Bible as inspired by God 'for teaching, for reproof, for correction, and for training in righteousness' (2 Tim. 3.16), will want to look for the answers to such questions with a listening mind, in order to gain a clearer understanding of the word of God and its meaning for our own time. There is no word in scripture against such study if it is done in faith, 'Where the Spirit of the Lord is there is freedom' (2 Cor. 3.17).

The quotations from the Book of Isaiah which we find in the New Testament are like those from the Psalms and the Pentateuch. Quotations from this book are often (though not always) accompanied by the words 'as Isaiah said'. But this was not in order to answer the modern question of authorship, it was simply to identify the source of the quotation from the book of Isaiah. See, for example, the following passages:

> Matt. 3.3; 4.14, 15; 8.17; 12.17–21; 13.14, 15; 15.7–9;
> Mark 1.3; 7.6, 7;
> Luke 3.4, 5; 4.18, 19;
> John 1.23; 12.38, 40, 41;
> Acts 8.32, 33; 28.25–27;
> Rom. 9.27–28, 29; 10.16, 20–21; 15.12.

In order to look for an answer to these questions which people of today ask, it is necessary to study each section of the book of Isaiah for evidence of the time from which it comes and the person who wrote it. Attentive readers will note a clear connection between Isaiah 1—39 and 40—66. A title used fourteen times for God in chapters 40—66 is 'Holy One of Israel'. This title appears 12 times in Isaiah 1—39. The similarity between chapters 35 and 40—55 is so marked that some scholars have thought that they must come from the same author (compare 35.10 with 51.11). The prophecies about the coming of the Messiah in 9.2–7 and 11.1–9 are written in a style something like that in chapters 40—55, though there are differences. The world-wide view of 40—66 is found in 2.2–4, as well as in 24–27. The author of 44.28 and 45.1, who described Cyrus as God's shepherd, may have been developing the thought of Isaiah in 10.5 about Assyria as God's battering ram. The author of 65.25 repeats words and phrases found in 11.6–9.

Some scholars have concluded from these similarities that a single author composed the entire sixty-six chapters of the Book of Isaiah in the eighth century BC. Others have examined the evidence and have thought it more likely that the book reflects a continuity of tradition which was carried on for several hundred years by a group of disciples such as those mentioned in Isaiah 8.16. While they waited and hoped for God's 'time of favour' (49.8), when the light of deliverance would shine on those in darkness (9.2; 42.6; 49.6; 58.8; 60.1–3), they made it their task to preserve and expand on the words of the great prophet Isaiah. According to this view, Isaiah 40—66 forms the latter part of a stream of prophetic writing which began with Isaiah in the eighth century and continued for several hundred years before it was collected in a single scroll as we have it today.

Evidence for this view is of three kinds.

1. First is the *historical background* reflected in chapters 40—66. In chapters 1—39 the historical background is the kingdoms of Judah and Israel at the time of Assyrian power about 740–700 BC. The background of chapters 40—66 is the fall of Babylon, the victories of Cyrus, and the rebuilding of Jerusalem in the period before and after 538 BC. It seems reasonable, therefore, to think that they were composed at that time.

2. The *message* of chapters 40—66 also points to the sixth century BC. In chapters 40—55 the prophet speaks words of comfort and encouragement to a despairing people. They were suffering oppression (51.13), and thought that God had forgotten them (40.7). He proclaimed the day of deliverance to them, and told them that God had a mission for them to perform for the world of nations (42.6). This corresponds to the situation in Babylon before 538 BC

3. The *literary style* found in chapters 40—66 is different from that of chapters 1—39. The length of individual poems is longer in chapters 40—66. The composition is more polished. It is a dramatic, singing style. In addition there are certain characteristics which are typical of this writer such as the following.

The frequent use of *questions* beginning with 'who' (40.12, 13, 14, 18, 25, 26; 41.2–4, 26), 'what' (40.18; 45.9, 10), 'why' (40.27; 55.2), or 'where' (40.13, 15).

Frequent *repetitions* for emphasis, such as single words (40.1), key words like 'cry' (40.2, 3, 6), 'sit' (47.1, 5), or key phrases like 'fear not' (41.10, 13, 14), 'I am the first and I am the last' (41.4; 44.6; 48.12), 'I am the Lord and there is no other' (45.5, 6, 18, 22; 46.9), 'Redeemer and Holy One' (41.14; 48.17; 49.7; 54.5).

These marks of style give evidence of a person with great literary gifts. His way of speaking and writing was his own, and not the same as that of the author of chapters 1—39.

The view we take in this Guide is that the sixty-six chapters of the Book of Isaiah form a body of tradition beginning with the prophet Isaiah of Jerusalem and continued by his disciples over a period of two or three hundred years.

Here is a general outline of the book as it stands:

Chapters

1—12   Biographical notes about Isaiah, and Isaiah's prophetic messages of warning and promise to the people of Judah, mainly in the time of the Syro-Ephraimite war, 734–732 BC.

13—23   A collection of prophetic messages, some by Isaiah, some by later disciples, about what God will do to the nations.

24—27   A collection of prophetic messages by later disciples about the final judgement of the world and the victory of God.

28—32   Isaiah's prophetic messages of warning and promise to the people of Judah, mainly in the reign of Hezekiah, 715–687 BC.

33—35   Prophetic messages by later disciples about the glorious future, and the dark days which will precede it.

36—39   Historical notes on events in Hezekiah's reign related to the work of Isaiah, mainly repeated from 2 Kings 18.13—20.19.

40—55   Prophetic messages of hope by a later disciple for the Israelite exiles in Babylon, 541–539 BC.

56—66   Prophetic messages of warning and hope by one or more disciples for those who returned to Jerusalem, 538–515 BC.

STUDY SUGGESTIONS

REVIEW OF CONTENT

1. There are two different ideas about who wrote the Book of Isaiah. Some scholars have concluded that a single author composed the whole book. Others have thought that the book reflects a continuity of tradition carried on by a group of disciples for several hundred years (p. 116).
   What are the chief sorts of evidence on which each of these two different views is based?

2. How does Isaiah 8.16 help you to understand the preservation of Isaiah's teachings and spirit?

3. (a) What special title for God is used many times in Isaiah 1—39, and also in Isaiah 40—66?

(b) Read Isaiah 35, and list some of the similarities between that chapter and the ideas expressed in Isaiah 40—66.
(c) What words and phrases in Isaiah 65.25 are also found in Isaiah 11.6–9?
4. (a) What is the historical background to Isaiah 1—39?
(b) List two events referred to in Isaiah 40—66 which suggest that these poems were composed around the year 538 BC.
5. What are some of the ways in which the literary style of 40—66 differs from that of 1—39?

6. Read Isaiah 40.1–11 and make a list of all the words which mean communication by word of mouth, such as 'cry', 'speak', etc. Who is the communicator, who receives the communication, and what is the message in each case?
7. Read the following New Testament passages. Find the passage in Isaiah which the New Testament writer was quoting in each case, and say what you think his reason was for quoting it.
Matt. 3.1–3; Matt. 8.14–17; Mark 7.5–8; Luke 4.14–19; John 12.36b–41; Rom. 9.27–33.

49.1–26
The Mission and its Fulfilment
After April, 539 BC

BACKGROUND AND OUTLINE

Today many Christians ask questions about the mission of God's people in a world which does not know God. They ask what should be the message and the work of mission, and what sort of results should we hope for. As in the days of this prophet, there are people today who think in a self-centred way, and regard mission as an expansion of the power and influence of the sending Church. There are also those who believe that no mission is possible, because the Church is too weak, or too heavily burdened with past guilt.

The previous poem was for the self-centred ones among the Israelite exiles. This poem was for those who were discouraged. Their

118

discouragement is described in vv. 7, 14, and 24, and may be summarized as follows: (1) We have no 'name' or prestige among the 'nations'; (2) God does not care about us any more; (3) There is no way out of our present difficulties. The prophet had often referred to the discouragement of his people. He was urging them to stand up and prepare for their coming mission.

Main theme: The Mission and its Fulfilment

Part 1: Mission (vv. 1–12)

Vv. 1–3: A message to distant nations: God's call, care, and commission.
V. 4: Through weakness to strength.
V. 5: The new Israel among the 'nations'.
V. 6: Salvation in each nation.
V. 7: The first result: Kings turn to God.
V. 8a: A day of salvation.
Vv. 8b–9a: Four sorts of work.
Vv. 9b–12: The great procession.
Interlude: Hymn of rejoicing (v. 13)

Part 2. Fulfilment (vv. 14–26)

Vv. 14–16: God's mother love.
Vv. 17–19: The broad land needed for the new Israel.
Vv. 18, 20–21: The new children of Zion.
Vv. 22–23: The Covenant celebration.
Vv. 24–26: For all mankind to know the Saviour.

READING SUGGESTIONS

TIME REFERENCE

This poem is about future events. In Part 1 the author describes events which he thought would happen soon. The events in Part 2 would take place in the distant future, as a result of the work of the Servant described in Part 1. Vv. 14 and 24 tell us that the prophet was using this picture of future events to encourage the exiles in Babylon.

IMPORTANT WORDS AND THEMES

'Coastlands' and 'the end of the earth' in vv. 1 and 6 have the same meaning (see Glossary). The words of the servant to the people at the 'coastlands' are to explain why he was there – not as punishment, but as a commission from God. This prophet used the words 'from afar' only three times: twice in this poem, and once in 43.6. What was his purpose in using them twice here? For whom does God act to 'save' in vv. 6, 8, 25? Who are 'these' (used three times each in vv. 12 and 21)? Note the repetition of the words: 'strength', 'peoples', 'nations', 'kings', 'desolate' places, the idea of the children of the new Israel'.

KEY THEMES FROM PREVIOUS POEMS

Notice the following: 'Servant', 'from the womb', 'glorified', 'strength', 'light to the nations', 'covenant to the people', 'salvation', 'saviour', 'Holy One of Israel', 'God has forgotten me', 'recompense', 'sons and daughters', 'wait for' the Lord, 'all flesh', 'Redeemer'.

INTERPRETATION

At the end of the previous poem the 'redeemed rebel' was commanded to leave Babylon's ruins, go out to the farthest places of the earth, and proclaim redemption (48.20). The prophet meant that the Servant of God should carry the invitation to 'all the ends of the earth' to 'turn to God and be saved' (45.22). He had told the exiles that God would 'teach them to be effective' (48.17, see p. 111). In this poem he developed his ideas of 'effectiveness' in mission.

In the first part, the prophet used the word 'servant' to refer to the group of faithful exiles going out to the 'nations'. In the second part, he referred to 'Zion' as the mother of the 'new Israel' that would come to her from the 'nations'.

THE MISSION

The direction of mission: This poem begins with an imaginary address by the Servant to the distant nations. He did not think of the mission as an expansion of God's people from Jerusalem out to the nations and a gathering of the nations to Jerusalem. Some people call this way of thinking the 'centrifugal' (outgoing) and 'centripetal' (inbringing) directions of mission. This prophet thought of the mission as being *toward* a future Zion *by way of* the nations as far as the 'end of the earth'. He thought of the goal of mission as in the future. Until that time, all those who turn to God along the way would join in the mission, as in a procession toward the goal.

THE MESSAGE OF THE 'SERVANT' (vv. 1–6)

In this imaginary speech of the Servant, the prophet was teaching his people in Babylon what they should be prepared to say, and how they should understand their work.

1. *Your own life story is the beginning of your message* (vv. 1–3). The task of a witness (43.10, 12) is to tell what he or she has seen and heard. The servant would be a living witness to the reality of God. The prophet suggested six things from the Servants' life story:
    (a) God called them from the distant nations (the end of the earth, 41.8),

'This poem was for those who were discouraged. . . . All the sufferings of that time were only the shadow of God's hand' (pp. 118, 121).

It is easy for Christians to become discouraged about their mission when they see people oppressed by poverty like this woman in the slums of Santiago in Chile, or by the cruelties of war like these Bihari refugees in Bangladesh.

What should be the message and the mission of God's servants in that sort of situation?

and so they are really *brothers and sisters* of the people they will be talking to.

(b) *They belonged to God* and were absolutely loyal to Him because He gave them their name (43.1). Giving a name means that God has *a personal relationship* with the person He names.

(c) They had *important teachings* that would affect the lives of the nations. By 'sword' the prophet probably meant the law or revealed teaching (42.4, 42.21, 51.7) given to them at the Covenant ceremony at Mount Sinai – i.e. their chief weapon or tool for doing the Lord's work.

(d) *They had personally experienced the salvation of God* from the fires of the destruction of Jerusalem (42.25), and would experience deliverance by Him from the ruins of Babylon (49.24–25). All the sufferings of that time were only the shadow of God's hand.

(e) God had *prepared them* over these long years, as a warrior polishes an arrow and keeps it in his quiver for the *right time*. God would send them out among the nations like an arrow: 'The Lord's arrow of salvation' (2 Kings 13.17), for His 'day of salvation' (Isa. 49.8).

(f) To summarize, they are *God's ambassador* or Servant to the nations, so that the nations will praise Him.

These thoughts are helpful to Christians today when they consider their own witness among those who do not know God.

2. *Do not conceal your own failures* (v. 4). The prophet told the people that they must be honest about themselves. They must not pretend that a person who follows God has constant success. They should tell how their own nation was destroyed, and their religion became empty. They should go to the nations not as victors, but as weak human beings, whose only strength came from God. Paul was giving a similar witness when he said that God's power was 'made perfect in weakness' (2 Cor. 12.9).

3. *Tell them about the new Israel of God* (vv. 5–6). At first we may think it strange that the Servant's task of restoring Israel as a new people, was a part of the message of the Servant to the nations. It seems as though the restoration of Israel should be an internal affair, and no concern of the nations. But the prophet probably had two reasons for saying what he did:

(a) There were many Israelite exiles scattered among the nations. It would be natural for the Israelites from Babylon to make contact with their fellow Israelites in the nations. But the prophet wanted to emphasize to the exiles in Babylon that they had a more important task than to invite only other *Israelites* to join them on their way to Jerusalem. So he said 'it is too light a thing . . .'.

(b) The prophet also wanted to emphasize that the new Israel would not be a restoration of the kingdom of David. His model was 'the tribes of Jacob'. He seems to have thought that the tribal structure of Israel at the time of the Judges was a better pattern for the new Israel than the monarchy. In that pattern, each tribe could maintain its own customs and tradition, and at the same time share with the other tribes its faith in God and its membership in the covenant. All tribes could join in the yearly covenant renewal ceremony. They would also join forces in the campaigns against their common enemies. This pattern was well suited to the new Israel, because those groups in each nation who were faithful to God could become members of a covenant federation.

4. *Show them the reality of salvation* (v. 6). The focus of v. 6 is not on the new Israel, but on the new nations. Salvation is God's will for each nation, according to His design of creation for freedom, stability, and wholeness of life. The meaning of salvation in each society will depend on the cultural background and historical situation in that society. God sends His Servant people to be present in each society in order to listen and learn from that society. Then, in the light of God's revelation, they will show what salvation means in that particular time and place. Today we would ask questions like these: Where are human rights most violated? Where is stability most needed? Where is life most broken or crushed down? Where is it necessary to destroy the old, or to build the new?

THE WORK OF MISSION (vv. 8–9a)

The work of mission is to co-operate with God in His saving work. In this section the prophet gave the exiles a summary of what the saving work of God would be in the world after the fall of Babylon.

He told them that that period would be a 'day of salvation' for all nations, and that God would help His Servant people to take part in the work of salvation. Paul said that the 'day of salvation' was whenever a person or a group was open to God's saving work (1 Cor. 6.2). Probably the prophet thought that the people of the world would be especially open to God's saving work after the fall of Babylon.

The prophet mentioned four ways in which the Servant people would participate in the saving activity of God, thus summarizing what he had said before: (1) restoring a lost unity ('covenant to the people', as in 42.6), (2) restoring a disordered earth, (3) resettling desolate ruins, (4) calling prisoners out of darkness.

Today we can participate by working for better relations between races and nations, in industry, in homes, and between individuals; by helping slum dwellers or refugees to find housing; changing unjust laws; leading people to the inner liberation that comes from a true knowledge of the Saviour.

THE GREAT PROCESSION (vv. 9b–12)

Next the author took his listeners further on into the future, after the work of mission has begun to take effect. We see a numerous company of people walking over mountains and desolate places, on their way to 'Zion'. This procession is not like the first Exodus. The people are protected from heat and cold, hunger and thirst. God is in their midst to give them 'travelling mercies'. This beautiful picture inspired the writer of the Book of Revelation when he described the community of the saved from every nation standing before the throne of the Lamb (Rev. 7.16). By his use of the phrase 'from afar', repeated from v. 1, (see Glossary) the prophet was saying that this procession would be composed of people from the distant nations who had heard the witness, seen the life of the Servant, and turned to God.

Probably the prophet meant to include in this procession the 'kings and princes' of v. 7, who would see the light of salvation in the Servant, and turn to Israel's God. There would also be people like the temple slaves (44.5), and the merchants (45.14), who had already turned to God as their Saviour.

Perhaps the author meant his listeners to hear this procession singing the hymn of rejoicing in v. 13 as they went on their way! This verse leads us on to the fulfilment of the mission in Part 2.

FULFILMENT

In these verses the prophet took his listeners to the distant goal of the mission, the final formation of the new Israel as the 'children' of 'mother Zion'. Perhaps he was comparing this gathering of the new Israel with the convenant renewal ceremony of the period of the Judges. At that time all the tribes assembled at the religious centre to hear the law read, and take their vows of loyalty to God.

The land needed for the new Israel must be broader than the land of Canaan (17.19). The prophet: (a) emphasized the great numbers of the new Israel, as in 49.19, and (b) told them that a new idea of the 'land' was necessary for the new Israel. Perhaps he was thinking of the whole earth, as in the first part of the poem.

The new children of Zion will be from the 'nations' (18, 20–21). The new children would belong to 'Mother Zion', but they were not born in Israel, nor brought up by the mother. And the mother would not even recognize her own children! Perhaps the prophet was trying to explain that the work of the servant people in each 'nation' would result in the growth of a group of people who would be loyal to Israel's God, while remaining citizens of their own nations. Thus, the mother would not recognize her children because of their strange language, dress, skin-colour, culture, and manner of life.

Christians sometimes think of the Church as a mother whose children come from all nations and peoples, very much like 'Mother Zion'. They think of the Christian community in each land as the beginning of a renewed nation which will become a member of the family of the new Israel at some time in the future.

The nations will become members of the covenant community (22–23). Probably these verses describe a ceremony through which the nations will be accepted into the covenant community, as in the days of the tribal confederation in ancient Israel. The kings of the nations who have seen the light of God's salvation in Israel (v. 7) will bow down in deep respect before mother Zion, as they present their 'children' to her.

All mankind will be able to know the Saviour (24–26). The prophet assured the discouraged exiles once more that God was more powerful than the strongest tyrant (Babylonia). Then he told them that God's purpose in saving Israel is that all mankind should come to know Israel's Saviour. By these words at the end of the poem he emphasized once more Israel's mission to all the peoples of the earth.

ADDITIONAL NOTE ON THE INTERPRETATION OF ISAIAH 49

1. *Unity.* Some scholars believe that this chapter was put into its present form by an editor, for the Jerusalem community, after 538 BC. They say that he took shorter poems by the prophet and arranged them for his own purposes. In this Guide we agree with other scholars who believe that this chapter is a single poem composed by the prophet.

2. *The Servant in vv. 3, 5, 6.* (See Glossary, *Servant of the Lord.*) Some scholars believe that 49.1–6 was originally a part of a series of four poems about an individual called 'the Servant of the Lord', who was not the same as 'Israel'. Some scholars, who agree that 49.1–6 is a part of the larger group of poems, also say that the Servant in vv. 5–6 must be an individual, because he has a mission to gather all Israelites together. For this reason, they think that a later copyist or editor, must have added the word 'servant' in v. 3, to help readers apply these verses to themselves, even though the author was really speaking of an individual. It seems more probable that the author of this poem was referring in v. 3 to 'Israel' as the people of God, and in vv. 5–6 to the 'remnant' of Israel in Babylonia (as in 46.3), and that he used the word 'servant' in a flexible way.

NOTES

49.1. Listen to me: The Servant who can say these words to the nations must be careful to 'hear' God. This may be the reason for the strong emphasis on hearing in Isaiah 48, as well as in 42.18: 44.1: and 46.3.

49.1, 5. From the womb: This means 'before you were born', as in Isaiah 1.5, i.e., the people of Israel had a place in God's plan before they became a people. See note on 44.24 for a possible meaning of the 'womb' from which Israel was born.

49.4. But I said: The prophet used a special Hebrew pronoun to show the contrast between the action of God (vv. 1–3) and the reaction of the Servant.

I have laboured: These words may refer to religious practices in Israel. The prophet used the Hebrew word which is here translated 'labour', in 43.22–24 (RSV) 'weary', and 47.12, 15 (RSV) 'labour'. In the case of Israel, he meant false worship; In the case of Babylon astrology.

For nothing: The Hebrew word is translated as 'chaos' in 45.18–19 (Glossary, *Chaos*). The prophet was saying that the Israelites had met the same sort of disorders and breakdown as every other nation. This made them doubt the value of their faith in God.

Vanity: Jeremiah also used this word, to describe the emptiness of idols and idol worship (see Jer. 2.5; 8.19; 14.22). He was saying that Israel had tried out the way of idols, but found it was only vanity.

My right: The prophet wanted to make a comparison with 40.27. In that verse, the words 'my right' meant a narrow concern with their own future. But in 49.4, it means God's plan for Israel. The prophet wanted to show the difference between doubt (in 40.27) and faith (in 49.4).

My recompense: The only other time the prophet used this word was in 40.10 (see note on that verse p. 14). It meant new 'children' to make up for those lost at the time of the destruction of Jerusalem. The hope expressed in this verse is fulfilled in vv. 14–26.

49.8. A time of favour . . . a day of salvation: The prophet may have been using the tradition of the Jubilee year as mentioned in Leviticus 25. This was a time when slaves were freed, and all those who had lost their land because they couldn't pay their debts would get it back again. Similar ideas are expressed in Isaiah 60.1–3 and 61.1–4. Christians believe that the day of salvation came first through Jesus Christ (Luke 1.78–79; 2.30–32; 4.16–21). Jesus began His ministry with the words 'the time is fulfilled' (Mark 1.5).

49.8. To establish the land: The Hebrew verb may be translated as 'raise up', as in 49.6, or 'repair' as in 61.4, or 'restore' (Jerusalem Bible). The Hebrew word translated 'land' is usually translated 'earth', meaning the whole earth. The prophet used this word forty times. In every case except 49.8, 19 the meaning is clearly the whole earth. In 49.19 he says 'your . . . land'. But in 49.8 there is no possessive pronoun. The words 'end of the earth' (v. 6), and 'earth' (v. 13), and the other words with world-wide scope such as coastlands', 'peoples from afar', 'covenant of the people', 'salvation', 'the nations', all show the prophet's intention to refer to the whole earth in 49.8.

49.23. Lick the dust of your feet: This is an idiom from the court language of the time. We should not understand it literally. It means to bow low and pay respect.

49.15: Can a woman forget her sucking child? In most parts of the Bible, the writers speak of God as father. Here the prophet compared God to a mother because of the tender love 'He' had for 'His' child, Israel. In speaking about God we must use the accepted forms of speech in our various languages. Many languages have pronouns which do not express gender. God is like both 'father' and 'mother', and much more than that. Jesus compared himself to a mother hen caring for her little chicks (Luke 13.34).

49.24–25. This verse may have been the basis for Jesus's parable about the strong man (Luke 11.21–22).

49.26. Eat their own flesh . . . drunk with their own blood. The Good News Bible (TEV) helps us to understand this difficult passage:

> 'I will make your oppressors kill each other;
> they will be drunk with murder and rage.

49.26. All flesh: The prophet was careful to use this expression, meaning 'all mankind', only three times. Although 'all flesh' is weak and transient like grass (40.6), there is God's promise that 'all flesh' will one day see the glory of the Lord (40.5). Perhaps the prophet was suggesting in 49.26 that the deliverance of the Israelite exiles from Babylon would be the beginning of the fulfilment of the promise given in 40.5.

STUDY SUGGESTIONS

REVIEW OF CONTENT

1. What three things were the discouraged Israelites saying?
2. What words in Isa. 48 lead on to the message of Isa. 49?
3. What are the two titles for 'Israel' in the two parts of this poem?
4. How did the prophet understand the 'direction of mission'?
5. What were the six parts of the Servant's life story which the prophet mentioned?
6. What part of the message of the servant to the nations shows that the servant people were just like the people they were talking with?
7. For what reasons did the prophet think that the tribal structure of Israel was a good pattern for the new Israel?
8. Was the 'day of salvation' for (a) Israel, or (b) the 'nations'?
9. What four works of mission did the prophet mention?
10. Who were the people in the procession described in vv. 9b–12?
11. Why was the land of Israel too narrow?
12. Who were the 'children' of Zion?
13. What was the prophet's real emphasis in vv. 24–26?

APPLICATION, DISCUSSION, RESEARCH

14. Which of the following words or phrases best describes your Church's attitude towards its mission? Give reasons for your answer.

self-centred   discouraged   too broad   too narrow
open minded   not interested   enthusiastic
striving for effectiveness

15. Does this chapter (Isa. 49) give any suggestions for 'effectiveness' in mission? Explain your answer.
16. How would you reply to someone who said: 'The prophet tells us we should go to the end of the earth, but how can we do that? We live here and have our jobs here.'
17. Which of the six items in the life story of the Servant are most important for anyone who intends to speak to those who wish to know more about God?
18. How would you use Isa. 49.1–3 as an aid in answering someone who said: 'I do not like evangelists who always refer to themselves. It shows they are egotistic, and we probably cannot believe what they say.'
19. What Churches or denominations today have a structure (a) like a monarchy, (b) like a tribal confederation, (c) any other pattern? How effective is each for expressing the unity and the mission of the Church?
20. Look at the examples of the four works of mission, on p. 122.
    (a) Find examples from the life of Jesus that are like these four works.
    (b) What other agencies besides the Church does God use for these works?
    (c) If God uses other agencies for these works, should Christians also take part in them?
21. Compose a hymn of rejoicing based on Isa. 49.13, for use on a festival day.
22. Do you think that the planting of the Church in Asia, Europe, Africa, the Americas, and the islands of the sea is a fulfilment of the vision in 49.12, 18, 20–21? Give reasons for your answer.

50.1–11
A Call for Disciples
April–September, 539 BC

BACKGROUND AND OUTLINE

This poem is about the cost of being a disciple. The prophet's appeal to the Israelite exiles to become disciples came at a time of suffering.
1. All Babylonians were suffering during the last days of the empire.

There was not enough food or water. Social services had broken down. There was confusion and fear. The exiles shared this suffering, and those who were slaves suffered more than the others.

2. Divisions within the community of exiles brought suffering to the prophet himself and to those around him. Behind this poem there seems to be some kind of public trial. Some of the exiles made accusations against the prophet because of his teachings. It may have been like the unofficial trial of Jeremiah following his temple sermon during the reign of King Jehoiakim (Jer. 26.7–19, 24).

Here are some of the charges that may have been brought against the prophet:

He has called us idolaters (48.5).

He has called our fathers rebels (58.8).

He has called our religious life insincere (43.22–24).

He has criticized our ideas about the restoration of Jerusalem and the dynasty of David (48.1–2).

He has proposed the utterly impractical idea that we should go on a mission to the end of the earth *before* returning to Jerusalem (49.6).

He has said that God has chosen a foreign king to serve as His anointed prince (45.1).

He has said that the people of the whole earth can be children of God like us (45.11).

This chapter, then, reflects a disagreement about the mission of the Israelite exiles after the fall of Babylon, and about God's will for the nations of the whole earth.

Main theme: A call for Disciples

Part 1: A disciple's preparation (42.1–3)

Part 2: A disciple's training (42.4–6)

Part 3: A disciple's inner strength (42.7–9)

Part 4. A disciple's way, and its opposite (42.10–11)

READING SUGGESTIONS

Find out who the *speakers* are in each of the four parts of the poem. This will help you to understand the poem.

Find the eight *questions* in this short poem. The prophet used the word Behold! five times, each time to introduce an important statement.

The prophet repeated words for *emphasis*. Find repetitions of the following: 'The Lord' (3 times), 'The Lord God' (4 times), 'my hand', 'ear', 'face', 'helps me', 'shame', 'those who are taught'.

ADDITIONAL NOTE ON THE INTERPRETATION OF ISAIAH 50

Christian readers are particularly interested in vv. 4–9, because they contain a description of suffering very much like the experience of Jesus in the last days of His life. It is possible that Jesus Himself meditated on these verses as He prepared to go up to Jerusalem. The writers of the New Testament were attracted to these words because they helped them to understand the suffering of Jesus. It was not sinfulness in Jesus which caused Him to suffer; because He was obedient to God he suffered as a result of other people's sin.

Probably the prophet who composed these words was thinking of his own personal experience in Babylon. Yet, although he was not predicting a future suffering, God used these words of Scripture to inspire people in later times to accept suffering willingly.

Scholars are not agreed about the unity of Isaiah 50. Some believe that only vv. 4–10 form a single poem about the Servant of the Lord, which was originally separate from the poems of Isaiah 40—55 (see Glossary: *Servant*). More probably 50.1–11 form a complete poem, as shown by a study of style, emphasis, and structure.

INTERPRETATION

THE PROPHET'S CALL FOR DISCIPLES (v. 10)

Look first at the question in v. 10: 'Who among you . . . ?' This was the prophet's second call to the exiles. In 42.23, he had called for those who were ready to listen with concentrated attention as a preparation for future obedience ('the time to come'). In 50.10 he was aware that the future day of salvation was coming closer (see 46.13). He felt it was a time to gather a group of disciples.

In v. 4 the prophet twice (i.e. emphatically) referred to a group of people known as 'those who are taught'. The only other place in the Old Testament where this Hebrew word appears is Isaiah 8.16–18, where the translation is 'disciples' (RSV). In those verses, Isaiah of Jerusalem, who lived about 200 years before this prophet, told about a group of faithful people gathered around him, who were called 'disciples' or 'those who are taught'. Their task was to preserve the *torah* (teaching), wait in hope for God to act, and to be signs pointing to God's future salvation.

Probably this prophet had these verses in mind when he was thinking about the future. And when most of the Israelite exiles rejected his ideas, he too wanted to gather a group of 'those who are taught' to make God's teaching (*torah*) glorious among the nations (42.21). They would have to learn to 'wait for the Lord' in hope (40.31) and in spite of suffering. Like the

Servant in 49.1–6, they would have a double mission: (a) to 'raise up the tribes of Jacob', and (b) to be the light of God's salvation to all nations.

We cannot tell how many of the exiles responded to his call. From the question in 50.2, it is possible that he was all alone at the time of his trial. Probably some of those who were close to him returned to Jerusalem and composed the poems of Isaiah 56—66.

A DISCIPLE'S PREPARATION (vv.1–3)

1. *Repentance* (v. 1). It is only too easy to blame someone else for our troubles. The younger Israelite exiles who had not experienced the fall of Jerusalem seem to have been blaming God. They used two popular word-pictures for the covenant relationship.

(a) First, they remembered that the covenant was like a marriage. They complained that God had 'divorced' his 'wife' (Israel). No future relationship was possible.

(b) Second, they recalled that the covenant was like an adoption ceremony in which God as 'Father' adopted Israel as His 'son'. They complained that the father had sold his son to his creditors (Babylon) to pay off his debts. The covenant was ended, they said, and they claimed that it was God who had ended it.

The prophet did not agree with those complaints. In his two questions he taught the people that there was no 'bill of divorce', as the law required. He said that God was not a debtor to anyone, and did not 'sell' His people to Babylon. He used the word 'Behold!' to emphasize that these complaints were merely excuses to avoid repentance. He had told them many times about God's forgiving love (see 40.2; 43.25; 48.9). The problem was that they were not willing to leave their old ways. It was easier for them to blame God when things went wrong, than to repent.

A disciple must not approach God boasting of a special relationship with Him, but 'in a Spirit' of willingness to change.

2. *Commitment* (vv. 2–3). A second temptation for those in trouble is to doubt God's power. God may be ready to forgive, they feel, but is He strong enough to save? This question troubled the Israelite exiles, so we can learn from the second question in v. 2: 'Have I no power to deliver?' The prophet replied in two ways.

(a) He said that the exiles should try to understand what was going on around them. God would show His saving power in the defeat of Babylon (symbolized by 'sea' and 'rivers'). The present time of suffering (symbolized by 'darkness') was a demonstration of God's *power*, not His weakness, just as at the time of the Exodus from Egypt.

(b) The prophet said that the only way to experience God's power was to answer His call with whole-hearted commitment.

This is the meaning of the question in v. 2, 'Why, when I called, was there no one to answer?' Jeremiah heard God asking the same question just before the fall of Jerusalem (Jer. 7.13). Now this prophet was asking a new generation to answer God's call.

A disciple must come to God fully prepared to serve Him with his whole heart and life.

A DISCIPLE'S TRAINING (vv. 4–6)

These are the words of someone telling how he learned to be a member of the community of 'those who are taught'. Perhaps it was the prophet himself. He included it in his call for disciples to show what happens when anyone answers God's call. That is when the process of training begins.

1. *A trained tongue* (v. 4). In 49.2 the prophet told how God enabled His servant to speak words of judgement, as sharp as a sword. This verse refers to another gift: the ability to encourage weary and discouraged people with a healing word (Prov. 12.18), and to be a 'tree of life' for them (Prov. 15.4).

Learning comes with practice. So a disciple must seek out the weary and bring them the good news of God's salvation. In Isaiah 40—55 there are many word-pictures describing weary people: e.g. a 'bruised reed' or a 'smoking lamp wick' (42.3), those in 'prison or darkness' (42.7), 'the poor and needy' (41.17), 'straw blown by the wind' (41.2).

Think of the encouraging words which Jesus spoke to discouraged people:

'Take up your pallet and go home!' (Mark 2.11).

'Take heart, it is I, have no fear!' (Mark 6.50).

'All things are possible to him who believes!' (Mark 9.23).

'Come to me all who labour and are heavy laden, and I will give you rest' (Matt. 11.29).

2. *A sensitized ear* (v. 4). The speaker had learned to let God sensitize his ear, so that he could hear what God was saying to him. God's message may come through daily events, the observation of nature, observation of human life, study of Scripture, personal crises, national crises, dreams, visions, other people's words, or simply our own thoughts. A disciple is one who is learning from God how to listen, to understand what he hears, and to act in obedience when the message is clear. 'Morning by morning' is the time when the ear is sensitized, in times of prayer or meditation.

Jesus prayed early in the morning (Mark 1.39). His ear was sensitized to the cries of needy people for healing, for forgiveness of sins, and for liberation from demonic forces. He went through His own greatest crisis in prayerful obedience (Mark 14.32–36).

A disciple is one who is ready to let God sensitize his ear in regular prayer, and in obedience to what he hears.

3. *A willing back* (vv. 5, 6). The process of training moves from lessons in speaking to lessons in listening, and even to lessons in suffering. The final test of a disciple comes in his willingness to endure suffering. Probably the

'The final test of a disciple comes in his willingness to endure suffering' (p. 131).

Viktor Saneyev of the USSR has been described as 'one of the greatest athletes of all time'. His strength as a triple-jumper, like that of a disciple, is 'the result of training and discipline' (p. 133).

In what chief ways does the suffering of a disciple of God *differ* from that of an athlete in training?

experiences of the speaker in v. 6 came at the time when sentence of the trial was carried out. First came lashes on the back. The important lesson was in how to give one's back to the smiter, willingly, as a service to God. Jesus was able to do this (Mark 15.15); so was Paul (2 Cor. 11.24–25).

Modern disciples may have to learn to give their bodies to the torturers, to inhuman prison conditions, or to harsh labour camps. Or they may have to be ready to endure other kinds of hardship for the sake of others, in obedience to God's will.

4. *A disciplined face* (v. 6). A person convicted of a crime not only had to suffer physical pain (lashes on the back), but also psychological punishment, symbolized by things done to the face. These included slapping (Lam. 3.30), spitting in the face (Num. 12.14; Deut. 25.9), and pulling out the hair from the head or beard (2 Sam. 10.4; Neh. 13.23–27). Punishment inflicted on the face affects a person's self-esteem, his reputation among others, and his emotional health. The purpose of this sort of punishment is to break down a person presumed to be guilty.

The prophet was saying that a disciple must learn to accept humiliation, shame, and emotional shock as a part of his obedience to God. Jesus was able to endure spitting by priests (Matt. 26.67) and Roman soldiers (Matt. 27.30), as well as slaps (John 18.22). He taught His disciples to turn the other cheek. Paul endured the same treatment (Acts 23.2) and wrote: 'For it has been granted that for the sake of Christ you should not only believe in him, but suffer for his sake' (Phil. 1.29).

A disciple is one who is trained by 'insults, hardships, persecutions, and calamities' (2 Cor. 12.10) how to obey. Paul even said that it was possible to 'rejoice in our sufferings' (Rom. 5.3). The author of the Book of Hebrews wrote that Jesus 'learned obedience by what he suffered' (Heb. 5.8). Today, Christians from rich and powerful nations sometimes have to endure humiliation because of past or present injustices done by their nations. Both individuals and Churches need to cultivate a 'disciplined face'.

A DISCIPLE'S INNER STRENGTH (vv. 7–9)

The inner strength of a disciple is the result of the training, or discipline, described in vv. 4–6. The prophet showed his hearers: (1) the secret of inner strength, which was the sure knowledge that 'The Lord God helps me'. He also showed them: (2) the living expression of that strength: the steadfast enduring of insults, misunderstandings, false accusations by powerful enemies, and unjust legal procedures.

When Luke wrote that Jesus 'set his face to go to Jerusalem' (Luke 9.51), he was probably thinking of Isaiah 50.7: 'I have set my face like a flint'. Paul was certainly inspired by Isaiah 50.7–9 when he wrote Romans 8.31–39. He used the same style of writing, in asking questions. He spoke of the same secret of inner strength: 'If God be for us, who is against us?'

Christians have always been inspired by these verses to stand for unpopular causes, or to take risky minority positions, when they are convinced that it is God's will.

THE DISCIPLES' COMMUNITY (v. 10)

After describing the preparation, training, and inner strength of a disciple, the prophet invited his hearers to join the community of disciples. We have already referred to Isaiah 8.16–18 as giving a model for the new community of disciples. Isaiah 10.20–21 was probably another verse from the words of Isaiah of Jerusalem. According to those verses, there would appear at some future time a small group of Israelite survivors called the 'remnant', who would 'return to the mighty God'. The prophet in Babylon 200 years later probably thought of this community of disciples as the remnant of Israel on God's 'day of salvation' (49.8). This would then be the beginning of a new Israel.

The prophet described this new community in six paired phrases.

1. *Members of the community.*

(a) They would be *a community of God-fearers*. By 'fear', the prophet meant covenant loyalty to the covenant God, with full acceptance of covenant obligations. Those who answer God's call (v. 2) must be ready to become a part of a responsible community. By using the general word 'fear', the prophet probably meant that membership in the community would be open to people of other nations or tribes. These would be the ones who said 'I am the Lord's' (44.5), or those who would 'come over' to Israel's God (45.14), or those who would see the light of salvation in Israel and come to God (49.7). Disciples must be ready to accept people of other cultures on a basis of equality.

(b) They would be *a community of people who would help each other to find God's will*. Each member would be ready to listen to, understand, and obey the advice and counsel of the community (here called the 'servant'), instead of thinking only of themselves. (See the emphasis on 'I', 'my', and 'me' in vv. 4–6 and 7–9; they turn to 'we', 'our', and 'us' in the community. A disciple is committed to the members of the community, as well as to God.

2. *The mission of the community*

(a) *They would walk in darkness*. The mission of Israel was to 'open eyes that are blind, bring out from prison those who sit in darkness' (42.7; 49.9). This remnant community of disciples would be present in the darkness of chaos, confusion, suffering, and pain of their time. They would have to suffer shame, humiliation, and even physical torture. Jesus meant something like this when He said that disciples must carry the cross daily. Commitment to God means commitment in mission to those in darkness.

(b) *They possess no light of their own*. They are dependent on God's light while they walk in the darkness of suffering.

3. The faith of the community

(a) They would help each other to have sincere *trust* in the present and powerful Lord, in contrast to those who bear the name of Israel (48.1) but do not really trust God. Perhaps the prophet was thinking of the words of the psalm in Isaiah 12.2: 'Behold, God is my salvation. I will trust and not be afraid.' Those who fear the Lord will not need to fear the powers of evil and destruction (Isa. 41.10, 13, 14). Jesus showed this sort of trust on the cross when He said 'Into thy hands I commit my spirit' (Luke 23.46; Ps. 31.5).

(b) They would *rely on their God* to bring His righteous purpose to victory. They would gain strength to participate in God's work with the help of God's victorious right hand (41.10).

THE ENEMIES (v. 11)

Those Israelites who tortured and humiliated the disciple (v. 6), or who brought charges against him (vv. 7.8), are described here as those who 'kindle a fire' and walk in the light of that fire. The 'fire' may refer to the practices of idol-worship (see Jer. 7.18 and 19.5). More probably it refers to the fire of hatred and prejudice stirred up during the trial. The prophet was telling his hearers that the fire kindled by these enemies would in the end destroy them. He was saying that enmity is sure to arise in the course of the future mission of the community, but that there is no reason to fear the enemies.

NOTES

50.1. Bill of divorce: For the Israelite law, see Deut. 24.1–4. Both Hosea (2.2–3, 14–20) and Jeremiah (2.2, 23–25; 3.1–5) described the covenant relationship in terms of marriage.

Sold you: Israel is referred to as God's 'son' in Exodus 4.22; Hosea 11.1–4; Isaiah 1.2; Jeremiah 3.19, 22.

50.2. No one to answer: As in Jeremiah 7.13, we find this sort of disappointed reaction to the slow response of the people In Isaiah 59.16 and 63.5. Jesus also was disappointed in His disciples (See Mark 14.37, 40, 41, 50).

50.3. The sea, rivers, desert: See Glossary: *World-view.*

Blackness . . . sackcloth. The prophet used these words to express the idea that nature was sad, because of the chaos on earth. Blackness in the heavens would mean darkness on earth. These words are therefore related to 'darkness' in v. 10.

50.7–9. Contend: adversary: declare guilty: These are all words from the law courts of ancient Israel.

50.7. Like a flint: Flint is a very hard rock. To make one's face like a flint would mean that nothing can change the course of action one has set. Perhaps the author was using an idea from Ezekiel 3.8–9, which suggests that the prophet must have a very hard forehead in order to stand against the attacks of the rebellious Israelites.

50.8. Vindicates: The literal meaning of the Hebrew word is 'to cause to be righteous' (or innocent). The same verb-form is used in 53.11 to describe the work of the Servant to 'make many to be accounted righteous'. This is the root of the New Testament word, 'justify'. From Jeremiah 17.17–18 and Lam. 3.58–66, we learn that the Old Testament meaning of the word is 'to be delivered from persecution, shame, and destruction'.

50.9. Wear out like a garment . . . eaten by moths: Many Old Testament writers use this idea to describe the transience of human life and work, as for example in Job. 12.28. In Psalm 39.11, Hosea 5.12, and Isaiah 51.8, God's judgement is compared with the destruction caused by the sort of moth whose caterpillars bite holes in woollen cloth. God's work by contrast is permanent (Isaiah 40.8).

50.10. Fears the Lord: In Deuteronomy 7.13–14, fearing the Lord, serving Him, and taking oaths in His name are all part of the covenant obligations.

Obey: The same Hebrew word may be translated as 'listen to', 'hear' and 'obey'.

Relies on his God: The same Hebrew word is found in Isaiah 10.20, translated as 'lean on' in the RSV. The remnant will 'lean on the Lord, the Holy One of Israel in truth'. The prophet had already used the phrase 'not in truth' to describe the insincere religion of many Israelites (48.1). His use of these two words suggests that Isaiah 10.20–21 was a model for his thinking about the new community of disciples as the remnant of Israel.

STUDY SUGGESTIONS

REVIEW OF CONTENT

1. In what way were the experiences of the prophet as described in this chapter similar to those of Jeremiah?
2. List seven possible accusations which might have been brought against the prophet by Israelites who did not agree with him.
3. In which two verses do we find a call by the prophet for a response from his hearers?
4. What two passages from Isaiah 1—39 probably influenced the prophet when he thought about the future?
5. What two sorts of preparation were suggested for those who wanted to become disciples?
6. (a) What two word-pictures describing the covenant relationship are found in v. 1?
   (b) What was the mistake of the Israelite exiles?

7. (a) What four parts of the body were a part of the disciple's training?
   (b) What does each one represent?
8. What is the secret of a disciple's strength in times of difficulty?
9. What passage in the New Testament was inspired by Isa. 50.7–9?
10. In what six ways is the community of disciples described in v. 10?
11. What is the meaning of 'fire' in v. 11?

APPLICATION, DISCUSSION, RESEARCH

12. Read the list of accusations which may have been brought against the prophet (p. 128).
    (a) Which do you think were the most serious in the minds of the exiles in Babylon?
    (b) Which ones might be used against a prophetic preacher today?
13. Which of the words or phrases in Isa. 50.1–11 seem most applicable to the records of the life of Jesus?
14. Discuss the following ideas:
    (a) The prophet was consciously foretelling the suffering of a Messiah who would come in the future.
    (b) The prophet was describing the actual suffering of a person more than 500 years before Christ.
    (c) The prophet's words help Christians today to understand the sufferings of Jesus and their own sufferings.
15. Read the following passages and say in each case: (i) who is the teacher; (ii) who is being taught; and (iii) what is the lesson to be learned.
    (a) Deut. 4.10   (b) Isa. 1.17   (c) Isa. 50.4–5   (d) Jer. 12.16   (e) Matt. 5.1–3   (f) Matt. 11.29   (g) Phil. 4.11   (h) Heb. 5.8.
16. God's call for service comes through the voice of certain people. Read the following verses and say in each case:
    (i) who was calling; (ii) who was called; (iii) what was the task; (iv) how is each 'call' related to Christians in your own country.
    (a) Isa. 6.8   (b) Isa. 50.10   (c) Mark 1.16–18.
17. Repentance means a willingness to change from old ways. How does the practice of religion sometimes give us excuses for *not* repenting? What sort of repentance is most needed by Christians in your country today?
18. 'The way to know God's power is to answer God's call' (p. 130). In what ways do Christians sometimes (a) show that they doubt God's power, (b) show that they are trusting God's power by answering his call.
19. Imagine you are planning the programme for a discipleship class. How would you plan for training of the 'tongue', the 'ear', the 'back', and the 'face', along lines suggested by Isa. 50.4–6?
20. Give examples from your own society of Christians who have shown

their inner strength (Isa. 50.7–9) by standing up for unpopular causes, taking risky minority positions, or enduring opposition.

21. A disciple must be ready to 'walk in darkness'. Which of the following activities seem most relevant in your society? Can you suggest others?
(a) Sharing the struggle for social justice.
(b) Helping old people who are sick, weak, or lonely.
(c) Helping people who have been in prison, or been addicted to drugs, or been in a mental hospital, to find a useful place in society.
(d) Being friendly to refugees who have come to live in your community.

51.1–16
'My Words in Your Mouth'
October 539 BC

BACKGROUND AND OUTLINE

The prophet probably composed this poem during the battle of Opis in early October 539 BC. In that battle, on the bank of the Tigris river north of Babylon, Cyrus's army broke through the last defences of the city of Babylon.

The poem shows us the sufferings of some of the Israelite exiles at that time. They were starving, cruelly treated (v. 14), accused of treason (v. 7), and in fear of being massacred by desperate Babylonian forces (v. 13).

In the previous poem, the prophet called for volunteers to walk in 'darkness' without a light (Isa. 50.10). He wrote this poem for those who were actually experiencing the darkness, and told them that God had chosen them for His work in the new world which was to come.

Not all Christians are called on to go through that sort of experience. But we can learn much from this poem about how God works in the midst of a world crisis, and how His faithful servants can share in His work.

Main theme: 'My Words in Your Mouth'

Part 1: Remember who you are (vv. 1–3)

Part 2: God's words for the nations (vv. 4–6)

Part 3: God's words for His people (vv. 7–8)

Part 4: Come now, Lord! (vv. 9–11)

Part 5: Do not fear! (vv. 12–14)

Part 6: God commissions His people in a time of crisis. (vv. 15–16)

READING SUGGESTIONS

God's urgent message. Note the urgent Hearken! or Listen! at the beginning of each of the first three parts. What did the prophet want the people to hear? Note the three commands to look! What did he want them to see or consider?

Look for words repeated for emphasis: 'Deliverance' (4 times) and 'righteousness' are different translations of the same Hebrew word (see Glossary: Righteousness).

Look for the Key words (repeated *five* times). Think of what the prophet meant in each case.

Look for those repeated *four* times: 'heavens and earth'; *three* times: 'salvation', 'Zion'; *twice*: 'comfort', 'my people', 'peoples', 'oppressors', 'the sea'. Consider the meaning in each case, and ask yourself what the prophet's purpose was in using the word.

INTERPRETATION

MY WORDS IN YOUR MOUTH (v. 16)

The theme of this poem is God's 'commission' or calling of the faithful remnant of His people in Babylon. The prophet was using the call of Jeremiah as his pattern, as we can see if we read Isaiah 42.6 and 51.16 together:

Jer. 1.5:   I have commissioned you as a prophet to the nations.
Jer. 1.9:   I have put my words in your mouth.
Isa. 42.6: I have commissioned you as a light to the nations.
Isa. 51.16: I have put my words in your mouth.

According to Jeremiah 1.10, the effect of God's words among the nations would be both *destructive* – uprooting and tearing down, and *constructive* – planting and building. During Jeremiah's time the main emphasis was on the destruction of the old order (see Jer. 45.4; 25.29–31). This work of destruction came to a climax with Cyrus's attack on Babylon (see Jer. 24.26). The time had come for the work of planting and building among the nations. This was the task which God was giving to the remnant of His people.

'In your mouth' means two things:

(a) The words must be *eaten* (see Jer. 15.16), that is, understood and accepted, until they become a part of the life of whoever receives them.

(b) The words must be *spoken* in order to have an effect on society, on communities, and on people's lives (see notes on Isa. 55.10–11). The words must be a part of the life and witness of God's Servant, so that other people will understand and accept them.

140

REMEMBER WHO YOU ARE (vv. 1–3)

The prophet prepared his followers to receive God's words, by reminding them who they were. He had four urgent messages:

1. *You are God-Seekers* (v. 1a). God's promise through Jeremiah was: 'You will seek me and find me, when you seek me with all your heart' (Jer. 29.13). This prophet called his people 'God-seekers' in a strange land. He also called them 'you who pursue deliverance' (see Glossary: *Righteousness*). He meant that those who seek God in prayer and worship must be ready to offer themselves as part of His righteous purpose (see comments on 55.10–12). In plain language we would say: If you worship God, you must be prepared to obey His will and take part in His work. To be God-seekers means to accept responsibility as obedient servants.

2. *You are living stones!* (v. 1b). The prophet was thinking of Mount Zion as 'the mountain of the Lord' and the 'Rock of Israel) (Isa. 30.29), which some believed to be the centre where God laid the original foundation of the earth (Isa. 2.2; Ezek. 5.5; 38.12). When Solomon built his temple on that rock, he used stones cut from a cave below which is still called 'Solomon's quarry' (1 Kings 5.17; 6.7).

The prophet compared the Israelite exiles with stones cut from that quarry; they would be the living foundations for the new earth (51.16). He was saying to them: You are true Israelites, and God will build his new earth on you! (compare Isa. 28.16). This reminds us of what Jesus said to Peter (Matt. 16.18).

To be true Israelites, means willingness to be used in God's new world.

3. *You are descendants of Abraham!* (v. 2). The prophet reminded them that they were descendants of Abraham. Like Abraham they must have enough faith to answer God's call (Gen. 12.4) and to trust in His promises. To be Abraham's descendants means having a faith that is open to future possibilities.

4. *You are descendants of Adam!* (v. 3). The prophet reminded them that they were descendants of Adam, who had been expelled from God's beautiful garden because of pride, and had to live in a world where there was suffering and enmity. (Gen. 3.18). God's will for the descendants of Adam was that they should once again live in a beautiful garden. Zion would one day be that new garden, the beginning of a new earth.

In order to live as descendants of Adam, they must work in hope that the earth will be transformed into a garden of God.

Each of these messages linked them to the past, pointed to the future, and gave meaning to the present.

GOD'S WORDS FOR THE NATIONS (vv. 4–6)

God's words are His purposeful actions in the world, and they are expressed in the life and witness of His people. When God's people

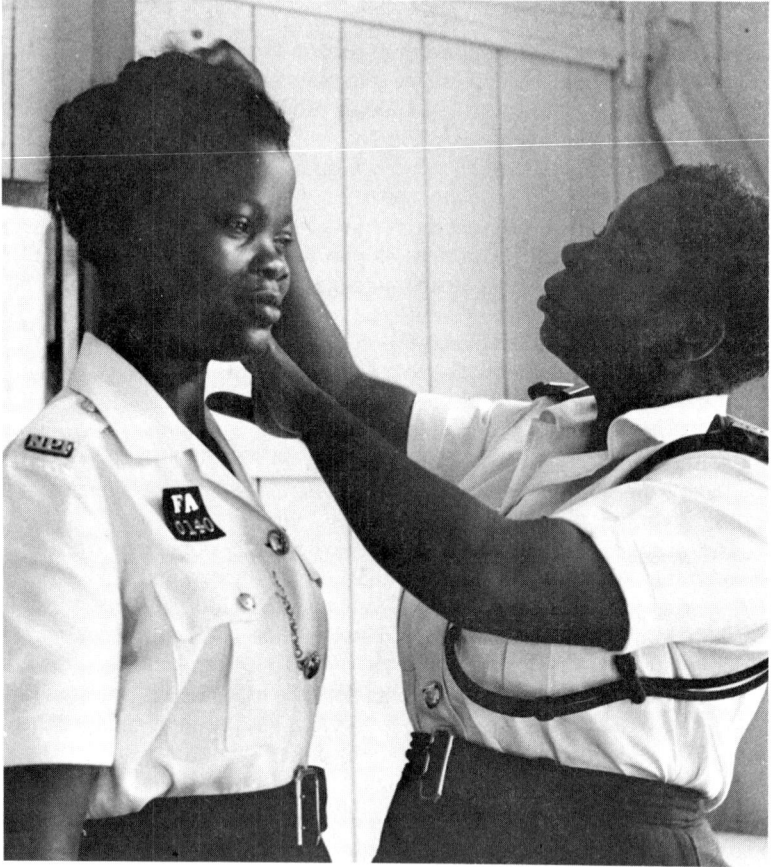

'The prophet prepared his followers to receive God's words . . . and to proclaim them . . . this was the fateful moment of commissioning. (pp. 140 and 143).

A woman police officer in Nigeria prepares a newly appointed recruit for her first day on traffic duty.

In what ways could she proclaim each of God's four 'words' (see p. 142) in the course of this duty?

understand who they really are, they are ready to receive His words, and to proclaim them among the nations.

1. *God's revealed teaching* (i.e. His law, see Glossary) was first given to His people as part of the Sinai covenant. But God intended it as a guide for all the nations, to show what their relationship should be, both with God and with each other (see Isa. 42.4, 21).

2. *God's justice* (Glossary) was demonstrated among His people (Isa. 5.16). He commanded them to make it the basis of their society (Deut. 16.20). It is His righteous resolve for all His creation, and the mission of His people is to bring it to all nations (42.1–4).

3. *God's deliverance* (Glossary: *Righteousness*) means liberation for all the poor and imprisoned people in every nation (see Isa. 42.7).

4. *God's salvation* (Glossary) restores wholeness (*shalom*) to individuals, groups, and nations.

The prophet used these four words to describe God's plan for the new world. He entrusted them to His faithful Servant at a time when the old heaven and earth (v. 6, Glossary: *World view*) were passing away, and when the whole earth was waiting for a new and true way (v. 5).

GOD'S WORDS FOR HIS PEOPLE (vv. 7–8)

The prophet then told his people that this 'new creation' must begin in their own lives. He was saying:

1. They must personally come to know God's power to save (RSV: 'know righteousness'). Such knowledge is not theoretical but practical. It comes from participation and experience (see notes on 53.11).

2. They must keep God's revealed teaching in their hearts, through practice and constant renewal of the covenant (Deut. 5.3; Jer. 31.33).

3. They must trust in God's power to save (RSV: 'deliverance, salvation') in every situation and in every generation. They would show this trust by fearless courage when faced by opposition and personal danger.

COME NOW, LORD! (vv. 9–11)

At this point, possibly when the battle of Opis had just begun, the prophet was so excited that he burst out in a hymn! He called on God to act in this time of danger. This moment in history was like God's struggle at the time of creation (v. 9, Glossary: *World view*) *and* at the time of the Exodus from Egypt through the sea (v. 10, compare Exod. 15.13, 16). It was the moment of redemption (Glossary: *Redeem*). In his imagination the prophet could see the joyful procession arriving at the new Jerusalem with songs of joy on their lips (Glossary: *Jerusalem-Zion*).

DO NOT FEAR! (vv. 12–14)

The helpless exiles were like Jesus's disciples in the storm when they thought their boat would sink. The exiles were afraid that their captors would kill them. Starvation had made them weak. The prophet was calming their fears as Isaiah had calmed King Ahaz: 'Take heed, be quiet, do not fear . . . these two smouldering stumps of firebrands' (Isa. 7.4). He told the exiles that:

(1) God was in control of what He had created; (2) God's purpose was to comfort His people, and comfort was not far off; (3) Their oppressors were not gods but ordinary human beings (compare Isa. 31.3).

With such a God, why should they fear?

GOD COMMISSIONS HIS PEOPLE IN A TIME OF CRISIS (vv. 15–16)

At this turning-point in West Asian history, when the final battle for Babylon was at its fiercest (in poetic language, 'the waves of the sea were roaring'), the prophet told the faithful remnant that this was the fateful moment of God's commissioning. This commissioning set the direction for their future. They were to be God's new people (Zion), following God's plans for laying the foundation of His new world among the ruins of the old.

NOTES

51.5. Vanish like smoke . . . wear out like a garment: The prophet did not mean that the sky would actually disappear, or the earth become useless (Glossary: *World view*). He was probably remembering that the empires of Egypt and Assyria had come to an end. Babylon was about to vanish like smoke, and its social structure was to become a thing of the past. A new world order was coming into existence as a result of Cyrus's victories.

Yet these words have a special meaning for our own day. Polluting 'smog' may blot out the sky in some of our industrial cities. And as we use up the world's resources of oil, coal, water, and forests it may seem that the earth can really 'wear out'.

STUDY SUGGESTIONS

REVIEW OF CONTENT

1. Where was Opis? At what date was an important battle fought there, and what was the result?
2. What four kinds of suffering did the prophet mention in this poem?
3. What other prophet's call formed the pattern for this prophet's description of God's 'commissioning' of the Israelite exiles?
4. What two things does a person who receives God's words have to do?
5. What were the four messages which reminded the exiles who they were?

6. What rock and what quarry was the prophet thinking of when he called the Israelite exiles 'living stones'?
7. What four words did the prophet use to describe God's plan for the new world?
8. What three things did God require of His servants before they were ready to proclaim His words in life and witness?
9. With what two events did the prophet compare Cyrus's victory at Opis?
10. With what three words of advice did the prophet encourage the frightened exiles?

APPLICATION, DISCUSSION, RESEARCH

11. Does God still 'put His words in the mouth' of His people today? If He does, who receives them – whole Churches? local congregations? ministers? individual Christians? small groups of Christians? How can an individual or a group of Christians 'eat' and 'speak' these words from God?
12. In what ways does this prophet's idea of 'God's words in our mouth' differ from the idea of 'speaking in tongues' as described in the New Testament?
13. God's revealed teaching is one of the foundation stones of the new world (see vv. 4, 7). Each religion and culture has its own teaching. What is the relation, if any, between the revealed teaching of God and the teaching of other religions? Discuss the following ways of describing the relationship. Which ones, if any, do you agree with?
(a) The teaching of other religions and cultures is false, and therefore has no value in God's new world.
(b) Christians should discuss the revealed teaching of God and the teaching of other religions.
(c) Christians should try to combine the revealed teaching from God as found in the Bible with teaching from other religions.
(d) Christians should look for revealed teaching from God in the teaching of other religions.
(e) Christians should use God's revealed teaching to help them decide what is true or false in the teaching of other religions.
14. It is important for Christians today to know who they are (see 51.1–3). How do the four messages in these verses help us to understand who we are? What additional insights come to us from the New Testament?
15. Compare 1 Pet. 2.4–5 and Eph. 2.20–22 with Isa. 51.1b. Who are the stones? What is the building?

51.17—52.12
Our God Has Begun to Reign!
October 539 BC

BACKGROUND AND OUTLINE

The death of Nabonidus, the last king of Babylon, on 13 October 539 BC was the fulfilment of the prophet's words about the fall of Babylon (see 47.11, and Note on Historical Background, pp. 41–43). It was also the beginning of the fulfilment of his words about deliverance for the Israelite exiles (46.13) and the nations (51.4–5).

The prophet had been trying to prepare his people for this moment from the beginning. As he saw them, they were like prisoners who had given up all hope. He wanted to wake them up to face the dawn of the day of salvation.

For Christians, this poem is suitable for the Advent season, when those who are asleep or in darkness must wake up to face the challenge and hope of Christ's coming.

Main Theme: Our God Has Begun to Reign!

Part 1: The cup of suffering (51.17–23)

Part 2: Recalled to life (52.1–2)

Part 3: God's assurance: 'Here I am!' (52.3–6)

Part 4: The herald of salvation (52.7–8)

Part 5: The song of salvation (52.9–10)

Part 6: A command to the herald (52.11–12)

Note: In this Guide we take the view that 51.17—52.12 form a single poem. However, some scholars do not agree with this. In addition, some scholars believe that 52.3–6 is not by the author of Isaiah 40—55. They are probably correct, because these verses are in prose style, and their contents do not seem to fit in with this poem as a whole.

READING SUGGESTIONS

This poem contains at least twelve *commands* to the Israelite captives. Find them, and try to think what they mean, and why they were spoken.

There are five references to Jerusalem, and four to Zion. Read the Glossary note on Jerusalem-Zion, and try to decide which of the six meanings apply to each reference in this poem.

Use a concordance and the Glossary notes to find other references to the following words from this poem in Isaiah 40—55. This will help you to find and trace major themes of the whole set of poems. 'Jerusalem and Zion', 'joy and singing', 'comfort', 'redeem, redeemer', 'salvation', 'Peace', 'Herald of good tidings', 'The ends of the earth', 'The nations'.

INTERPRETATION

OUR GOD HAS BEGUN TO REIGN! (52.7)

The unifying theme of this poem is the message of the herald. The poet thought of God's reign as having three stages:

1. The first victory, marking *the beginning of God's reign*. Humanly speaking, Cyrus was the victorious conqueror of Babylon. However, the prophet believed that God's 'holy arm' (52.10) was the hidden and decisive cause of Cyrus's success. He saw the fall of Babylon as God's victory over the power of death and destruction.

2. *The proclamation of God's reign*. During this period, God's people were to go as a herald among the nations to show the meaning of God's reign (52.7). This was the prophet's idea of the new Exodus.

3. *The fulfilment of God's reign*. At the end of the new Exodus, God himself would return to the new Jerusalem (52.8) at the head of His redeemed people (52.12), and in the sight of all the nations, as a demonstration to them of salvation.

Christians have a similar view of God's kingdom which was announced by Jesus:

(a) The first victory over the forces of evil was in the life, death, and resurrection of Jesus;

(b) The proclamation of the Kingdom is by the Church;

(c) The fulfilment of the Kingdom will come when Jesus reigns over all (Rev. 11.15) in the New Jerusalem, and all the people of the world live in peace (Rev. 22.2–3).

Christians reading Isaiah 51.17—52.12 can learn to recognize the victories of God's reign in such historical events as the end of an empire, the defeat of a tyrant, or the victory of righteousness.

The three Zions: The prophet spoke of Zion in three ways, corresponding to the three stages of God's reign:

1. As *Captive Zion* (52.2): i.e. the Israelite exiles in the Babylonian captivity.

2. As *Herald Zion* (40.9; 52.7): i.e. the group of Israelites moving out

among the nations to proclaim the reign of God to remnants of captive Zion (52.7) and to the nations (49.6, 8–9). We could also call this 'Exodus Zion', or Missionary Zion'.

3. As *Perfected Zion* (52.8–9): i.e. the new Jerusalem at the end of the mission of *Herald Zion.*

We can compare these ideas to three ways of describing the Church: i.e. as captive, missionary, and triumphant.

THE CUP OF SUFFERING (51.17–23)

For the Israelites, the fall of Jerusalem and the captivity in Babylon had been an experience like death. Their land and cities had been 'devastated', and the people 'destroyed' by 'famine and sword' (51.19). They were like condemned men who had drunk a cup of drugged wine. The nation was weak and had lost control of its future.

The prophet was referring here to a vision seen by Jeremiah. His message was this: (1) The cup was given to Israel by God because of her sinfulness (see Jer. 25.17). (2) All the nations of the earth had to drink this same cup because of their sinfulness (see Jer. 25.15, 17). This meant that the suffering of the Israelites was a shared suffering. (3) God's plan to judge the whole earth came to its climax with the defeat of Babylon ('After them the king of Babylon shall drink' Jer. 25.26). He meant that the defeat of Babylon was the beginning of a new period in history, the 'day of salvation' (Isa. 49.8). Thus it was a time for *Captive Zion* to return to life, and become *Herald Zion.*

RECALLED TO LIFE (51.17; 52.1–2)

The prophet told the exiles that life could come out of death. His words are like a call to the dead: he told them to stand up, to rise from the dust, to wake up from sleep, and to come back to consciousness. He believed that God was ready to give them strength instead of weakness, freedom instead of chains, dignity instead of oppression and degradation, purity instead of pollution.

Christians share this faith. We say that a totally new beginning is possible if we are united with Christ (Rom. 6.4–5; 2 Cor. 5.17). This poem reminds us that new life is possible in each new generation for groups of people, such as families, Churches, tribal groups, or nations, as well as for individuals.

THE HERALD OF SALVATION (52.7–8)

The words of Isaiah 52.7 are well known to Christians, because Paul quoted them in Romans 10.15 to support the sending of missionaries to proclaim the Gospel of Christ. In these two verses we can find all three Zions:

1. The herald is *Herald Zion*, as in Isaiah 40.9, proclaiming God's reign among the nations.

2. The message is directed to *Captive Zion*, meaning the exiles still scattered among the nations. The prophet's message would recall them from death to life, and then they too would become *Herald Zion*.

3. The content of the message was that world history had come to a turning point with the fall of Babylon. God's reign had begun. He is both the God of Zion 'your God', and the Saviour of the nations (Isa. 45.21–23). Therefore the message is meant for 'all the ends of the earth'. God's reign brought wholeness or *shalom* (peace), the goodness of the first creation (Gen. 1.31), and salvation (see Glossary). The prophet called the act of proclaiming 'beautiful', because it brought hope to the nations (51.5 and 42.4).

4. Between v. 7 and v. 8 lies the whole mission of *Herald Zion*, leading up to the establishment of *Perfected Zion*. V. 8 tells of the return of the Lord to a *Perfected Zion*, or a new Jerusalem.

THE SONG OF SALVATION (52.9–10)

This is the song which the *Perfected Zion* will sing when the Lord arrives at the head of the Exodus procession (40.10–11; see also Rev. 4.6–11; 5.9–14; 15.2–4; 9.1–8). People in thankfulness for a time of fulfilment, and those who can see this time in faith, can sing now. The prophet mentioned three reasons for joyful song:

1. *The earth restored.* The ruined land at the centre of the earth will become a garden like Eden (51.3), a symbol of the restoration of the whole earth. The relationship between God the creator, mankind, and nature will return to its original good and proper state ('tidings of good', 52.7). For this reason all nature will join in the song (44.23; 49.13: 55.12).

2. *Israel redeemed.* This verse sums up the whole meaning of redemption (Glossary). Liberation from slavery, forgiveness of sin, a new covenant relation with the Lord, and a new family of descendants will all be complete in *Perfected Zion*. The message of *Herald Zion* to the nations (48.20) is redemption. In this song, it is completed.

3. *The nations saved.* All nations will 'see' (Glossary) and share in God's salvation (Glossary; 40.5; 51.4–5).

This song shows us the prophet's view of the climax of history of the whole world. These are the goals of God's righteous and victorious purpose in every generation. They are the keys to the understanding of history.

A COMMAND TO THE HERALD (52.11–12)

After the vision of the fulfilment of God's reign, the prophet returned to the immediate situation. He told the newly liberated *Captive Zion* to become

'The prophet told the exiles that life could come out of death . . . the ruined land become a garden like Eden' . . . 'Christians share that faith' (p. 147).

An experimental well-drilling project in Egypt has turned many hectares of lifeless desert into fertile garden and farmland.

How does God work in today's world to bring 'life out of death'?

Herald Zion. It was the time for the New Exodus to begin. As in the first Exodus, the Lord would go with them (Exod. 33.16; Num. 14.14). But this time they would not be running away from a pursuing army. They would be beginning the mission of heralding God's reign among the nations with the new Jerusalem ahead of them.

STUDY SUGGESTIONS

REVIEW OF CONTENT

1. What two prophecies were fulfilled when Nabonidus died?
2. What three stages in God's reign did the prophet describe?
3. What are the three 'Zions' in this chapter?
4. What were the three messages of the 'cup of suffering'?
5. What changes would take place when the 'prisoner' (the exiles) heard the words of the prophet?
6. What important New Testament writer used the words of Isa. 52.7?
7. Who is speaking and who is hearing in 52.7?
8. What was the message of the herald?
9. What is the time difference between v. 7 and v. 8?
10. What are the three reasons for the 'song' of salvation?
11 (a) In what ways would the new Exodus be similar to the first Exodus?
   (b) In what ways would it be different?

APPLICATION, DISCUSSION, RESEARCH

12. Isa. 47 and 51.17—52.12 could be called 'a tale of two cities'. Read both poems, and from what you read draw parallels and contrasts between Babylon and Jerusalem.
13. The reading suggestions refer to the many imperative verbs, or commands in this poem. Why do you think the prophet used these imperatives, some of them with special emphasis, like 'awake! awake!'? Are such imperatives necessary for the Church today? Which of the imperatives in this poem would be appropriate for your own congregation?
14. Read Matt. 24.14; Mark 13.10; Luke 24.47; Rom. 1.5; 16.26. Compare the ideas expressed in these verses with the prophet's ideas about heralding God's reign before its fulfilment.
15. What events in modern history, if any, make you think of the fall of Babylon. Give reasons for your answer.
16. Which of the three 'Zions' would apply to your Church?
17. (a) Read Jer. 25.15–31. Compare this with Isa. 51.17–23. Did the author of Isa. 51.17–23 believe that God's word to Jeremiah was fulfilled in his time?
   (b) Compare the vision of the cup in Jer. 25 and Isa. 51 with the cup Jesus spoke of in the Garden of Gethsemane (Mark 14.36).

18. Listed as (i)–(vii) below are examples of people or places where the reign of God does not seem to be visible.
    (a) What would the message of peace and salvation mean there?
    (b) What would the idea of being 'recalled to life' (as in 51.1–2) mean?
    (c) What action could be taken by those proclaiming God's reign?
      (i) A prisoner suffering torture because of his witness to God's love and justice.
      (ii) A country girl forced to be a prostitute in a guarded house in a large city.
      (iii) A crippled girl needing medical care.
      (iv) A village where people are afraid of many evil spirits.
      (v) A rural community where many farmers have lost their land to money-lenders.
      (vi) A Christian congregation in a communist land.
      (vii) A lonely person in a big city.
19. In what ways is your own Church's work of proclamation like, or unlike, the work of the herald in Isa. 52.7?
20. Are Christian hymns like the 'song of salvation' in 52.9–10? Which of the three themes do we chiefly find in our hymns? Give some examples of hymns, in support of your answer.

52.13—53.12
The Suffering and Victory of the Lord's Servant
November 539 BC

BACKGROUND AND OUTLINE

This is one of the best known passages in the Old Testament, because Christians have believed that it foretells the death and resurrection of Jesus Christ. When we look at it in its historical setting, just after the fall of Babylon, however, we find that the prophet intended it to be a message for the Israelite exiles. He wanted to prepare them for the mission of suffering which awaited them among the nations, and for the victory which lay at the end of the mission, when the Lord would return to Zion (52.8).

By trying to find out what this poem meant at that time, Christians will gain a better understanding of its meaning in the New Testament, and for today.

Main theme: The Suffering and Victory of the Lord's Servant

Part 1: Future glory (52.13–15)

Part 2: The Servant's suffering for the nations (53.1–9)

Vv. 1–3: The mission of the exiles.

Vv. 4–6: The Servant's pain is our healing.

Vv. 7–9: The innocent victim.

Part 3: The fulfilment of God's will (53.10–12)

Note: The last paragraph of the Glossary article on 'Servant' gives the opinions of some scholars about this poem.

READING SUGGESTIONS

To understand this poem we need to answer two questions: (a) who is the speaker in each part? (b) what time or period is he referring to?

(a) *The speaker* in parts 1 and 3 is *the Lord*. The speakers in part 2 are *the nations*, as shown by a careful comparison between 52.13 and 53.1.

(b) Parts 1 and 3, with their verbs in the *future* tense, such as 'shall prosper . . . shall startle . . . shall see . . . shall bear . . . shall divide', are prophecies written in 539 BC about what will happen at the end of the mission.

Part 2, with its verbs in the *past* tense, such as 'grew up . . . was wounded . . . was oppressed . . . was cut off', presents the words of the nations who will come to believe in the Lord at the end of the mission, telling about the life and death of the Servant of the Lord during the mission. For those who tell the story, it is the past.

To state this in another way, in Part 2 the prophet was telling the exiles what was ahead *during* their mission, and, in parts 1 and 3, what was waiting for them *at the end* of their mission.

Important words to look for:

(a) words for *suffering*: 'sorrow' (twice), 'grief' (twice), 'afflicted' (twice), 'bruised' (twice), 'stricken' (twice), 'despised' (twice), 'wounded', 'chastisement', 'stripes', 'marred appearance', 'cut off', 'death'.

(b) words for *sin*: 'transgressions, or transgressors' (4 times), 'iniquity' (3 times), 'sin' (twice), 'the wicked', 'oppression'.

(c) words for *salvation*: 'made whole', 'healed', 'accounted righteous'.

(d) Words telling about the *action of the Servant* on behalf of the nations: 'bear' (3 times), 'carried', 'laid on him', 'the travail of his soul', 'poured out his soul', 'made intercession'.

(e) pronouns referring to the *nations* in vv. 1–6: 'we', 'our', 'us' (14 times).

(f) Pronouns referring to the *Servant* in 52.13—53.12: 'he', 'his', 'him', (47 times).

Major themes in this poem are explained in the Glossary: 'Servant', 'nations', 'see', 'arm of the Lord', 'will of the Lord' (Glossary: purpose), 'judgement' (Glossary: justice).

INTERPRETATION

THE SUFFERING AND VICTORY OF THE LORD'S SERVANT

Who is the servant? This poem is a description of an individual whom God calls 'my servant' (52.13; 53.12). The question asked by the Ethiopian court official (Acts 8.34) shows how an ordinary reader might be confused about the identity of that individual. 'About whom, pray, does the prophet say this, about himself, or about someone else?'

Why did the prophet not name the individual? Here are some suggestions:

(a) He was talking about the future (see Reading Suggestions) and could not give him a name.

(b) He was showing the Israelite exiles what their mission of suffering for the world would be like. He did not have any particular individual in mind.

(c) He was thinking of a person who could be a representative Israelite, fulfilling the whole meaning of Israel according to God's purpose (Glossary: *Servant*).

(d) He wanted future generations to recognize, from this general description, individuals who fulfilled the mission of God's people in their own time.

These suggestions help us to see why Christians think of Jesus as the representative Israelite, and find in His life, death, and resurrection a perfect fulfilment of what the prophet wrote in 539 BC.

Where would the Servant suffer? Although the prophet did not mention any particular place, he said that the Servant would suffer, die, and be exalted in the sight of the nations. Part 2 of this poem (53.1–9) is like a mourning song, to be sung at the funeral of the Servant by those who knew him. The mourners in the poem are the kings who represent the nations (see Reading Suggestion, 1(a)). In 52.15, the prophet said, 'kings shall see'. The same idea is found in 49.7. Perhaps the prophet was giving a new interpretation of a similar idea from the first Exodus (see Exod. 15.14–16).

FUTURE GLORY (53.13–15)

The dry tree (53.2). The Servant would be like a young tree transplanted in very dry ground, where it could hardly grow because of a lack of water. Ezekiel had used this picture of Israel 'transplanted in the wilderness, in a dry and thirsty land' (Ezek. 19.13). By 'dry ground' (41.18; 53.2) the prophet meant the world destroyed by war, as Jeremiah had described the

Babylonian Empire after the destruction of Babylon. It was a place where 'cities have become a horror, a land of drought and desert, a land in which no one dwells, and through which no son of man passes' (Jer. 51.43). The prophet was telling the exiles that they would be transplanted into a world full of problems and difficulties.

The green tree (53.13). In the future, however, God would make the dry tree grow very tall and green. The prophet agreed with Ezekiel that God could 'make the dry tree flourish' (Ezek. 17.24). He was probably also thinking of the fruit and leaves as good for healing (see Ezek. 47.12). Perhaps he thought of the tree as a picture of a king, as in Daniel's interpretation of the king's vision: 'The tree . . . which grew and became strong so that its top reached the heaven, and it was visible to the whole earth, whose leaves were fair and its fruit abundant, and in which was food for all . . . it is you, O king . . . Your greatness has grown and reaches to heaven, and your dominion to the ends of the earth' (Dan. 4.20–22). The prophet was saying that in spite of the difficulty of the mission (dry ground), God will raise up some representative of Israel like a great tree, to bring blessing to all the earth.

This picture of the miraculous growth of the great tree helps us to understand why the prophet said that 'many nations' would all see and be surprised (52.15).

THE SERVANT'S SUFFERING FOR THE NATIONS (53.1–9)

The mission of the exiles (52.2–3). These verses make us think of Paul's words: 'death is at work in us' (2 Cor. 4.12). The prophet's hearers must be ready to suffer violence (52.14) and rejection (53.3). To understand these words, we may think of those crippled by war, disfigured by torture, broken by cruelty, dehumanized by oppression, left alone in their misery.

Outwardly, these verses suggest that the mission would be a complete failure. The servant would not have any influence on those who met him.

The prophet was warning the exiles that their mission would be a continuation of the sort of life they had already experienced. They would continue to be exiles among the nations until all came to see the salvation of God.

The Servant's pain, our healing (53.4–6). According to 52.15, however, the nations would gain a new understanding or insight: 'They shall see . . . shall understand.' In 53.1 the prophet said that this would be a new revelation of God's way of ruling (Glossary: *Arm of the Lord*). And here in 53.4–6 he describes the new revelation. If we read these verses aloud, special attention to the pronouns will show the prophet's poetic skill, and the moving beauty of the passage.

The new revelation which became the basis for the Christian faith was this: The undeserved suffering of Israel, whether of the whole people or of individuals, brings relief from suffering for others, whether nations or individuals.

The traditional understanding of suffering in all religions, including the religion of Israel, was that it was a punishment from God for sin, or perhaps a test of faith. This view is stated in v. 4: 'stricken, smitten by God, afflicted' because of sin. But the prophet was telling the Israelites something new as he prepared them for their mission. The whip-lashes, extreme pain, affliction, and grief which they would experience were part of God's plan to save others, both nations and individuals. 'The Lord has made the punishment fall on him, the punishment all of us deserves' (v. 6, TEV). To put it in a Christian way, those who proclaim God's rule must be ready to carry a cross, for that is God's way of ruling.

For the nations, the new revelation would mean a way out of the dead-end caused by war, destruction, brokenness, and sin, into wholeness (*shalom*) and healing.

The innocent victim (53.7–9). In these verses the prophet was saying that the final and most extreme form of suffering for the nations would be death itself (v. 9), the result of an unjust sentence by a corrupt court of justice (v.8).

There was nothing special about one more victim of injustice in a world where corrupt courts were often part of an oppressive system. The prophet was warning the people not to ask God for special treatment or protection from injustice, just because they would be engaged in mission. In fact, suffering from injustice was one way of witnessing to the true justice of God (see Isa. 42.1–4).

The Servant's innocence was not a reference to Israel's past sinful history, but to Israel's future mission as a forgiven sinner and redeemed rebel (see Isa. 43.25; 44.22; 48.9). The prophet was telling the people that in their mission they must not themselves use violence or lying of any kind (v. 9). Their silent witness would speak loudly for true justice, and help to speed it among the nations (Isa. 42.1–4).

The prophet's description of death was probably meant to cover other experiences like death which Israel would suffer, either as a people (see comments on Isa. 51.17—52.2), or as a representative individual (Ps. 88.3–12). Being 'cut off from the land of the living' (v. 9) could also mean enslavement, exile, oppression, separation from friends, injury, poverty, and trouble.

As Christians we think of these words as referring not only to Jesus's undeserved death, but to the experience of 'losing one's life' for Jesus's sake (Mark 8.35), or 'giving oneself up to death' (2 Cor. 4.11). To engage in mission means continuing to experience the suffering of God's Servant (Col. 1.24; Phil. 1.29–30).

THE FULFILMENT OF GOD'S WILL (53.10–12)

God's will entrusted to His Servant. These verses show us, not the passive lamb of 53.7, but the active, struggling Servant working with God to achieve the fulfilment of His will. His strenuous efforts are a description of what the prophet called 'pursuing deliverance' (51.1). We can see the close relationship between God and the servant in the two references to God's will: 'Yet it was the will of the Lord to bruise him . . . the will of the Lord shall prosper in his hand' (v. 10).

Knowledge of God. The Servant's 'travail of soul', meaning his inner suffering with and for the nations, and his bearing of their punishment, will give him an intimate 'knowledge' of God. In this he is contrasted with Adam (Gen. 3.6–7) and Israel (Hos. 4.1), who had lost such knowledge (see comments on 51.7). This knowledge of God, gained through sharing in the struggle for the salvation of the nations, makes it possible for the Servant to lead the nations back to God (v. 11).

Intercession. The Servant's intercessory prayer for God's enemies (v. 12) is another way of sharing in God's own struggle, and of belonging to God's 'kingdom of priests' (Exod. 19.6).

Sacrificial love. The Servant is willing to devote his whole life ('pour out his soul') and to die as an offering for sin (v. 10), in order to free the nations from the consequences of their sin, and allow them to begin again in wholeness and peace (v. 12).

The prophet was saying that the exiles' mission was part of God's will (Glossary) for the whole world. They must accept it with complete dedication and self-sacrifice. God's purpose would be fulfilled through their knowledge of Him, their priestly intercession, and their sacrificial self-giving in life and death.

God's will for the nations. The effect of the Servant's life and death would be to 'make many to be accounted righteous' 'v. ii). That is, those who were enemies of God ('transgressors') would be accepted by God as members of His people. The prophet had said that Cyrus's victories would bring outward deliverance from Babylon's power, and create conditions for a new order of nations. God's real purpose in supporting Cyrus, however, was that people all over the world would 'know . . . that I am the Lord and there is no other' (Isa. 45.6). True wholeness and healing can only come from 'knowing' the true Saviour through the sacrificial ministry of the Servant. This would be the fulfilment of the mission.

The continuing mission. Those among the nations who are accepted as a part of God's people will become 'offspring' (v. 10), or the next 'generation' (v. 8) of the Servant. It is they who will carry on the mission among the nations and across the 'generations' (51.6, 8) until it is finished. The prophet was telling the exiles to prepare a future community of 'Servants of the Lord' (54.17) in every place to continue the work. We compare this with what Christians call 'Church planting', when they think of the Church as continuing the mission of Jesus.

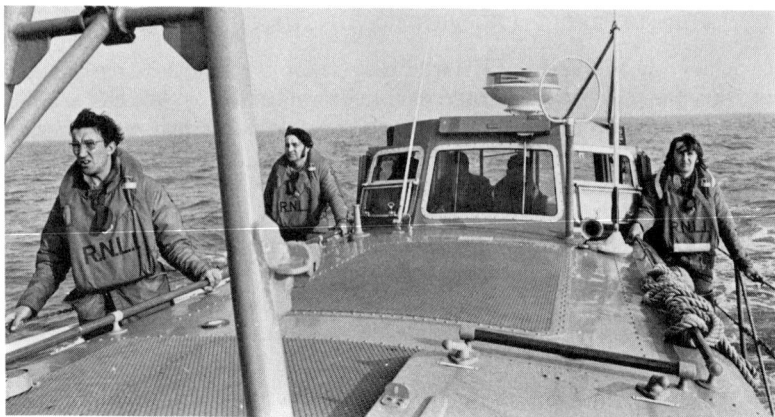

'The Servant is willing to devote his whole life . . . and to die in order to free the nations' (p. 156).

The crew of the Walmer lifeboat in southern England have volunteered for a service in which they risk their lives to save others from shipwreck.

In what parts of the world today do God's servants risk death in order to liberate others?

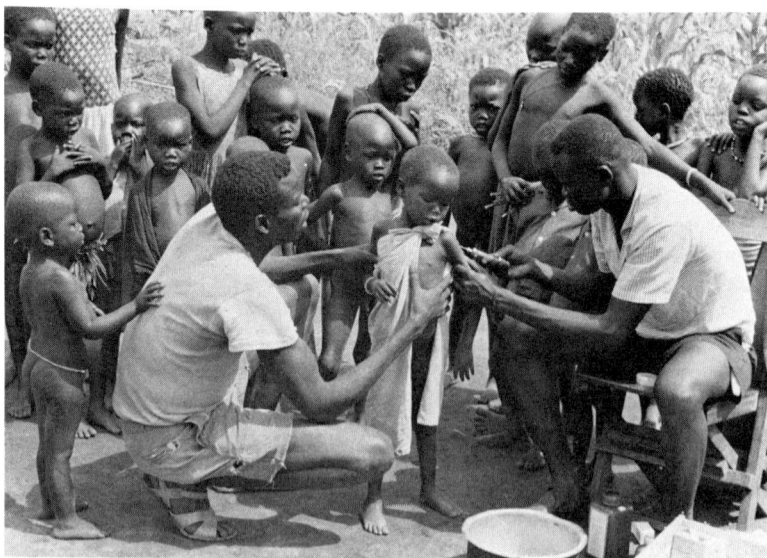

'God's promise . . . gave them hope and made them strong' (p. 162).

'During an epidemic in the southern Sudan a doctor and his assistant give injections to protect children and make them resistant to the disease.

What difference, if any, is there between the hope and strength we get from doctors and medicine, and that which God's promise gives us?

WHAT ABOUT THE FUTURE?

This poem began with a picture of the future glory of the Servant, as a beautiful green tree in a garden, giving blessing to the whole earth (52.13).

The picture in the last part of the poem is different. Now the Servant is in a place of honour, surrounded by his many descendants, living a long life. But the prophet was not referring to resurrection as we know it from the New Testament, or a life in heaven after death. It would be a new life here on earth after the sacrificial death of the Servant. Christians interpret this as meaning the 'next life' which they enjoy as a result of the life and death of Jesus.

We have seen above that the prophet may have been describing an experience *like* death rather than death itself. His picture of future glory is something like that of the *Perfected Zion* of the previous poem (51.17–52.12). He was telling the exiles that a glorious future lies at the end of the mission, therefore they could be joyful in this hope. This leads directly to the next poem.

ADDITIONAL NOTE ON THE IMPORTANCE OF ISAIAH 52.13—53.12 IN THE NEW TESTAMENT

Many passages in the New Testament show the great influence this poem had on the early Christian community. Some scholars believe that Jesus himself must have known it well, and in some way used it as a pattern for His own life.

WORDS ATTRIBUTED TO JESUS

'The Son of Man came to serve and give his life as a ransom for many' (Mark 10.45). 'He makes himself an offering for sin . . . shall make many to be accounted righteous' (Isa. 53.10, 11).

'The Son of Man must suffer many things.' (Mark 8.31). 'It was the will of the Lord to bruise him' (Isa. 53.10).

'This is my blood of the covenant which is poured out for many' (Mark 14.24). 'He poured out his soul to death . . . bore the sin of many' (Isa. 53.12).

'When I am lifted up from the earth . . .' (John 12.32). 'My servant shall be . . . lifted up' (Isa. 52.13).

QUOTATIONS OR REFERENCES BY
WRITERS IN THE NEW TESTAMENT

'He gave them no answer, not even to a single charge' (Matt. 27.14). 'He opened not his mouth' (Isa. 53.7).

'He took our infirmities and bore our diseases' (Matt. 5.17). 'He has borne our griefs and carried our sorrows' (Isa. 53.4).

'Behold the lamb of God who takes away the sins of the world' (John 1.29). 'Like a lamb that is led to the slaughter . . . he bore the sin of many' (Isa. 53.7, 12).

'. . . that Christ died for our sins in accordance with the scriptures, that he was buried, that he was raised in accordance with the scriptures' (1 Cor. 15.3–4). 'He made himself an offering for sin . . . they made his grave with the wicked . . . my servant shall be exalted and lifted up' (Isa. 53.9–10; 52.13).

'. . . who was put to death for our trespasses and raised for our justification' (Rom. 4.25). 'He was cut off from the land of the living . . . an offering for sins . . . he shall be exalted . . . my servant shall make many to be accounted righteous' (Isa. 53.8, 10; 52.13; 53.11).

'. . . delivered up according to the definite plan and foreknowledge of God' (Acts 2.23). God 'did not spare his Son but gave him up for us all' (Rom. 8. 32). 'The Lord has laid on him the iniquity of us all. . . . It was the will of the Lord to bruise him, he has put him to grief' (Isa. 53.6, 10).

'. . . having been offered once to bear the sin of many' (Heb. 9.28). 'He bore the sin of many' (Isa. 53.12). 'He is the expiation of our sins . . . also for the sins of the whole world' (1 John 2.2). 'He made himself an offering for sin . . . bore the sin of many' (Isa. 53.10, 12).

'He emptied himself, taking the form of a servant . . . humbled himself and became obedient unto death. . . . Therefore God has exalted him' (Phil. 2.7–9). 'A man of sorrows . . . he opened not his mouth . . . was cut off from the land of the living . . . My servant shall be exalted' (Isa. 53.3, 7) 52.13).

'Yet they did not believe in him. It was that the word spoken . . . might be fulfilled, "Lord who has believed our report and to whom has the arm of the Lord been revealed?"' (John 12.38, quoting Isa. 53.1).

'My ambition is to preach the gospel not where Christ has already been named . . . as it is written, "They shall see who have never been told of him, and they shall understand who have never heard of him"' (Rom. 15.21). Paul was using Isa. 52.15 to explain why he planned to go into new regions to preach the gospel.

These and other New Testament verses show us how Isaiah 52.13—53.12 helped the early Christians to understand Jesus's life of service and suffering, His sacrificial death, and His resurrection, as part of God's plan for the salvation of the nations. For them, the Servant was none other than Jesus Christ. Christians today reading this passage find both a prophecy of Jesus and a description of the continuing mission of suffering to which we are called.

STUDY SUGGESTIONS

REVIEW OF CONTENT

1. For what reason did the prophet write this poem?
2. Who are the speakers in (a) 52.13–15; (b) 53.1–9; (c) 53.10–12?
3. For what four reasons did the prophet not name the Servant?
4. What was the prophet's picture of the glorious future of the Servant in 52.13? Where did he get these ideas? What is the contrasting picture in 53.2?
5. In what way would the mission of God's people be like their life during exile in Babylon?
6. What was the new revelation about the meaning of suffering which the prophet described in this poem?
7. Why did the Servant not receive justice in the court?
8. What is meant by 'experiences like death'?
9. What did God put in the Servant's hand?
10. What kind of knowledge did the Servant have, and how did he get it?
11. (a) How did the Servant fulfil the vocation of Israel as a 'kingdom of priests'?
    (b) How did the Servant finally fulfil his mission?
12. How did the mission of Cyrus differ from the mission of the Servant?
13. Who would the 'generation' of the Servant be?
14. What was the picture of the future glory of the Servant in 53.10–12? In what way is it like the picture of Zion in the previous poem?

APPLICATION, DISCUSSION, RESEARCH

15. Christians have many different ideas about the past or present identity of the Servant in this poem. Which of the following seems to you the most likely? Give reasons for your answer. The servant of the Lord in this poem is (a) Israel, (b) Jesus Christ, (c) the Church, (d) a small group within the Church, (e) the pastor, (f) a radio envangelist.
16. What can Christians learn from the experiences of Israel in exile that will help them to understand their own mission today? Ought such a mission to be carried on by specially committed and equipped groups within the Church? What kind of spiritual or other equipment would be needed?
17. Read Rom. 5.6–11. What similar ideas, if any, do you find in that passage and in Isa. 52.13—53.12?
18. How would you interpret the missions of Cyrus and the Servant in relation to your own community today?
19. In what ways can this poem be of help to Christians today in thinking about their own mission? What would a 'Servant life-style' mean for Christians in your country?

20. Read 2 Cor. 4.7–12; Phil. 3.10; and Col. 1.24 and show how these passages can be related to Isa. 52.13—53.12.

54.1–17
Israel's Heritage of Hope
November–December 539 BC

BACKGROUND AND OUTLINE

The prophet composed this poem to encourage the Israelite exiles after the fall of Babylon. He had observed their great insecurity (see v. 11), their inner divisions (v. 15), and their feeling that God had turned away from them (v. 1). They were not yet ready for the mission of suffering described in the previous poem (52.13—53.12). They needed hope which could give them strength and courage to go forward into the unknown future.

Many Christians today are experiencing insecurity and inner conflicts, and have doubts about God's power and love. This poem can still give hope to those who need strength and courage to live into the future. 'In this hope', wrote Paul, 'we are saved' (Rom. 8.24).

Main theme: Israel's heritage of hope

Part 1: Hope for a new people (vv. 1–8)
Vv. 1–3: The new people and the nations.
Vv. 4–5: A heartwarming welcome back home.
Vv. 6–8: A love which never fails.

Part 2: Hope for a new world (vv. 9–17)
Vv. 9–10: Firm foundations.
Vv. 11–15: The beautiful city of the future.
Vv. 16–17: Security in a violent world.

READING SUGGESTIONS

Look for the following 'pictures' of a troubled Israel, and compare each one with the other references given:
A mother whose children are dead (compare 51.18).
An unfaithful wife whose husband has left her (compare 49.14; 50.1).
Survivors in a time of chaos like an earthquake or flood (compare 42.16; 51.6).
A ship in a storm.
A people under attack (compare 41.11–13; 51.13).

Find the ten commands of God in vv. 1, 2, 4. They show God's will for his people. Following each group of commands God gives His reason, introduced by the word 'for'. Most of these reasons are God's promises for the future.

Themes in this poem which appear many times in Isa. 40—55 include the following: 'descendants of Israel' (Glossary), 'nations' (Glossary), 'redeemer' (Glossary), 'Holy One of Israel' (Glossary), 'mountains and hills' (Glossary), 'righteousness' (Glossary), 'peace'.

INTERPRETATION

ISRAEL'S HERITAGE OF HOPE (v. 17.)

The heritage. At the time of the Exodus from Egypt, the Hebrews were encouraged to endure hardship, division, and danger by God's promise to give them a land.

The promised land was their 'heritage', or inheritance from God 'see Psalm 136. 21, 22). The prophet who composed this poem used the same word, 'heritage', to describe God's promise to the Israelite exiles in Babylon at the beginning of their new 'Exodus'. He told them of God's promise to make them a new people and give them a new world. This promise gave them hope, and the hope made them strong.

The servants of the Lord. This is the only time that this prophet used the plural form 'servants'. Except for this verse, he always used 'servant' in the singular form. Here he was probably referring to the 'offspring' or 'generation' of the Servant of Isaiah 53.8, 10. He was thinking about the communities of faithful people in every nation who continue the work of the Servant. 'Servants of the Lord' is a good description of Christian communities today in every nation.

Their vindication. In the RSV 'vindication' is here used to translate the Hebrew word which is elsewhere translated as 'righteousness' or 'deliverance' (see Glossary, *Righteousness*, para. 3). Here it means the final fulfilment of God's promises, when the hope of a new people in a new world will come true.

HOPE FOR A NEW PEOPLE (vv. 1–8)

The new people and the nations (vv. 1–3)

(a) *Many new descendants* (v. 1). The prophet was 'comparing' the Israelite exiles with 'Captive Zion' (see p. 146), and gave them hope for many new children. In previous poems he had told them that these children would be born among the nations (49.20–23), and would become sons and daughters of Israel through faith (44.5).

(b) *The world, your promised land* (v. 3a). When the prophet said that the Israelites would 'spread abroad', he was referring to a tradition about Jacob. God had promised Jacob in a dream that he would 'spread abroad' in all directions and bring blessing to the nations. (Gen. 28.14).

One way to interpret that promise was that the Israelites would occupy the whole land of Canaan. But the prophet saw a different meaning. He thought of them spreading abroad over the whole earth, so that they could bring blessing to the nations. This interpretation of the promise came true when the early Church began to 'spread abroad', and is coming true in the present day.

(c) *The nations, your covenant family* (v. 3bc). The Hebrew word which is here translated 'possess' can have two meanings: either (a) to drive out by conquering, or (b) to receive as an inheritance. Both meanings are present in Deuteronomy 9. 1, 6. This is a tradition about the conquest of Canaan. Israel would 'dispossess' the nations of Canaan, and 'possess' the land promised by God.

The prophet applied the second meaning of the Hebrew word to the nations. He meant that Israel would one day receive the nations as members of the covenant family. Thus the descendants of Israel would themselves be fellow members of the nations among whom they lived. Loyalty to the God of Israel would not make them any less loyal to their own nation, because the God of Israel is also the 'God of the whole earth'. When the prophet said they would work to make desolate cities full of people once again, he was referring not only to Judah, but to the cities destroyed by war in every nation.

We find the same idea in the command of the risen Christ to 'make disciples of all nations' (Matt. 28.19); that is, to make the nations members of God's covenant family. In Ephesians 3.6, this is proclaimed as a surprising discovery that 'the nations' (the word is translated 'gentiles' in the RSV) are fellow heirs, members of the same body.'

A heartwarming welcome back home (vv. 4–5)

Today if a young person leaves home because of a quarrel, the parents put an announcement the newspaper: 'Mr and Mrs So-and-So appeal to their son or daughter to come back home. All is forgiven.' The prophet was saying once again to the Israelite exiles that God was fully prepared to welcome them back into His love and His service.

He used six titles of God, five of which explain God's welcome for Israel, and one, the last, refers to a welcome for all nations. (1) God was like Israel's *husband*, ready to take the unfaithful wife back and forgive everything (see Isa. 40.2). (2) God was like Israel's *close relative* or *'redeemer'* (Glossary), who was ready to rescue her from captivity. (3) God was like a *craftsman ('maker')*, ready to remake his people. (4) God was Israel's *Holy One* (Glossary), who would make His people holy once again, and use them for His holy purpose. (5) God was *Lord of Hosts,* ready to use all the forces of nature and history to help His people. (6). He was *God of the whole earth,* and one day all nations would worship Him.

A love which never fails (vv. 6–8)

The most important truth about God is not that He punishes sinners, but that he loves His people (see Isa. 43.4) with a love that will never change. Love is action. Three verbs describe God's love in action:

1. God will *gather* them from the nations to make them a people once again (see notes on Isa. 49.5–6). God showed this same sort of love-in-action in Jesus, the good Shepherd (John 10.11) who came 'to gather the lost sheep of the House of Israel' (Matt. 10.16), and make them into a new people (1 Pet. 2. 9, 10).

2. God will *have compassion* on His people like a mother (see Isa. 49, 15 and 43.2) when they face troubles (Isa. 49. 10–11). God showed this same compassion in Jesus who healed and cared for the sick (Matt. 14.14), the lost (Matt. 9.36), the hungry (Matt. 15.30), and the sorrowing (Luke 7.13).

3. God has *called* His people to have a part in the works of love – gathering the lost, showing compassion on the suffering.

HOPE FOR A NEW WORLD (vv. 9–17)

Firm foundations (vv. 9, 10). The prophet was comparing the West Asian world of the sixth century BC with the world in the time of Noah. In Noah's day the waters of the flood covered all the mountains and hills (Glossary). In the sixth century BC the wars fought by Assyria, Babylon, and Persia had destroyed the foundations of the old order. In Noah's day God's foundation for a new order was His covenant with Noah and his descendants (Gen. 9.8, 18–19). In the sixth century God's new foundation would be His covenant of peace with the remnant of Israel and their descendants, the nations (see notes on Isa. 42.6 and 49.8).

The beautiful city of God (vv. 11–15). The prophet began by describing the Israelite exiles as 'storm-tossed' in a small boat on a stormy sea. As a contrast to their present extreme insecurity, he showed them a picture of the city of the future. He described this city as built with beautiful precious stones, green as the forest, blue as the sky, and gold as sunrise. Probably the author who described the new Jerusalem in Revelation 21.18–21, borrowed some of his ideas from this chapter of Isaiah. As in Revelation, this city would also be open to the nations (Rev. 21.24; 22.2).

In that city, all the sons of Israel, as members of the covenant family of nations, will become disciples, and the Lord will teach them how to help those in trouble, and to stand with courage for the right (see notes on Isa. 50.4, 5). In a society where everyone is a disciple of the Lord, there will be wholeness and peace for all (RSV 'prosperity', see Isa. 53.5), and the righteousness mentioned in Isa. 45.8 will fill the city (see Isa. 48.18).

Oppression and terror will disappear, and everyone will live in complete security.

Security in a violent world (vv. 16, 17a). At the end of the poem the prophet turned once again to the actual situation. Peace was being destroyed by evil-speaking and violence. The metal-smiths were making weapons of war. For the servants of God, however, there is the promise that none of these destructive powers can succeed against God's covenant of peace.

RESPONSE TO HOPE

When the prophet described the hope of the Israelite exiles for a new people and a new world, he wanted to strengthen them to go forward into the future.

Instead of weeping, they sing and rejoice (v. 1). Instead of turning inwards and trying to preserve their own lives, they should turn outward and prepare to accept new peoples and nations into their 'tent', even changing their traditions and way of life if necessary ('stretching out the curtains, and lengthening the cords', v. 2). Instead of forgetting their own faith and identity, they should renew their commitment ('strengthen your stakes', v. 2). Instead of giving in to despair or defeat, they should accept God's forgiveness and respond to His call to practise love (vv. 6–8). Instead of standing hopeless because the foundations of the old order had been destroyed, they should build for the future city of God with acts of peace and righteousness, and work for the end of oppression, terror, and enmity.

STUDY SUGGESTIONS

REVIEW OF CONTENT

1. Why did the prophet feel it was necessary to remind the exiles of their hope for the future?
2. What was the heritage promised to Israel at the time of the Exodus from Egypt? In what ways was this idea changed in this poem?
3. What did the prophet mean when he used the plural form 'servants of the Lord' in Isa. 54.17? How is it related to 52.13. 53.12?
4. What three promises did this prophet mention, describing the hope for a new people?
5. (a) What six titles of God did the prophet use to explain God's warm welcome to the Israelites?
   (b) What three verbs tell of God's love in action?
6. With what was the prophet comparing what happened in 'the days of Noah'?
7. How is Isa. 54.10 related to Gen. 9.8, 18–19?

8. Describe the society of the city of God.
9. List five ways in which God's people should respond to the heritage of hope.

APPLICATION, DISCUSSION, RESEARCH

10. Which of the five descriptions of a troubled Israel in this poem would best fit any congregation you know? (See the Reading Suggestions.)
11. Compare the ideas about hope in Isa. 54 with those in 1. Pet. 1. In what ways are they similar or different? In what ways, if any, is each related to the Exodus idea of salvation?
12. One of the hopes for Israel in this poem is that the nations will be the 'covenant family' of Israel. Read Matt. 28.19 and Eph. 3.6. Compare the ideas there with this idea from Isa. 54.3. What is the responsibility of God's people in making this hope come true? What changes in Church structures or attitudes would be needed to enable the Church to become a real 'covenant family' of all peoples and classes in the world today?
13. According to Isa. 54.4, 5, God is ready to receive His sinning people back. What do these verses tell us about what happens to a person or congregation when they do return to God in faith and hope? How would you use these verses in a renewal service for Christians?
14. God promises to 'gather' His people into a single flock (v. 7). What does this mean for the following problems: (a) denominational separateness, (b) racial discrimination in the Churches, (c) differences based on caste, (d) laws concerning racial segregation?
15. Discuss ways in which (a) individual Christians, and (b) your congregation show God's compassion for the sick, lost, hungry, or sorrowing?
16. Discuss God's covenant of peace as described in v. 10.
   (a) For whom is this covenant intended?
   (b) In the Old Testament there are several covenants which may have been in the prophet's mind. Which of the following express the same ideas as those in 54.10? (i) The covenant with Noah in Gen. 9. (ii) The covenant with Abraham in Gen. 15.18 and 17.2–7. (iii) The covenant with Israel in Exod. 24.8 and Deut. 5.2–3. (iv). The covenant with David in Psalm 89.3. (v). The covenant with Levi in Mal. 2.4–7. (vi) The new covenant in Jer. 31.31–34 and Ezek. 37.26.
   (c) What did the covenant described in Isa. 54.10 mean for the future?
   (d) What are the obligations of those who are included in this covenant?
   (e) How can this covenant be understood as the foundation for a new world?

17. Compare the picture of the city of God in Isa. 54.11–15 with the picture of the New Jerusalem in Rev. 21–22.
    (a) Make a list of the similarities and differences between them.
    (b) Why is there no temple in either city?
    (c) In what way does each picture give strength for living in a world where there is oppression and terror?
18. Read the 'response to hope' (p. 165) and say how this poem might be of help in interpreting the Christian hope to Christians in your country.

55.1–13
Signs of Salvation
January 538 BC

BACKGROUND AND OUTLINE

This passage contains what may well have been the last recorded words of the nameless prophet of Babylon. The likely time of its composition is early in the year 538 BC, before the first group of Israelites set out from Babylon to return to the ruins of Jerusalem. The aim of this group was to rebuild the temple and once again appoint a descendant of David as King.

The prophet did not agree with these aims. He described a different vision of Israel's future. In his final words he did not mention the city of Jerusalem, the temple, or a Davidic king. Instead of working to get a new king, he told them they should accept the mission which God had given to David.

They were to be signs of God's salvation among the nations.

Main theme: Signs of Salvation

Part 1: An invitation to the covenant feast (vv. 1, 2)

Part 2: The mission of David's heirs (vv. 3–5)

Part 3: A call to repentance (vv. 6–9)

Part 4: God's word at work in a needy world (vv. 10, 11)

Part 5: The joyful procession bringing salvation (vv. 12, 13)

READING SUGGESTIONS

STRUCTURE AND EMPHASIS

Note the words which are repeated: come (4 times), buy (twice), money (twice), eat, eater, (3 times), words related to hearing (3 times), thoughts and ways (8 times), go out or go forth (twice).

Note the following words which show that the author wanted to emphasize something: in vv. 4, 5 'behold' (twice), followed by 'because of' and 'for'.

Note the important word 'for' in vv. 5, 7, and especially in vv. 8, 9, 10, 12.

CONNECTION WITH OTHER PARTS OF ISA. 40—55

See Glossary notes on 'Holy One of Israel' (v. 5), nations (v. 5), purpose (v. 11), and mountains and hills (v. 12).

References to water (v. 1): 41.18; 43.20; 44.3, 4; 48.18, 21; 49.10. See also Isaiah 35.6–7 and Ps. 84.6. How do these references help you to understand Isaiah 55.1?

References to a garden in the wilderness (v. 13): 41.19; 42.9; 44.3, 4; 45.8; 51.3; 52.9. See also Isaiah 35.1, 2; 32.15–17; Psalm 107.35–38. How do these references help you to understand this poem?

References to joyful song (v. 12); 42.11; 44.23; 48.20; 49.13; 51.3, 11. How is 55.12 related to these verses?

RELATION TO OTHER PARTS OF THE BIBLE

God's feast: Psalm 23.5; 36.6, 7; Isaiah 25.6; 65.13; Proverbs 9.5; Matthew 5.6; Luke 22.29, 30; Revelation 19.9; 21.6; 22.17.

Covenant with David: Psalm 89.3–4, 15–37.

Thorns and briars: Genesis 3.18; Isaiah 5.6; 7.23–25; 10.17; 34.13.

INTERPRETATION

SIGNS OF SALVATION (v. 13b)

In this poem also the main theme is found in the last line. A 'sign' may relate either to the present or the future. For example, the words 'coffee shop' on a sign tell us that food is ready for customers at any time. But a roadside sign reading 'Hotel and Restaurant 50 kilometres ahead' tell us that food and drink will be available when we reach that place in the future.

One of the signs referred to in the Bible is the rainbow. It is a sign that the rain falling now is for life, and not for death as it was in the time of the flood (see Gen. 9.12). But it is also a sign pointing to the future blessing which God intends for all the descendants of Noah. When the prophet Isaiah walked like a slave in Jerusalem, he was a sign pointing to the future defeat of Egypt, and a warning to the people of Jerusalem not to make an alliance with Egypt (see Isa. 20.1–6). The disciples of Isaiah were also signs, warning the present generation to turn to God, and pointing to God's coming judgement and grace (Isa. 8, 16–18).

This prophet wanted the Israelite exiles to think of themselves as signs pointing to present blessings and future hope for the nations. He told them of five ways in which they could be signs.

AN INVITATION TO THE COVENANT FEAST (vv. 1, 2)

1. *The invitation is from God but brought by His people.* For God's invitation, see Isaiah 45.22. For the mission of the servant community, see 49.6, 9.

2. *The invitation was for the hungry and thirsty.* The prophet believed that those who worship idols can never find satisfaction. Such worship is like feeding on ashes (Isa. 44.20). He was probably thinking of the deep longing in people's hearts for truth, or for the true God (see Ps. 42.2; 63.1). Many people today would speak of this as 'the search for truth', or 'for meaning', or 'for life'. The prophet was saying that any substitute for truth, any twisted meaning or false values, are like ashes instead of real food. See also Isaiah 51.1 and Matthew 5.6.

3. *The feast was a celebration of the covenant.* In ancient times people celebrated the making of a covenant by eating a meal together. One example is the meal shared by Jacob and Laban (Gen. 31.44, 54). Another is the covenant meal on Mount Sinai (Exod. 24.11). The prophet was thinking of this feast as a celebration of the 'covenant of peace' (Isa. 54.11), in which the nations would participate as members of the covenant family.

4. *The covenant meal is real nourishment.* This is the food and water of life which satisfies the deep longing of the heart for truth and meaning.

5. *The covenant meal is a sign.* For those who accept the invitation now, it is a sign of present grace and blessing. At the same time it is a sign of future blessing for all, in the day when all nations will sit at the feast as sons of Abraham.

THE MISSION OF DAVID'S HEIRS (vv. 3–5)

According to Israelite tradition, God promised to protect the kings of David's line from all their enemies, and to keep a descendant of David on the throne in Jerusalem for ever (see Ps. 89.21–23, 34–37). Many Israelites could not understand why God had allowed the Babylonians to bring the dynasty of David to an end. They thought that this meant that God was unfaithful to His covenant (see Ps. 89.39).

The prophet said that God's covenant with David could not be separated from His covenant with Abraham. God's purpose in both cases was to bring His blessing to the nations of the whole earth (see Gen. 12.3).

He used three words to describe God's purpose in choosing David:

(a) *Witness.* The prophet said that God wanted the Davidic kings to tell the nations about God's love and power. Probably he was familiar with this idea from Psalm 18.49, 50.

(b) *Leader.* The kings of David's line should lead the nations in such a way that they would receive God's blessing in fulfilment of the promise to Abraham. This idea is expressed in Psalms 18.43 and 72.17 (see note below).

(c) *Commander.* The Davidic kings were to inherit the nations as part of God's kingdom (Isa. 54.3, see Ps. 2.8). The kings should teach the nations to obey God (Isa. 45.14; 53.11, see Ps. 18.43), so that they would become a part of the covenant family of Abraham (Isa. 54.1, see Gen. 17.5 and Ps. 47.9).

The prophet believed that the mission which God had entrusted to David was more important than the dynasty. Even though the dynasty had come to an end, the mission continued. He was saying that the Israelite exiles were David's heirs, and that God was not unfaithful to His side of the covenant with David.

The prophet had already explained to the people their mission as witnesses (Isa. 43.8–13), as bringers of blessing (Isa. 42.6, 7; 49.6; 52.5), and as leaders of the nations to God (Isa. 45.14–17; 49.7; 53.12). Herald Zion (see 51.17; 52.13) was to carry on the mission of David among peoples of whom they had never heard, with history, customs, cultures, and world-views completely different from their own.

A CALL TO REPENTANCE (vv. 6–9)

In order to prepare his people to avoid mistakes in their mission among strange nations, the prophet called on them to turn to God in prayer and submit themselves to His guidance. He said three things:

(a) God makes Himself available to those who seek Him with a humble heart (v. 6).

(b) God is ready to remove what is self-centred and destructive from the thinking and life-style of those who turn to Him (v. 7).

(c) The Israelites must not make the mistake of imagining that their thoughts are God's thoughts. They must even be ready to admit that their thoughts might be wrong or sinful, as they try to lead the nations to God. They must be modest in their claims, and try to avoid thinking too much of themselves or their own race and culture.

The prayerful community turning to God, and avoiding self-glorification in their mission, is a sign of God's present salvation and future hope for the nations.

GOD'S WORD AT WORK IN A NEEDY WORLD (vv. 10–11)

The Israelites believed that God puts His thoughts or plans into action by

171

means of His word. The word becomes effective when it is heard, proclaimed, and acted upon by the people of His choice (see 51.16).

In order to explain how God's word becomes effective, the prophet compared it to rain: (a) Rain soaks into dry ground and softens it so that growth can take place; (b) Rain brings the buried seed to life so that it sends up green sprouts; (c) Rain keeps the sprouts growing until at harvest time they bear grain for this year's food and next year's planting.

In the same way: (a) God's word penetrates into the life of a nation or individual, softening obstacles to growth, such as self-centredness, class or caste divisions, prejudices, cruelty in human relations, dehumanizing customs or laws, and creating conditions for growth. (b) God's word brings to life hidden possibilities, such as goodwill, reconciliation, freedom, love, compassion, courage. (c) God's word supports the growth of these hidden possibilities so that they bring about real changes in human relationships; justice (Isa. 42.4), righteousness, and salvation (Isa. 45.8).

The prophet was saying that when God's word is heard, proclaimed, and acted upon, it penetrates into the lives of individuals and of society as a whole to bring about real changes. This is a sign of God's present salvation and future hope for all.

THE JOYFUL PROCESSION BRINGING SALVATION (vv 12, 13)

The last words of the prophet were full of joy. He described a procession going from place to place bringing about a real transformation everywhere. Instead of hatred and bitterness (briars and thorns), love and peace (cypress and myrtle) will grow up. The true foundations (mountains and hills, see Glossary) of society will appear as justice, law, righteousness, salvation (Isa. 51.4, 5), and God's covenant of peace (54.10). Nature ('the trees of the field') will no longer be exploited and destroyed, but will be restored to its proper place in God's creation.

The prophet was describing the new Exodus of God's people from Babylon to the New Jerusalem by way of the ends of the earth, carrying out the mission given to David for all nations.

The covenant feast, the mission to the nations in fulfilment of God's call to David, the repentant community, the effective word, and the joyful procession are signs showing to all that God's salvation is a present reality, and a future hope.

NOTE

55.4. Leader: The Hebrew word here translated as 'leader' is translated as 'prince' in other passages. In 1 Samuel 9.16 and 10.1 we can see that this leader was supposed to save his people from their enemies. According to 2 Samuel 7.8, God appointed David as a 'prince' over His people. Perhaps

'Signs pointing to present blessings and future hope' (p. 171).

These Bolivian farmers are holding 'signs of blessing and hope' – letters of ownership of land distributed to them under a government land reform scheme.

Do you think the farmers would think of these letters as blessings from God?

'To believe that a person's life is determined by the stars at the time of birth is to deny the power of God to work new things in the future' (p. 180).

At a school for fortune tellers in Japan, students are taught that a person's life is determined – and can be predicted – from the lines in the hand.

How can we tell which practices in our own or other religions will tempt us to deny the power of God?

the prophet was quoting this verse as a basis for his new interpretation of the mission of David as a 'leader for the peoples'.

The prophet was using several psalms related to the king in his new interpretation of God's covenant with David. These are the 'royal psalms', which were used for special occasions, such as a coronation, and for weddings and anniversaries. Some of them are Psalms 2, 18, 20, 21, 45, 72, 89, 144.

STUDY SUGGESTIONS

REVIEW OF CONTENT

1. In what way did the prophet's ideas differ from those of the Israelite exiles who were planning to return to Jerusalem?
2. What are two possible meanings of a 'sign'?
3. Give three examples of a 'sign' in the Old Testament.
4. In this passage the prophet refers to a feast.
   (a) Who would carry the invitation to the feast?
   (b) What sort of hunger and thirst was the prophet referring to?
   (c) Give two other examples of covenant meals in the Old Testament.
5. Why did some Israelites believe that God had broken His covenant with David?
6. What were the three sorts of mission which God entrusted to David?
7. In what way were the covenants with Abraham and with David related?
8. Who are David's heirs, according to the prophet?
9. What three things did the prophet say in his call to repentance?
10. In what three ways can God's word be compared with the action of rain?
11. What sorts of changes were to take place among the nations to whom the people of God would go?
12. What are the five 'signs' mentioned in this poem, and what do they mean?

APPLICATION, DISCUSSION, RESEARCH

13. Each of the following could be understood as a 'sign' pointing to something present and future. Explain the meaning of each:
    (a) a mushroom cloud caused by an atomic blast.
    (b) A green tree in a city slum.
    (c) A well in a drought-stricken area.
    (d) A member of a war-like tribe who is converted to Christ.
14. Compare the covenant feast in Isa. 55.1, 2 to the Lord's Supper of Christians. Say in each case who is invited. What is the meaning of the meal? What kind of food is offered? In what way is the meal a sign for the present and the future?

15. Should Christians today think of their mission as a continuation of the mission entrusted to David? What are the dangers of a wrong understanding of the words 'witness', 'leader', 'commander'? How can the 'call to repentance' help to correct these mistakes?

16. In Isa. 53.8, 9, the prophet seems to be saying that human beings can never fully understand God's truth.

(a) Do you think that any religion or ideology can rightly claim (possess) 'absolute truth'?

(b) How would you account for the seeming contradiction between these verses and the words of Jesus, according to John 14.6 and 16.13?

Special Note C
Historical Background to Isaiah 56—66

These twelve poems belong to the twenty-three-year period between the first return of exiles from Babylon and the time when work on the second temple was completed.

THE FIRST SIXTEEN YEARS, 538–522 BC

This was a time of discouragement and frustration. After Cyrus's decree permitting a return to Judea (see 2 Chron. 36.22–23; Ezra 1.1–4), he appointed Sheshbazzar as Governor of the Persian Province of Judah (Ezra 5.14). Sheshbazzar was a 'prince of Judah' (Ezra 1.8), and was probably son of the deposed King Jehoiakin (see 2 Kings 25.27–30 and 1 Chron. 3.18, where 'Shenazzar' is probably another form of the name). It was he who led the first small group back to the ruined land.

A number of people were already living there. Some of them were Israelites who had been left behind by the Babylonian army in 587 BC (see Jer. 52.16). Others may have come back from Egypt (see Jer. 44.14, 28), or from other lands (see Jer. 40.11–12). Some may have come from the northern areas of Samaria (see Ezra 4.2). These people were referred to as the 'people of the land' (Ezra 4.1) or the 'peoples of the lands' (Ezra 3.3). They claimed to be worshippers of *Yahweh* (Ezra 4.2), but those who returned from Babylon considered that their worship was not a true worship (see 2 Kings 17.41).

Some sort of religious ceremonies had probably been held at the ruins of the temple (see Jer. 40.5) during the exile. Faithful Jews may have held services to recall the fall of Jerusalem and the destruction of the temple, and to pray for a new display of God's power and grace (see Lamentations,

Ps. 74 and 79, and Zech. 7.5). However, there were also other practices which the people of the land had adopted from Canaanite, Egyptian, or other religions of that period (see Isa. 57.3–10; 65.2–5).

The group from Babylon began by laying a foundation for the temple (Ezra 5.16). They were not able to do more however, because they were few, and found it difficult even to get enough to eat and to build houses for themselves.

Cyrus died in 529 BC on the eastern borders of his empire, in what is now Afghanistan. His son Cambyses expanded the borders of the empire by conquering Egypt in 525 BC.

The high hopes of many of the exiles from Babylon were not fulfilled. There were no signs of the New Jerusalem.

THE SECOND PERIOD, 522–515

This was a time of excitement and hope. Cambyses died in 522 BC without leaving an heir. For six months a man claiming to be his brother tried to rule, but in August Darius, a relative of Cambyses, took power. Darius's campaigns to put down revolts and independence movements lasted until the end of 521 BC. Peace was finally restored after almost two years of turmoil.

The news of these events revived hope among the Jews that the last days were at hand, when God would come and establish His kingdom. Just at that time Zerubbabel, a grandson of Jehoiakin, was appointed as the new governor, probably by Darius. He led a second and much larger group of Jews from Babylon back to Judea (see Ezra 2), in hopes of being in Jerusalem for the Day of Salvation. A priest named Joshua and the prophets Haggai and Zechariah were with him. The prophets encouraged the people to stop working on their own houses and begin rebuilding the temple. They said that God would overthrow the Persian Empire (Haggai 2.21–22), and anoint Zerubbabel as a new David (Haggai 2.23) and Joshua as a new Zadok (Zech. 2.4–5; see 1 Chron. 29.22).

They began in 520 BC by rebuilding the altar so that their sacrificial worship could start again. Then they relaid the foundations of the temple (see Ezra 6.11; 3.2–3, 8–10), and five years later, in 515 BC, work on the temple was completed, and they were at last able to celebrate the Passover (Ezra 6.11–15, 19–22).

56—59
Reform and Renewal
535–515 BC

BACKGROUND AND OUTLINE

These five poems reflect the concerns of the new community which grew up in the ruins of Jerusalem and Judah after 538 BC (see Note on Historical Background of Isaiah 56—66). This community was neither the *Herald Zion* nor the *Perfected Zion* about which the prophet in Babylon spoke (see Isa. 51.17; 52.12). It was a group of very ordinary people who faced the tasks of rebuilding their society as well as their temple, and of reshaping their theology as well as their religious practices.

In these poems we see discouragement (59.11), guilt (59.12, 13), injustice (59.14), divisions (58.9b), poverty (58.10), corrupt religion (57.3–10), confusion about fasting (58.6–9) and sabbath observance (58.13, 14).

Similar problems face Christians today. The poems contain practical guidance for the reform and renewal of our own lives.

Main theme: Reform and Renewal

First poem: God's house is for all people (56.1–8)

Second poem: Wrong worship (56.9; 57.13)

Third poem: God cares for all, far and near (57.14–21)

Fourth poem: Right worship (58.1–14)

Fifth poem: A call to repentance (59.1–21)

READING SUGGESTIONS

Some passages in these poems are worth marking in your Bibles for easy reference:
   56.6–7: The inclusiveness of worship. Jesus Himself quoted part of v. 8.
   57.12b: The relationship between land and people.
   57.15: God is highest and nearest.
   58.6–14: True worship.
   59.9–15: Confession of sins.

INTERPRETATION

This first group of five poems deals with three questions which the discouraged people were facing in their daily life: (1) Who is a true Israelite? (2) What is true worship of God? (3) When will God save us? For Christians these questions might be stated as follows:
 (1) What restrictions should there be for Church membership?
 (2) What is the relationship between worship and life?
 (3) When will Christ come?

WHO IS A TRUE ISRAELITE?

The problem was whether 'foreigners' or 'eunuchs' (56.3, 4) should be welcomed into the community and allowed to worship God with the Jews who had returned from exile. We learn from Ezra 6.21 that they accepted some from the 'peoples of the land'. It is possible that some of those who returned from Babylon were not Jews by birth (see Isa. 44.5; 45.14). The eunuchs may have been servants in the royal household in Babylon (see Isa. 39.7; 2 Kings 20.17, 18). According to the law, Moabites and Ammonites were excluded from membership in the worshipping community for ten generations (Deut. 23.3), and this law could be extended to include all who were not of Israelite descent. Another law made it impossible for eunuchs to become members of the Jewish community (Deut. 23.1; Lev. 22.4).

Some of the people insisted on the strict application of these laws. The prophet Haggai seems to have done so. Ezra and Nehemiah, 100 years later, also belonged to this group. Haggai said that any contact of the Jews with outsiders made the Jewish worship unclean (Hag. 2.10–14). Ezra and Nehemiah forced the Jewish men to put away their foreign wives (Ezra 9.1–10; Neh. 13.1–3, 23–27). This group believed that the 'holy race' should not 'mix itself with peoples of the lands' (Ezra. 9.2).

The prophet who wrote Isaiah 56.1–8, however, was opposed to this view. He said that God welcomed eunuchs and foreigners to membership in the covenant community and to worship in the temple. Paul agreed with this prophet when he wrote, 'He is not a real Jew who is one outwardly . . . He is a Jew who is one inwardly, and circumcision is a matter of the heart, spiritual, not literal' (Rom. 2.28, 29). Jesus quoted Isaiah 56.7 when he cleansed the temple (Mark 11.17), and He was probably thinking of Isaiah 56.8 when He spoke of other sheep 'not of this fold' (John 10.14).

How wide should the community of faith be? This prophet tells us that there can be no restrictions of race, 'nationality', sex, condition of life, social class, or political views. *All* are welcomed by God.

WHAT IS TRUE WORSHIP OF GOD?

God gave the Israelites the covenant regulations as a guide to show them how to approach Him in worship. But the people in every generation were continually failing to fulfil the covenant law. For this reason, God sent prophets to bring them back to the true worship.

Some were corrupting their worship by adopting popular practices from other religions. Others were worshipping God according to the covenant law, but were corrupting their worship by living selfish lives. In these poems the prophet spoke to both groups.

Popular practices from other religions which corrupt worship.

The prophet condemned three sorts of religious practices (see 56.9—57.13; 63.3–5, 11; 66.3–4).

1. *The use of sexual relations to influence God.* Many people at that time believed that they could get abundant crops, large flocks and herds, and many children, by having sexual relations with persons dedicated to a fertility god or goddess. The usual place for such practices was at garden shrines (57.5; 65.8; 66.17). Another custom related to sex was for parents to sacrifice a child as a burnt offering to the nature gods (57.7; 66.3). They believed that this costly act was necessary in order to influence the gods to answer their prayers.

The prophet said these practices were a wrong way to approach God. They were forbidden by God's law (Deut. 18.10; 23.17). Israelites before the Exile had followed them (2 Kings 23.7; Jer. 7.31; 19.5), and the Exile was the result. Jeremiah had said that such practices were not directed toward God at all, but were usually a way of satisfying sexual lust with the approval of religion (see Jer. 2.20, 23–25). We can see three main reasons why the prophet opposed the use of sex to approach God:

Firstly, sexuality is not a possession which men and women can safely use as they like. It is a gift from God (see Gen. 1.26, 27). Men and women are responsible to God for the ways in which they express their sexuality.

Secondly, to use sex in order to influence God or another person to do what we want is a misuse of God's good gift, because we say to God, 'my will be done', instead of 'your will be done'. Sexual relations in the garden shrines were a misuse of sexuality. Today we allow commercial advertising to sell products by exploiting sexual desire; men's domination over women in society; prostitution; pornography; marriages that are arranged by parents for selfish purposes such as preservation of family property, without regard to love; selling children as prostitutes or slaves. All these involve a wrong use of sexuality.

Thirdly, sex may become a 'substitute god', to which people give more honour than they do to the true God. In the ancient world the gods and goddesses of sex had names. Today there are no such names, but the temptation to turn to sex instead of to God is still present. More effective methods of contraception, the breakdown of traditional marriage customs, changing moral values, the continual emphasis on sex in books, newspapers, radio, and TV programmes, all these have brought a new freedom in sexual relations and new temptations to forget God. Paul reminded the Christians in Corinth: 'The body is not for immorality, but for the Lord. . . . Your body is the temple of the Holy Spirit within you' (1 Cor. 6.15, 19).

2. *Consulting the dead* (57.9; 65.4). People spent the night in tombs among the bones of their ancestors. They shared a sacred meal in which they ate the meat of pigs and mice, which was forbidden by Jewish law. They hoped in these ways to contact the spirits of their dead relatives, either through dreams, or though a medium who, they believed, could visit the land of the dead. They believed that the spirits of the dead were powerful and could influence living people. Sometimes they tried to persuade the dead to curse and bring harm to their enemies.

The prophet gave three main reasons why consulting the dead is wrong:

Firstly, it is based on wrong ideas about the power of the dead. They are not strong but weak (see Isa. 14.10). They return to dust, a symbol of weakness (see Gen. 3.19). This means that they do not have power to influence living people. Mediums who consult the dead can only 'chirp and mutter' (Isa. 8.19), without saying anything.

Secondly, it was for their own selfish purposes that the living tried to use the dead: either to preserve their own power, to dominate others, or to prevent change. For this reason, consulting the dead leads to 'distress, darkness, gloom of anguish and cursing' (Isa. 8.21–22), rather than to peace and love.

Thirdly, it turns people away from the true God and toward themselves instead. 'Should not a people consult their God?. . . . to the teaching and to the testimony' (Isa. 8.19, 20). For this reason, necromancy, that is, consulting the dead, was absolutely forbidden in Israel (Deut. 18.11, 12).

The proper way to think about the dead in our worship is in the 'communion of saints' We thank God for them. We honour their memory. We learn from their example. We are bound to them by ties of love and faith. But we should not consult them or try to use their love and power for our own purposes.

3. *Star worship.* Star worship also was popular in Israel. In 65.11, the Hebrew words translated 'fortune' and 'destiny' are probably the names of two star gods: Gad (male) and Meni (female). Those who joined in their worship took part in communion meal with mixed wine. They believed that the star gods of good luck and bad luck could affect the lives of individuals and nations.

Worship of the star gods was common in Israel before the exile (2 Kings 17.16; 21.3–5; 23.4, 5). The law condemned it (Deut. 4.19; 5.8; 17.3), and

the prophets opposed it (Amos 5.26; Zeph. 1.5; Jer. 8.2; 19.13; 44.17–19).
There were three reasons also for opposing star worship.

First the sun, moon, planets, and stars are not themselves gods, but were created by the one true God to serve His purposes (see Gen. 1.16; Ps. 8.3; Isa. 40.26). Even if scientists in the future discover that the magnetic fields of the other planets or of stars do influence human behaviour, they remain a part of God's good creation, and are under His control.

Secondly, the stars have no power in themselves to save people or nations from disaster, or to control the future (see Isa. 47.12–15; 57.10–13). God alone is in control of the future (see Isa. 12–24; 44.7). He alone can save from disaster (see Isa. 45.12–22; 45.15, 21–22). To believe that a person's life is determined by the position of stars at the time of birth is to deny the power of God to work new things in the future (see Isa. 42.9).

Thirdly, star worship turns people away from the true God toward themselves, because it makes them forget God's demands for repentance and obedience.

The prophet who wrote these lines spoke out strongly against these practices (66.3). Those who take part in them, he said, are children of witches (57.3). They provoke God to His face (65.3), because they are choosing their own way instead of God's (65.2; 66.4). These popular practices borrowed from the customs of other nations corrupt the true worship which God expects from His own people.

Christians in each land have the difficult task of deciding what customs of their own country should be adopted for use in Christian worship. One example is the rice harvest festival, which is held by many Asian peoples. Christians often celebrate this festival, using some of the traditional customs of their own people. But they do not follow any of the practices which might turn them away from the true God.

Selfish acts which corrupt worship.

Many Jews were faithfully carrying out their religious practices in the belief that following these rules would bring them close to God. They prayed daily (58.2) and fasted regularly (58.3; see Zech 7.5; 8.19). Yet something was wrong. Their worship had no effect on the life of their community. The problem was that the outwardly correct practice of worship brought them no understanding of their sins. The community was torn with divisions (58.4; 65.5). There was great inequality between the rich and the poor (58.3; 59.3–8). Those who tried to do right became victims of greedy people (59.15). No-one cared if a good person was wrongly punished (57.1). This sinful condition of society was a barrier which separated the people from God (59.2). They were like blind people who could not understand their own condition (59.9, 10).

The prophet pointed out that worship of God must result in doing His will. True repentance (59.12, 13) will result in caring action to liberate the oppressed, feed the hungry, shelter the homeless, and clothe the naked (58.6–10). When worship and life are brought together in this way, God is pleased (56.7).

These words remind us of Jesus's description of the Pharisees, who kept all the details of their religious duties but neglected justice, mercy, and faith (Matt. 23.23). James echoed this teaching when He said that faith without works is dead (James 2.17), and so did John; 'If anyone says "I love God" and hates his brother, he is a liar' (John 4.20).

Christians are in danger of this kind of corrupting influence in their worship when they fail to prevent injustice and care nothing for its victims.

True worship will turn a person from self to the true God, and to caring for others.

WHEN WILL GOD SAVE US?

Many in the community of returned exiles in Judea hoped and believed that God would miraculously intervene to establish a Jewish kingdom and make the land fertile once again. However, as year followed year with no change for the better, they became more and more discouraged. They wondered when God would come to save them from all their troubles. The prophet gave them three answers to this question:

1. God is always able to save (see 59.1, and compare with 50.2), and He will come with salvation that is world-wide (59, 16–20). The prophet did not say *when* God would come, but tried to give the people a new understanding of their present situation.

2. God's gift of salvation is available in the present. God will revive humble people who turn to Him now with true worship (see 57.15). God's covenant bond of love (compare 54.10), His powerful spirit (compare 42.1), and His commission to His servant people ('my words in your mouth', compare 51.16) are present realities. These are God's gifts for His people and their children's children (59.21). The prophet was telling the Jews to open their eyes to the reality of salvation in the present.

3. The people must respond to God's gift of salvation by deeds of love according to His will. God intends His salvation to change the present world and society.

Those who meet the needs of the afflicted will find that God will satisfy their desires and make them a blessing (see 58.10, 11). Those who heal the hurt of their neighbours will find comfort in God (see 58.6; 57.18). Those who answer the cry of the hungry will hear God's answer to their cry (see 58.7, 9). Those who open the house of God to all peoples (56.7, 8) will receive the mountains of Palestine as God's gift (see 58.14). Those who give the light of kindness to the hungry and homeless will see God's light for them (see 58.7, 8).

The prophet was saying that salvation is not just something we receive; it is a way in which we walk (see 57.14). Those who walk in that way will bring peace to their community. They walk in hope of the coming of God's future great salvation.

STUDY SUGGESTIONS

REVIEW OF CONTENT

1. What is the historical background for the five poems in Isa. 56.9?
2. What was the Jewish law about Moabites, Ammonites, and eunuchs?
3. What verse did Jesus quote when He cleansed the temple?
4. In what chief ways do we corrupt the true worship of God?
5. What three sorts of religious practice did the prophet condemn?
6. Why did the prophet criticize the worship of the faithful Jews?
7. What three things did the prophet say about God's salvation?
8. What is the right response to God's salvation?

APPLICATION, DISCUSSION, RESEARCH

9. What would be the attitude of congregations you know towards accepting the following people as members? Do you share that attitude? In what ways is it related to Isa. 56.1–8?
   (a) A person from another caste or tribe,
   (b) A person with a different skin colour,
   (c) A bar-tender,
   (d) A night club singer,
   (e) A member of the police force,
   (f) A member of the communist party,
   (g) A person who does not behave according to accepted social customs.
10. In what ways does human sexuality: (a) help us to remember God, (b) tempt us to forget God?
11. What are some ways in which (a) traditional customs, and (b) modern customs in your country, encourage people to misuse human sexuality for selfish purposes?
12. Study the beliefs and practices of another religion concerning the spirits of the dead and their relationship with the living. Compare these with the views of Old Testament writers. Do you think that Christians should observe the strict laws of ancient Israel against trying to contact the spirits of the dead?
13. When a person accepts Jesus Christ and is baptized, what happens to his or her relationship with parents who have died without knowing or accepting Christ? Discuss the following ideas:
    (a) We commit our parents to God's love.
    (b) Although we rejoice in our salvation, we feel sad that we shall not see our parents after we die, because they will be in another place.

(c) We try to do as much good as possible so that God will use our good deeds to save our parents.

(d) We pray to God to accept their sincere faith in their own religion.

14. Which do you think is more dangerous to true worship: (a) adopting practices from other religions, or (b) selfish behaviour by regular Church members? Give reasons or examples to support your answer.

15. Are all practices of other religions in conflict with the Christian faith? What is your opinion of the following statements?

(a) Some practices in other religions are related to the agricultural year, such as planting and harvesting, or to the events in the life of an individual, such as birth, marriage and death. We should try to adapt these to the Christian religion, since all human life is under God's care.

(b) Christians should say a firm 'no' to all practices from other religions, because they would lead away from God.

(c) Christians should borrow as many customs and practices as possible from the culture and religions of their country, in order to make Christianity really at home and understandable to their fellow countrymen, and lead them to the true God.

(d) Christians should attend the ceremonies of other religions as a sign of common humanity with them under one God.

60—62
Living Toward the Future
520–515 BC

BACKGROUND AND OUTLINE

These three poems about the glorious future which God will bring to His people were composed during the turmoil at the beginning of the reign of the Persian King Darius. They express the hope which stirred in the hearts of the people during the building of the temple in Jerusalem. (see Note on the Historical Background, p. 175). The prophets Haggai and Zechariah were urging the people to work on the temple, and were giving them hope that God would establish His kingdom very soon. This prophet showed them a different kind of hope.

The 'darkness' mentioned in 60.2 may be a poetic description of the wars and rebellions throughout the Persian Empire in 522–521 BC. The

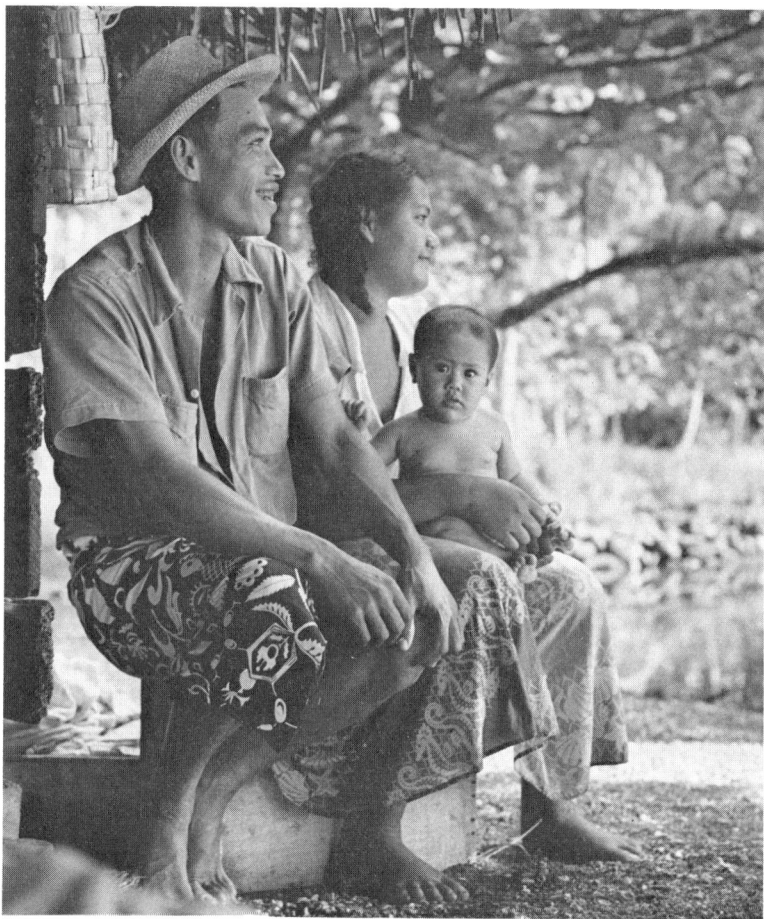

'A vision of the future in their hearts' (p. 185).

Their baby son is one 'vision of the future' which these Tahitian parents keep in their hearts.

What are some other 'everyday' things which give people a vision of the future, and what sort of vision is it likely to be in each case?

promises about the future also show us what condition the land of Judah was in at that time. The land was in ruins (61.4; 62.4). The walls of Jerusalem and the temple had been broken down (60.7, 10, 17, 18; 62.9). Violence and robbery by unfriendly neighbours was a common experience (60.18; 61.8; 62.8).

The prophet's purpose was to encourage people living in those difficult times to keep a vision of the future in their hearts.

Main theme: Living toward the future

First poem: A light to the nations (60.1–22)

Second poem: The wealth of the nations (61.1–11)

Third poem: A torch of salvation (62.1–12)

READING SUGGESTIONS

The interpretation given below deals with themes rather than with each poem separately. Therefore you should read the poems through before going on to the interpretation.

It will help your understanding if you take time to look up the references to these poems which are mentioned in the interpretation.

Some passages worth underlining in your Bible are:

60.1–3. Israel as a light to the nations. Compare 49.6, 7: 60.21; and 61.11. The People of God as a beautiful garden. Compare 41.18–20; 44.3–4; 45.8; 55.12, 13.

61.1–2. Jesus's programme for His ministry (see Luke 4.16–21).

61.10. Israel as the bride of God.

62.1–2. Jerusalem as a torch for the nations (compare 60.1–3).

62.11. The coming Saviour (compare 40.10, 11).

INTERPRETATION

GOD'S INTENTION

The prophecies which we find in these poems show God's intention for the future and the present. This does not mean that the details of the prophecy came true at a later time. It was the inner meaning that was fulfilled. For example, the fulfilment of the prophecy in 60.6, 9 is not in sailing ships and camels. That was simply the poet's way of describing (a) the prosperity to come, and (b) a future relationship between God's people and the nations.

When Jesus said that the words of Isaiah 61.1, 2 were fulfilled (Luke 4.21), He meant that God's intention had come true in His ministry to the poor, the blind, and the captives, as the beginning of the time of salvation.

This means that we must look behind the prophetic words for God's intention, which may be partially fulfilled in our own time. The words in

60.4, 'They all gather, they come to you from afar', are partially fulfilled in a Church service in Northern Thailand in which many hill tribe Christians join with Thai Christians in worship. And the same is true on similar occasions in other countries.

Again, the words in 61.9, 'Their descendants shall be known among the nations', are perhaps fulfilled in the witness of joy, faith, and hard work for national construction by Christians in China. God's intention is that the gates of Jerusalem should be opened for all nations (60.11). This intention is partly fulfilled when Christians plan for dialogue and social action with people of other religions and cultures. God's intention that ruins should be rebuilt (61.4) makes Christians eager to help rebuild what has been broken down by war or disaster.

In these poems we find a description of God's intention for a new Jerusalem, a new people of God, and new nations.

A NEW JERUSALEM

When the Israelites were slaves in Egypt, or wandering in the wilderness, they had a dream of the promised land – good, broad, and fertile (Exod. 3.8). The community living among the ruins of that land dreamed another dream – a new Jerusalem.

The first to experience this dream was the prophet Isaiah. Jerusalem in his time was like Sodom and Gomorrah (Isa. 1.10; compare Gen. 18.20, 21; 19.24), which had to be destroyed. Although he later came to believe that God would not destroy His holy city, Isaiah proclaimed that God was working to build a new Jerusalem (10.2), with a new foundation of faith and a plumbline of justice (28.16, 17, compare Amos 7.7–9). The new city would arise, he said, and would be called the city of righteousness (1.26), full of God's spirit (32.15). The people would live there in quietness, trust, and peace, and the land would be very fertile (32.15–18). God's intention was that all nations should come to this new city to learn the ways of peace (2.2–4). This was Isaiah's dream.

This dream inspired the disciples of Isaiah in later generations. The prophet in Babylon saw a *Perfected Zion* of the future, at the end of the mission of *Herald Zion* (see 51.17; 52.12). Perfected Zion would be the bride of the Lord (54.5), with many children coming from the nations (54.1–3). It would be built on a covenant of peace (54.10); its people would live in righteousness and security (54.11–14).

The prophet who wrote these poems continued to dream of a new Jerusalem. He thought of it as a burning torch of salvation for all nations to see (62.1–2, compare 60.1–3). In this city there would be no need for the sun or moon, because God Himself would give eternal light as on the first day of creation (60.19, 20, compare Gen. 1.3 and Rev. 22.5). The new Jerusalem is the beginning of God's new creation, the new world!

In this city there will be no violence (60.18, 21), corruption (65.16), sorrow (65.19), disease, or other cause of early death (65.20). There will be no more enmity between nations (65.25), and all will be reconciled with God (65.24). The gates of the city will be open day and night for all nations to come in and go out (60.11).

This description cannot fit any actual city, not even the Jerusalem of history. The picture of a new Jerusalem is in fact a poetic description of God's intention for the whole earth. It is the *goal* of history. For this reason, the writer of Revelation did not locate it in heaven but on earth (Rev. 21.2, compare 21.22–27; 22.1–5). Others have dreamed of this kind of society. The Chinese call it the Ta T'ung, 'the great harmony' of all mankind. Revolutionary idealists call it the 'classless society'. Jesus called it the 'Kingdom of God'.

A NEW PEOPLE

The prophet continued to see the vision which the prophet of Babylon had seen about God's intention for His people. They were God's covenant people (61.8; compare 54.10), God's 'bride' (62.4; compare 54.6–8), wearing robes of salvation (61.10; compare Rev. 7.9), and full of everlasting joy (61.7; 60.15; 61.10; compare 51.3). God would give them a new name (62.2, 4, 12; compare 43.1 and Rev. 2.17; 3.12; 14.1; 22.4). This new people would belong to the Lord.

Although the people were small in numbers, God's intention was to multiply them (60.22) with new sons and daughters (60.4, 9) in place of those lost in the disasters of former years.

THE NEW NATIONS

Although the small community was living in Judah, the prophet said that they would go out among the nations, as a visible example of righteousness and praise (61.9, 11). Because of their example the nations would come from great distances to Jerusalem (60.11), bringing fine wood for the temple (60.13), and flocks of animals and incense for the temple worship (60.6, 7). Their 'wealth' which they bring to Jerusalem (60.5, 11) must include not only silver, gold, and material things, but their cultural and spiritual treasures as well. The sons and daughters of Israel who have been born among the nations (60.4, 9) would interpret the inner meaning of this heritage to the people who live in Jerusalem. All enmity between Israel and the nations would disappear. Former oppressors would gladly help build the walls of the city (60.10), and tend their flocks and herds (61.5).

What will the nations think of Israel? They will speak of Jerusalem as the city of God (60.14), and recognize the people of Israel as priests for them before the Lord (61.6; compare Exodus 19.6). They will know that Israel has been blessed and brings them the blessing of covenant with God (61.9). They themselves will praise the Lord (60.6).

The circle of salvation seems to grow wider and wider, as the nations and the descendants of Israel living among them pass in and out of the gates of Jerusalem, to and from their homelands.

LIVING TOWARDS THE FUTURE

Prophecies about an ideal future tell us what God is working for (God's intention), and what He wants us to work for in this very imperfect world. Hope helps us to understand our present world and society, *and* inspires us to change it. Prophecy about the future is thus a call to action in the present.

Worship towards the future. God's intention is to make us His new people, living among the nations as bearers of blessing and priests for them (see above). This hope inspires us (a) to rejoice now in our salvation, (b) to pray for our society and for all nations, (c) to work for the welfare of our society, and (d) to show in our lives the meaning of righteousness and salvation for others to see.

Living towards the future in society. God's intention is that all peoples should take part in building His new society, and contribute to it from their own cultural richness (see above). This hope inspires us: (a) to appreciate the value of all societies and cultures, (b) to welcome the contribution which people from different classes, castes, economic groups, racial groups, ideologies, and religions can make to the new society which God is creating, and (c) to seek opportunities to engage with all sorts of people in dialogue, and so help to break down the barriers of prejudice and misunderstanding.

Mission towards the future. God's intention is that there should be an end to violence, corruption, sorrow, disease, and hatred (see above). This hope inspires us, (a) to change the conditions and attitudes which lead to these evils, (b) to be concerned with the victims of them and to help rebuild ruined lives and societies.

God's intention is that communities of faith should increase among the nations (60.4, 9, 22). This hope inspires us (c) to work for the growth of the Christian community in every part of society in order to serve as the light of God's new creation.

STUDY SUGGESTIONS

REVIEW OF CONTENT

1. (a) When were the poems in Isa. 60—62 composed?
   (b) What was the condition of the land at that time?
2. What three descriptions of God's intention do we find in these poems?
3. Who was the first to dream of a new Jerusalem?
4. What did the prophet mean by the words, 'The sun shall no more be your light by day'?

5. What are God's intentions for the society of the future, as we find them in the prophet's description of the new Jerusalem?
6. What words or phrases used by other peoples express the same sort of idea as 'the new Jerusalem'?
7. What is God's intention for 'sons and daughters of Israel'?
8. Why will nations travel great distances in order to reach Jerusalem?
9. What is meant by 'the wealth of nations'?
10. What are *two* ways in which the hope of future salvation influences us in the present?
11. What *four* things does the hope of being God's new people inspire us to do?
12. In what *three* ways does hope affect our attitude towards other peoples?
13. What *three* sorts of mission task are demanded of us as a result of our hope for the future?

APPLICATION, DISCUSSION, RESEARCH

14. What is the difference between, (a) a prediction of what God will do at a certain time, and (b) a description of God's intention for the future? What does 'fulfilment' mean in each case? What should be our response to each?
15. 'The picture of the New Jerusalem is a poetic description of God's intention for the whole earth' (p. 5).
(a) Do you agree?
(b) Compare the pictures of the new Jerusalem in these poems with other pictures by (i) Isaiah, (ii) the prophet to the exiles in Babylon, and (iii) the author of Revelation. Are they the same in every detail? If not, in what ways do they differ?
(c) Would you agree that these pictures all show God's intention for the whole earth? Give reasons for your answers.
16. Do you think that the Christian Church as you know it, (a) already is, (b) is becoming, (c) is not now but one day will become, (d) is not now and never will become, the 'new people of God' as described in these poems? If your answer is (c) or (d), who do you think is, or will become, the 'new people of God'?
17. 'The wealth of nations shall come to you' (Isa. 60.5). What meaning can this statement of God's intention have, for Christians who are a small minority of the population in their country?
18. Write a prayer for society based on God's intention as described in these poems.
19. 'The future of the Church in my country depends on how actively she contributes to the solution of urgent social issues here.' This is the opinion of an Asian priest of the Roman Catholic Church. How would you relate this to the descriptions of God's intention for society in

these poems. In what ways does this statement help Christians to understand what it means to 'live toward the future'?

20. Do you think that evangelism and Church-planting are a fulfilment of God's intention as seen in these poems? Give Bible references to support your answer.

63—65
The Hidden God
520–515 BC

BACKGROUND AND OUTLINE

As we have seen, the Jews in Jerusalem were not only feeling discouragement. There was also hope in their hearts. They were not passive recipients of God's word, like cups receiving water. They were like their ancestor, Jacob. They were wrestlers with God, struggling to understand His ways, and crying out for blessing. They were asking questions. God also asks questions and gives unexpected answers. Through this wrestling dialogue between God and His people, they came to know God in new ways.

Main theme: The Hidden God

First poem: 'Who is this'? The unrecognized God (63.1–6)

Second poem: 'Where is He'? The silent God (63.7—64.12)

Third poem: 'I will not keep silent!' The God who answers (65.1–25)

READING SUGGESTIONS

The interpretation deals with each poem separately. It will be helpful if you read each poem through before reading the interpretation.

Some passages worth marking in your Bible:

63.7–14: A beautiful summary of Israel's history.

64.5b–7: A moving confession of sin.

64.8: God is the potter, we are the clay.

64.12: Israel's bitter question to God.

65.1–2: God's free grace to sinners.

65.13–14: A striking contrast between the fate of God's servants and that of the unfaithful Jews.

65.17: A new heaven and earth.

INTERPRETATION

WHO IS THIS? THE UNRECOGNIZED GOD (63.1–6)

God was coming to save the people (v. 1.), but they did not recognize Him. They expected God to come directly from heaven to save them only (see 64.1), dressed as a bridegroom for his bride (see 61.10). But God came in an unexpected way: 'from Edom' (see note on 63.1), wearing 'blood-stained garments' (see note on 63.2) from a struggle to set things right among the rebellious nations (vv. 2–4). This reminds us of the words about Jesus: 'His own people did not receive him' (John 1.11).

The prophet was criticizing his people's narrow view of salvation. He said that the time of restoring wholeness to the world of nations (see note on 63.4) was also God's time of *redeeming* His own people (v. 4, see also 61.2). They could not recognize God when He acted in a way they did not accept. Yet, in spite of their blindness, God was saying, 'It is I, announcing salvation, mighty to save!' (v. 1).

WHERE IS HE? THE SILENT GOD (63.7—64.12)

What do we do when it seems that God does not answer our prayer? What should we advise others to do when there seems to be no end to their suffering? These are the questions the prophet was facing in the discouraging time when Judah, Jerusalem, and the temple were in ruins (64.10–11). He composed this poem for people in the depths of despondency. Seven questions show the people's misery (see vv. 63.11, 15, 17; 64.5, 12). Answering these questions, he told them that they should do three things: (1) remember the past, (2) confess their sins, and (3) prepare for God's future action.

1. *Remembering the past* (63.7–16). The prophet recalled God's past grace for them by summarizing the Exodus story: 'God made us His people and became our Saviour by covenant agreement (63.8); He carried us as a father carries his child over dangerous places (63.9); He guided us through the wilderness by His servant Moses to a land of rest and peace (63.11–14). In every crisis God Himself was present with us by His 'angel' or His Holy Spirit, sharing our suffering (63.9, 11). When we rebelled He punished us (63.10) and then redeemed us by His covenant love (63.7, 16).

When it seems to us that God does not answer prayer, the first thing we should do is to remember the past. That will help us to find our identity (as God's people). It will remind us who God is (Father, Saviour, present Spirit), and what salvation means (His sustaining, judging, forgiving us, sharing our suffering, guiding us to a place of peace).

2. *Confessing Sin.* An honest look at the past made it clear to the Jews that there had been frequent rebellions, judgements, and deliverances. For this reason it was necessary for those living in Jerusalem to realize that

they needed to repent and confess their own rebellious nature. This poem contains one of the most sensitive and profound descriptions of sin in the whole Bible. We can see how it influenced Paul's thinking. Here is what the prophet said to his people:

We blame God for hardening our hearts as He hardened Pharaoh's heart, instead of accepting responsibility ourselves (63.17 and Exod. 14.8).

We have forgotten that God rules us. We have become lawless and selfish (63.19; compare Rom. 1.28; 2.22).

We do not worship God any more (64.7; compare Rom. 1.21).

Our sinfulness is like a disease that infects all our deeds and thoughts, and dries up our strength so that we cannot do any good (64.6; compare Rom. 7.15).

We are caught in the power of sin like being caught in a trap, so that we cannot even reach out our hands to accept God's offer of help (64.7; compare Rom. 7.23).

The prophet might have called out, as Paul did four hundred years later: 'Who will deliver me from this body of death?' (Rom. 7.24).

The people's only hope, said the prophet, was to return to the Father and depend completely on His grace. Three times he said, 'Thou art our Father!' (63.16; 64.8); and referred to Israel as God's people (63.8, 14; 64.9): 'Behold, consider, we are all thy people!' The prophet told them not to depend on their physical descent from Abraham or from Jacob (63.16; compare Matt. 3.9), but only on God's mercy.

When it seems that God does not answer our prayer, the second thing to do is confess our sins, depending only on the gracious love of our Father, in order to open the way for His healing action (see Ps. 32.5). Only by such a self-searching can we see the deep inward nature of sin, and our own need for God's forgiving grace.

3. *Preparing for God's future action.* An honest look at the past gave hope for the future. The prophet described four kinds of future action by God for which the people should prepare.

(a) When God comes to save He will shake the foundations of the present order (64.1). God's future will not be a repetition of the past.

(b) When God comes to save He will destroy useless and evil things, as fire burns useless brushwood (64.2, compare 10.17). Those who prepare for His coming should be ready to do without such things.

(c) When God comes to save, He will stir up the passive community to action as fire causes water to boil (64.2). His people must be ready for the heat of His presence stirring them to action.

(d) When God comes to save He will remake His people like a potter who works soft clay into a pot of whatever shape and purpose he chooses. Those who pray for God's coming must prepare to become something new which they cannot now imagine.

When it seems that God does not answer our prayer, the third thing to do is to prepare ourselves for the time when He will act, because that will mean changes at which we can only guess.

'I WILL NOT KEEP SILENT!' THE GOD WHO ANSWERS (65.1–25)

Sometimes we think that God is silent. But in fact it is we ourselves who fail to listen when He calls, or turn away when He wants to help us. That is what the prophet told his people in this poem (65.1–2, 12).

We can see how the community was divided into two groups. One group was unfaithful to God (vv. 1–7). For them God's answer would be hunger and thirst, disgrace, a broken heart, and a living death (vv. 6, 12–14). On the other side were the repentant, faithful, and obedient people. For them, God's answer would be a feast of good things, great joy, and life in the new heaven and earth which He was creating (vv. 13–14): 'Before they call I will answer, while they are yet speaking I will hear' (v. 24).

Some scholars believe that this poem reflects a division between the returned exiles who were from the 'tribe of Judah' (see v. 8), and the 'people of the land' who included Israelites from other tribes (see Ezra 4.1–5). Probably the division affected the returned exiles themselves. As we have seen (see Isa. 43, 48, 50), there were serious differences among the exiles in Babylon.

The choices offered in this poem are for all Christians. We are free to refuse God's call for service, to neglect prayer, to worship the popular false gods of our culture whether ancient or modern, to follow the way of our stubborn hearts. If we choose any of these ways, God's answer will be unexpectedly hard. He will 'burn up useless brushwood' (see 64.2).

We are also free to seek God through prayer, worship, confession, and repentance; to answer His call for dedicated service. The good news is that God is always holding out His hands, always ready to say 'Here I am, ready to help!' His help means that He forgives our sins, and gives us a place at His covenant feast (see Isa. 55.1–2), and a part in His new creation, which is as wide as the earth and as solid as the new Jerusalem (see chapter on Isa. 60—62).

NOTES

63.1. From Edom: To the Jews Edom was a symbol of the hatred and enmity between nations, peoples, and classes which results from self-centred pride (Obadiah v. 2). The people of Edom were cruel slave traders (Amos 1.6, 9), and pitiless and revengeful neighbours (Amos 1.11). Although 'the Edomite is your brother' (Deut. 23.7), the Israelites had special reason to hate them. The Edomites prohibited the Israelites from passing through their territory on the way to Canaan (Num. 20.14–21), and took advantage of them in their time of defeat, to loot their goods (Obadiah vv. 10–14). This accounts for the terrible curse against the

Edomites in Psalm 137.7–9. The Edomites also had reason to hate the
Israelites, because David's military commander Joab had killed every
adult male in Edom (1 Kings 11.4–15). God wanted to put an end to this
sort of undying hatred.

63.2. Why is . . . thy garment like his that treads the wine press? At grape-
harvest time, the juice is extracted for wine-making by the harvesters, who
trample the grapes with their feet so that the juice runs out into vats. Some
of the red juice would splash and stain their clothes as if with blood. The
prophet used this picture to describe God's struggle with the peoples, with
'their lifeblood sprinkled on his garments' (Isa. 63.3). This is a rather
shocking picture, which seems to imply that God Himself was killing many
people. Probably the meaning of the picture is this: Behind the seemingly
meaningless wars and mass suffering in the world, a judgement process is
going on. God is not far away from the people's sufferings, but there in the
midst of them, where His garments may be stained with their blood.

63.4. Day of vengeance: The Hebrew word translated 'vengeance' does
not mean 'revenge' in the sense of paying someone back for harm that
person may have done to one. God is both loving and righteous. His
'wrath' (v. 6) is against wickedness and evil which destroy the wholeness of
the community and individual persons. One explanation of His 'wrath' is
that He permits evil deeds to bring their own destructive results. God's
'vengeance' means that He is not indifferent to suffering and evil. He
intervenes to set things right so that the community can enjoy wholeness
(*shalom*) and integrity (truth) once again. God's intention is not to destroy
but to prepare for rebuilding (see Jer. 1.10).

STUDY SUGGESTIONS

REVIEW OF CONTENT

1. In what way was the Jerusalem community like Jacob?
2. For what reason did the people not recognize God?
3. What *three* things should a discouraged people do when God does not
   seem to answer their prayers?
4. What *four* things will happen when God comes to save, according to
   these poems?
5. What were the *two* groups in Jerusalem, and what would be God's
   answer for each?

APPLICATION, DISCUSSION, RESEARCH

6. Suggest situations in which God may be working in the world today in
   ways which Christians do not expect, and perhaps may not even be
   able to accept. How can we recognize God in such situations?
7. Which of the following should be included when Christians 'remember

their past' (p. 3)? In what ways would each help you to remember who you are, and to learn who God is, and what salvation means?
(a) The events of Old Testament history.
(b) The events of New Testament history.
(c) The events of Church history after the New Testament.
(d) The events of Church history in your own country and home town.
(e) Your own life story.

8. Compare the description of sin in 63.7—64.12 with other descriptions in the following verses: Gen. 3.6; Isa. 1.18; 30.16; 43.22; 47.10; Rom. 7.
Which of these passages describe outward acts, which the inward condition of the sinner, and which the effects of sin?

9. Complete the following prayers (see page 192):
(a) O God come and burn up the useless brushwood in my life, such as ....
(b) O God come and kindle a fire in my heart and help me to
....

10. Write a short essay on 'The clay and the potter', using Isa. 64.8, Gen. 2.7, and Jer. 18.1–12, and applying the theme to your Church or to yourself.

11. According to Isa. 65 there were serious divisions in the Jerusalem community after the exile. Find as many possible causes of this division as you can from reading that chapter, and other parts of Isa. 56—66. Which if any of these problems cause divisions in the Christian community today? What suggestions do these chapters offer which might be of help in healing the divisions?

66.1–24
The Saviour of the World
520–515 BC

BACKGROUND AND OUTLINE

The last chapter of the Book of Isaiah is the prophet's answer to the question the people asked in 63.1, 'Who is this . . .?' It is also the conclusion of the collection of prophetic poems for the Jews after their return from exile. More than that, this chapter looks back across the whole book of Isaiah and forward to the New Testament. Here we find many of the themes of the whole book of Isaiah: God as Ruler, Judge, and Saviour.

We also find words which seem to foretell the coming of Christ and the beginning of the Church.

It may well be, as some scholars have suggested, that an editor has collected a number of prophetic oracles to serve as a summary and conclusion for the entire book.

Main Theme: The Saviour of the World

Vv. 1–2: God's universal dominion.

Vv. 3–4: The corruption of worship.

Vv. 5–6: Judgement on corrupt worshippers.

Vv. 7–8: The birth of a new people.

Vv. 10–14: The joy and plenty of the coming age.

Vv. 15–16: The nations judged.

Vv. 17–24: The nations saved.

INTERPRETATION

As many of the themes of Isaiah 66.1–24 have been discussed in previous chapters of this Guide, we shall only look at the three answers to the question 'Who is God?'

1. GOD IS RULER (vv. 1–2)

The career of the prophet Isaiah of Jerusalem began with a vision of God 'seated on a throne, high and lifted up,' (Isa. 6.1). The prophet of the exiles began his ministry with a vision of God sitting 'above the circle of the earth' (Isa. 40.22), ruling all nations. In the same way the book of Isaiah ends with a majestic vision of God seated on His heavenly throne, with His feet firmly planted on the earth. This in turn looks forward to the Book Of Revelation, with its vision that 'the kingdom of this world has become the kingdom of our Lord and of His Christ, and He shall reign forever and ever' (Rev. 11.15).

The words in 66.1 had a special meaning for the returned exiles when they were starting to rebuild the temple in Jerusalem in the year 520 BC (see note on historical background). God's footstool meant that place where He is present and powerful as ruler. There is a similar tradition in Buddhism about the 'footprint' of the Lord Buddha. Buddhists revere a rock formation that resembles a footprint, or an artificially made footprint, because they believe it is a sign of the presence and lordship of the Lord Buddha in that place.

According to Israelite tradition, God's footstool was the temple in Jerusalem (see Isa. 6.1; 1 Chron. 28.3; Ps. 132.7; Ezek. 43.7). Those who were rebuilding the temple believed that they were making a 'footstool' for God, from which He could rule the earth. But the prophet said that God's 'footstool' was not the temple, but the whole earth. He wanted the returned exiles to understand the real meaning of the temple (66.1). He was opposing *'temple nationalism'*, that is, use of the temple or any religious institution to increase the power or glory of the nation. He warned them that they could not force God to be present in a particular place, or to begin His kingdom, by building a temple.

The prophet was probably opposing not the temple itself (see 56.7; 60.13), but a narrow nationalistic interpretation of its meaning. Perhaps he was familiar with the picture of the new Jerusalem without a temple (Isa. 54.11–14).

New Testament writers shared this critical view of temple nationalism. Stephen quoted Isa. 66.1–2 in criticizing the Jews of his time, who had the temple, but resisted God's will (Acts 7.46–51). The author of the Gospel of John said that the true temple was the 'temple of Christ's body', that is, the followers of Jesus (John 2.19–21) The same thought is repeated in Ephesians 2.14–21 and 1 Peter 2.19–21. See also the discussion of Isaiah 51.1.

Today we would say that God is above all nations and religions, and does not make any Church headquarters or national capital His 'footstool'. Buildings and institutions like the temple may be necessary for congregations, denominations, and social organizations. However, God's rule is not brought about by erecting buildings, but by those who turn to Him in their hearts and obey His word. 'I am pleased with those who are humble and repentant, who fear me and obey me' (Isa. 66.2).

GOD IS JUDGE (vv. 15–16)

These verses picture God's judgement on all the peoples of the world ('all flesh') by the fire of war. The prophet had observed the wars and revolutions of the beginning of King Darius's reign (see Special Note C). In that crisis of 522–520 BC, he saw a vision of world judgement.

Isaiah of Jerusalem had spoken about 'a Day of the Lord', in which God would pass judgement against the rich and powerful of Judah (Isa. 2.12–19), against the Assyrian oppressor (10.12, 15–16), and against all the nations of the whole world (14.25; 30.27–28). He described the crisis of the 8th century BC in West Asia in words that seem to refer to a universal judgement.

The prophet of the exile described God's judgement and salvation in relation to the victories of Cyrus and the defeat of Babylon in the sixth century BC. But his words also seem to refer to a final age of judgement and salvation for all the nations of the earth. Isaiah 24.1–13, 17–23 also describe God's judgement in great detail, in words that sound even more like a last judgement.

Each of these prophets described, in poetic terms, God's intention to set things right by punishing the wicked and blessing the righteous. They saw God's day of judgement in times of unrest, wars, and social or personal crises; and these crises made them think of God's intention for the whole world and for all mankind.

When Jesus said that He came 'to set the earth on fire' (Luke 12.49, TEV), He meant that His preaching, deeds, death, and resurrection would bring the fire of God's judgement into the life and society of those who heard His message. In other words, the preaching of the Gospel brings a partial fulfilment of God's intention to judge the world (2 Thess. 1.7; Heb. 10.27; Rev. 17—20).

GOD IS SAVIOUR (vv. 7–9, 18–23)

God's rule and His judgement on sin and evil in the midst of crises, both great and small, are part of His purpose of salvation. The chief emphasis in this chapter is on God's saving work for Israel and the nations. The chapter is like a high mountain from which we can look back over the Book of Isaiah, and forward to the New Testament.

The birth of a new people. V. 7 describes the birth of a child in words that make us think of Isa. 7.14: 'A young woman shall conceive and bear a son.' The original meaning of those words for King Ahaz in 734 BC was no longer remembered 200 years later among the ruins of Jersalem, yet the prophetic force of the words continued on across two centuries.

Vv. 8–9 give the prophet's interpretation of Isa. 7.14 for his time. The 'woman' in v. 7 is 'Zion', i.e., the people of Israel chosen and sustained by God from the Exodus to the fall of Jerusalem and the Exile in Babylon. The male child (v. 7) is the 'new people' ('sons' v. 8) who will be born from 'Israel' for the new age. The 'doctor' attending the birth with personal attention and intention, is God Himself.

The prophet to the exiles in Babylon pictured Zion as a surprised mother of many children (see Isa. 49.20–21). Perhaps he, too, was thinking of the young woman in Isa. 7.14. In any case the prophet who wrote Isa. 66.7–9 put Isa. 7.14 and 49.20–21 together as a picture of the birth of a new Israel.

He was explaining that God intended them to become a new people, and that He wanted to give them rich abundance and joy (vv. 10–14, see discussion of the new Jerusalem in the chapter on Isa. 60–62).

The New Testament writers interpreted this theme in their own way. Matthew 1.22–23 presents the birth of Jesus as the fulfilment of Isa. 7.14. According to the symbolic pictures in Revelation the Messiah is the male child (Rev. 12.5) born from mother Zion (the woman with child, Rev. 12.1). This is obviously a reference to Isa. 66.7–9. Possibly the words of John 3.3 are related to the same passage: 'Unless one is born anew, he cannot see the Kingdom of God.'

We may see in Isa. 66.7–9 a prophecy of the birth of the Christian Church from Israel as part of God's purpose for His people. This emphasizes the continuity which Christians have with the People of God in the Old Testament. We may also see this birth story as foretelling the formation of new congregations as 'daughter churches' from older 'mother churches'.

The salvation of the nations (vv. 18–23). God's last great unfinished task as described in the Old Testament is wider than the redemption of His people. It extends beyond His work of judging the world. It is the salvation of the nations. With this theme the book of Isaiah comes to an end. The prophet who wrote these words wanted to remind the returned exiles that the birth of a new people and the joys of a new Jerusalem were a part of God's 'purpose concerning the whole earth' (Isa. 14.26). He described God's purpose, or intention, in seven stages:

1. *The first gathering of the nations* (v. 18). In his vision of the future, the prophet saw a group of representatives from all nations gathered in Jerusalem to understand ('see') the glory of God as Creator, Ruler, Judge, and Saviour. The light of God's glory is on His people (Isa. 60.1–3).

Probably the prophet was thinking of people from the nations who would come to believe in the true God through the Jewish communities among them. This picture reminds us of the gathering from every nation at Pentecost (Acts 2).

2. *God's sign among the nations* (v. 19a). See discussion of the meaning of a sign (pp. 168, 169). Here the prophet was summarizing several passages:

The new people of Israel will be a sign (Isa. 7.14 and 66.7–9).

The new descendants of David will be a sign (Isa. 11.10–11; 49.22; and 55.3–5).

The new Exodus community will be a sign (Isa. 8.16–18 and 55.12–13). He meant that the faithful disciples in every place will draw the people of that place to God.

We may think of the cross as this sort of sign among the nations. Christians lift up the cross which will 'draw all men' to Christ (John 12.32).

3. *God's mission to the nations* (v. 19b). From the first gathering, God will send a selected group of non-Jewish missionaries to proclaim His glory to peoples who have never heard of Him. This was a further development of the thought of the prophet in Babylon (see Isa. 48.20; 52.12; 55.12), who saw the mission as beginning with the Israelite exiles.

The prophet selected place-names from a much larger list in Ezekiel 27, or possibly from Genesis 10 (see Ezek. 27.10, 12, 13 and Gen. 10.2, 3, 6, 13). This was in order to emphasize distant lands beyond the Persian Empire where there were as yet no Jewish communities. Tubal is in north-eastern Asia Minor, along the Black Sea coast. Lud is in western Asia Minor (now part of Turkey, but a part of the Persian Empire at that time). Javan refers to Greece and the Greek colonies on the Aegean coast. Put is northern Africa, now Libya. Tarshish is Spain, the furthest westward point known to the ancient world of that time.

We may recall the westward expansion of the early Church into Asia

'The community was divided into two groups' . . . there was 'a judgement process going on' (pp. 194 and 195). 'God's rule and His judgement are part of His purpose of salvation . . . They bring a harvest' (pp. 199 and 202).

As farm women in Taiwan sieve the harvested rice, they divide the precious grain from the straw.

In what ways do you see God's judgement process going on in your own community today? In what ways do you see His 'harvest' being gathered in?

Minor (Acts 13–14) and Greece (Acts 16–18), and Paul's desire to go to Spain (Rom. 15, 24, 28) and 'regions beyond' (2. Cor. 10.16).

4. *The harvest of first fruits* (v. 20). The prophet pictured the missionaries returning from distant lands in a long caravan, to participate in the wheat harvest festival. Instead of the cereal offering of the first fruits of their grain harvest, (see Num. 28.26), they bring a harvest of new brothers and sisters in faith (see Isa. 44.5) to celebrate the covenant feast (see Isa. 55.1–2). As in Isaiah 19.24–25, these new brothers and sisters in faith will have equal status with the Jews.

We may think of the Ethiopian court official (Acts 8.38), the cripple at Lystra (Acts 14.8–10), Lydia (Acts 16.14–15), the Philippian jailer (Acts 16.30–32), and many others as 'first fruits' in New Testament times, as well as those in every land who were the first to believe.

5. *Priests from non-Jewish nations* (v. 21). The prophet was not referring to the official priests of the temple like Joshua (see Ezea 3.2). He was thinking of priests belonging to other nations who could interpret the revealed teaching of God to their own people (Glossary: *Law*), and lead them into God's presence. At an earlier stage of the mission, the Jews would fulfil this responsibility (see Isa. 61.9). But now God Himself (contrast 1 Kings 12.31) would take individuals from the non-Jewish nations and make them into religious leaders for their own people.

We may think how Paul appointed and trained elders in every congregation (Acts 20.17–28), and how the Church today gives theological training to selected people in every place, so that they can lead their own people to God.

6. *The permanent mission* (v. 22). The active missionary people of God, going out and coming back to celebrate the harvest with new brothers and sisters in the faith from all nations, will always be a part of God's work of building a new heaven and earth.

7. *The fulfilment* (v. 23). The mission will go on until all people of the world ('all flesh') worship the true God in fulfilment of the vision of Isaiah 2.2–4; 11.9; and 40.5. God's great vow (Isa. 45.22) will finally come true. This vision points ahead to the vision of the author of the Book of Revelation:

'After this I looked and, behold, a multitude which no man could number, from every nation, from all tribes and peoples and tongues, standing before the throne and before the Lamb, clothed in white robes, with palm branches in their hands, crying with a loud voice, "Salvation belongs to our God who sits upon the throne and to the Lamb".' (Rev. 7.9–10).

STUDY SUGGESTIONS

REVIEW OF CONTENT

1. What three themes from the whole Book of Isaiah do we find in Isa. 66?
2. In what way is Isa. 6.1. like 66.1?
3. (a) What tradition in Buddhism is similar to the idea of God's 'footstool'?
   (b) Why did the prophet say that the *earth* was God's 'footstool'?
4. What passages in the New Testament support this prophet's view of the temple?
5. In what way is the Gospel a partial fulfilment of God's 'day of judgement'?
6. The prophet who wrote Isa. 66.7–9 was giving his hearers an interpretation of another verse from Isaiah. What verse was it, and how many years earlier was it spoken?
7. What are the seven stages in the process of the salvation of the nations, as described in Isa. 66.18–23?

APPLICATION, DISCUSSION, RESEARCH

8. Suggest present day examples of 'temple nationalism'. What is the proper response to it?
9. (a) The prophecies of God's judgement are descriptions of God's intention which may be partially fulfilled in times of crisis (p. 197). Discuss this in relation to the Second Coming of Christ.
   (b) Could 'one of the days of the Son of Man' (Luke 17.22) be a partial fulfilment of the 'day when the Son of Man is revealed' (Luke 17.30)? What sort of crisis might be considered as 'one of the days'?
10. There are three or possibly four interpretations of Isa. 7.14 in the Bible (p. 198). Do you think they can all be true? Are they contradictory? What does this tell us about the prophetic power of words spoken in a particular situation, but applied in other situations?
11. Apply Isa. 66.7–9 to your own Church. Who is the 'mother'? Who is the 'child'? Who is the attending 'doctor'?
12. Write a song or a poem about the seven stages of the salvation of all peoples, as applied to your own situation.

Glossary Notes on
Important Themes and Ideas
in Isaiah 40—66

The Arm of the Lord: In Isaiah 40—55 this is a picture of God's power to rule and to save.

1. God's 'arm' will rule the nations (40.10; 51.5), and many will look forward with hope to His coming reign (51.5). His arms will gather the weak and helpless in tender care (40.11).

2. God's arm will defeat present and future oppressors, just as He defeated Egypt at the time of the Exodus, or as He defeated the chaos monster at the time of the creation of the world, in order to make a way for His people (51.9–10).

3. All nations will see God's ruling and saving power over His people (52.10), but they will be surprised when they see the victory of His arm through the weakness and suffering of His Servant (53.1).

Chaos, nothing, emptiness: These words describe the results of personal or social breakdown. They are the opposite of 'salvation', 'redemption', 'justice'. The most important Hebrew word used by the prophet for these ideas in Isaiah 40—55 is *tohu*. Probably he was thinking of Genesis 1.2 and Jeremiah 4.23–26, where this word is also used. In Genesis, *tohu* describes the chaotic state of the world before God began His work of creating breathing space, living place, and a garden of life for mankind. Jeremiah used the word to describe the chaotic state of a society in which order and the rule of law has broken down.

In Isaiah 40—55, the word describes the breakdown of society in the sixth century BC (45.18–19), and the breakdown of national or political order (40.17; 40.23). The prophet thought that this breakdown came because 'nations' depended on empty gods (*tohu*, 41.29) who brought those who constructed them to 'nothing' (*tohu*, 44.9). So he often associated *tohu* with defeat or disgrace (45.16).

Coastlands: In Isaiah 40—55 this word is used four times to mean the peoples living on the whole surface of the earth (41.1, 5; 42.4; 51.5), and three times to mean peoples who live in the distant parts of the earth, on the border between earth and sea (42.10, 12; 49.1). The Hebrew word is used once in a special way to mean the ridge around the flat earth, to keep out the salt water of the ocean (40.15).

Some scholars think that the prophet was referring to the coastal areas of the Mediterranean sea, as in Psalm 72.10, rather than the whole earth, as in Psalm 97.1. However, the prophet always gives us a hint about the meaning, in parallel or twin words in the same passage.

Create: This verb (Hebrew: *bara*) is used in the Old Testament only to describe God's action, never for man's action. (Other verbs, such as 'form' and 'make' are used for both man and God.) In Isaiah 40—55 the prophet used it 15 times, more than any other writer of the Old Testament. The writer of the priestly tradition in Genesis 1—6 also used this word to describe God's action. In Isaiah 40—55, the word relates to four actions of God:

1. Creating the heavens (42.5), the stars (40.26), the earth (40.28), man (45.12; compare Gen. 1.27), and the garden of life (45.18).

2. Creating Israel (43.1, 7, 15).

3. Creating a new garden (41.20; a community of salvation and righteousness (45.8), and a new possibility of life (48.7).

4. Creating woe and darkness (45.7), and the power of judgement (54.16). Notice that God's work of creation goes on continuously.

End of the Earth, Ends of the earth: A geographical term. As used in Isaiah 40—55 it has a different meaning according to whether it is singular or plural.

1. In the *singular* form, *the end of the earth* means the distant places, far from a city like Jerusalem or Babylon. The prophet uses it to emphasize the mission of the Israelite exiles. They must send out the message of redemption, and be the light of salvation *to* the most distant places (48.20; 49.6). They must find new sons and daughters of God *from* the most distant places and bring them to God (43.6). This does not mean that these new members of the family of God will actually leave their homes. They will praise God there, where they live (42.10).

The prophet probably also used this term to refer to those in trouble (42.7), i.e. those who are for some reason 'distant' or separate from God or from their family or friends. Note that in this phrase the word 'end' does not relate to time, as it does in the phrase 'end of the world'.

2. In the *plural, the ends of the earth* means the totality of the earth's surface from one end to the other. The emphasis is not on distance, but on inclusiveness. God made the whole earth for His loving purpose (40.28), but the peoples of the earth are continually following their own purposes instead (41.5). So God chose out Israel from all the peoples of the earth (41.9; compare Exodus 19.5: 'All the earth is mine', and Psalm 24.1: 'The earth is the Lord's') to carry His invitation to all peoples on the earth to turn to Him and be saved (45.22; compare Psalms 22.27; 67.7). Finally, all the peoples of the earth will see God's salvation when He establishes the new Jerusalem (52.10; compare Psalm 98.3).

Glory of the Lord: In Isaiah 40—55, this means the visible manifestation of God's hidden grace and power in His people. It is not primarily a bright light behind a cloud (Exod. 16.10), or on Mount Sinai (Exod. 24.16), or in the tabernacle (Exod. 40.34). It is not God's revelation in nature as in Psalm 19.1. The prophet used two words for this idea, both translated by the English word 'glory'. One means a shining brightness like a beautiful sunrise. The other means beauty like a crown or a garment. We will look at various verses where these two words appear.

God will glorify (make beautiful) His people (55.5) who because of their suffering had no beauty of their own (53.2). God will give His people a beautiful garment (52.1), so that all may see His beautiful glory (46.13; 44.23; 49.3; 42.12). The reason why He calls new sons and daughters is to make His glory visible in all places of the earth (43.7). Finally, even though idols may show the beauty of the human form (44.13), they cannot possibly reveal the glory of God (42.8; 48.11).

In the New Testament, we find that Jesus Himself reveals God's glory (John 1.14; 1 Cor. 11.7), and gives it to His disciples (John 17.22; 2 Cor. 3.28). Yet the full revelation of God's glory will be in the future (1 Pet. 4.13).

The Hand of God: This is a picture of God in action to create, to punish, and to give help. It does not mean that God actually has a hand of flesh and blood:

1. God's 'hand' is big enough to hold an ocean, and to pick up mountains (40.12). His 'hand' laid the foundations of the earth, and stretched out the heavens (48.13; 45.12). His 'hand' created a garden in the wilderness (41.20), and He is creating new sons and daughters among the nations (45.11).

2. God's 'hand' punished His people by sending them into exile in Babylon (40.2; 51.17).

3. God's 'hand' symbolizes His care for His people in time of trouble (42.6; 49.2; 51.16), and the help He gives them (41.10, 13). His 'hand' will keep them from the power of the oppressor (43.13).

Holy One of Israel: The 'holiness' of God means: (1) His great power (Ezek. 38.23); (2) His distance and difference from human beings (Isa. 6.3–5); and (3) His righteous purpose in action (Isa. 5.16; 52.10). 'Holy One of Israel' means that this great power, purity, and purpose was turned toward Israel in grace. He is both distant and near (Isa. 57.15). If you wish to study this phrase in detail here are the verses where the author used it: Isaiah 40.25; 41.14, 16, 20; 43.3, 14, 15; 45.11; 47.4; 48.17; 49.7; 54.5.

Jerusalem and Zion: These words have six different but related meanings in Isaiah 40—55.

1. The actual holy city in Judah, built by David as the capital of the nation and the central place of worship. The temple was in Jerusalem, and Zion was the name of the rocky mount on which it was built. This city had been destroyed by Nebuchadnezzar (48.1).

2. The Israelite captives in Babylon (52.2). They heard the good news of God's decision to save them (40.1–2) by means of His herald (41.27). In their deep suffering they could not react normally (51.17), and they thought that God had forsaken them (49.12).

3. God's herald to the 'cities of Judah' who will announce the coming of God to rule and save (40.9–11).

4. The redeemed people. They will be the starting point of God's new creation (51.16). They will hear the good news of God's return to rule over them in the new age (52.7–8).

5. The mother of many new children to replace those lost in past destruction. They will come to her with singing (51.11), but she will not recognize them because they come from the other nations of the earth (49.19–22) and not from within Israel. (Glossary: *Nations*).

6. The new city with the 'cities of Judah' around it. God commanded that both Jerusalem and the cities of Judah should be rebuilt and inhabited again (44.26, 28; 54.3). Her wilderness will become like Eden, the garden of God (51.3; 52.9), the beginning of God's new creation. For discussion of individual occurrences, see the relevant chapters.

Justice: The Hebrew word is *mishpat*. In the RSV two other words also are used to translate it: 'right' and 'judgement'. The author of Isaiah 40—55 used the word with four meanings:

1. The design of the created universe. God made the physical, biological, and human world according to 'the way of *mishpat*' (40.14. RSV; 'justice'), i.e., in an orderly and balanced way.

2. The right of Israel under the covenant. According to the covenant agreement, Israel had the right to expect God's protection and blessing. In Isaiah 40.27 the prophet said that the Israelites in Babylon were complaining that God had forgotten their '*mishpat*' (RSV: 'right'). But in 49.4, he said that in the future they would leave their *mishpat* (RSV: 'right') to God's grace.

3. The verdict of a trial at law. In 41.1 the prophet presented his hearers with a picture of God calling all the nations of the world together '*for mishpat*' (RSV: 'judgement'). It was to be a trial between Yahweh and the gods of the nations over the question of who controls the events of history. In 53.8 the Servant of the Lord is condemned to death by a legal verdict called *mishpat* (RSV: 'judgement'). The word is used in a similar way in 54.17.

4. The prophet said that the mission of the servant of the Lord was to make *mishpat* (RSV: 'justice') a part of the life of the nations (42.1, 3, 4), that is, to carry the *mishpat* (RSV: 'justice') of God to them as a light (51.4). Here the word means the right ordering of society according to the design of the created universe. (See 1 above.)

King of Israel: The prophet called Yahweh by this title three times in Isaiah 40—55: In 41.21 he stressed the difference between Israel whose king was Yahweh, and the nations with their kings and gods. In 43.15 he reminded the Israelite exiles that the end of the Davidic dynasty through past failures (see notes on 43.25–28, p. 59) only meant a return to the days before the monarchy when Yahweh alone was their king (see Judges 8.23). Finally, in 44.6 he told them that the King of Israel, in contrast to the Babylonian gods, was also the Lord of history, both 'first' and 'last'. Although Yahweh had temporarily chosen Cyrus as His 'anointed one' (a term usually reserved for kings in Israel; see Isa. 45.1), David's mission as God's 'anointed' would pass to the people of Israel (55.3–4).

Law, or 'revealed teaching': The Hebrew word *torah* originally meant 'instruction' or 'teaching' given by God through parents and teachers (Prov. 1.8), priests (Mal. 2.6–7), and prophets (Isa. 1.10). Later, the word came to mean the collection of laws concerning ethical behaviour and worship practices in Israel, which is contained in the first five books of the Old Testament, or the first five books themselves, or even the whole Old Testament.

In Isaiah 40—55 the word *torah* means 'revealed teaching' rather than a body of laws. This teaching came to Israel through Moses, the prophets, the priests, and those who gathered traditions together in historical writing. Thus, the 'revealed teaching' was deep in the heart of Israel (Isa. 51.7). Many years before the time of this prophet, at a period when the nation of Judah had forgotten God's teaching, the prophet Isaiah preserved this teaching (Isa. 8.16) by gathering together a small group of disciples (Isa. 8.16). The author of Isaiah 50—55 said that it was God's sure and steadfast purpose to make His revealed teaching great among all nations (42.21). But the Israelite exiles were, he said, too blind to see this, and too deaf to hear the call to service (Isa. 42.18–20). Nevertheless, the prophet saw that in the future God would send out this 'revealed teaching' to the peoples (51.4); His faithful Servant would carry it to the farthest parts of the whole earth (42.4).

In 42.1–4, the prophet related the content of this 'revealed teaching' to 'justice' (see Glossary), in the sense of God's design of creation. A summary would be something like this: How to live together peacefully as a family of nations in covenant with God, and maintain the earth as a garden of life for human beings and all of nature.

Mountains and hills: 1. People of the ancient world thought that mountains were the foundation pillars of the earth, which seemed flat. The mountain peaks, they thought, held up the dome of the sky. The base of the mountains was in the underworld. They believed that there was one mountain in the distant north, where the gods lived. And whenever there was a particularly high mountain, it was thought to represent this mountain home of the gods. Sometimes people built artificial mountains to represent the 'world mountain' of the gods. The Buddhist *chedi* or *pagoda*, and the Hindu *stupa* are artificial models of the mythical mountain of the gods called *Meru*. Mesopotamia had no natural mountains. So in each city the people built an artificial mountain or tower called a *ziggurat*. They thought that the god of that city lived in the temple tower and gave blessing and prosperity to the city. The most famous of the temple towers was in Babylon. It was called Etemenanki. People today do not think of mountains as the foundations of the earth, because science has shown us that the earth is not flat but round.

When Christians began to erect special buildings for worship, they added a tower or a spire to symbolize man's reaching for God and God's coming down to man. So today, most church buildings have some sort of spire. Some people believe that there was a link between this idea and the earlier idea of a mountain where the gods lived. In some cultures, a tall tree is a symbol of this contact between man and the divine.

What do people in your country regard as symbols of the divine? Mountains? Trees? Sacred groves? Or what?

2. The Israelites shared many of these ideas with their neighbours. They thought that God put the mountains in place to keep the earth from being shaken by the forces of chaos (Pss. 104.5; 93.1; 96.10). Some thought that Mount Zion was God's holy mountain (Isa. 11.9) in the far north (Ps. 48.2).

3. Many Israelite writers also thought of mountains as symbols of the foundations of the social order. When Jeremiah wanted to describe the terrible chaos in Judah and in neighbouring lands, he said 'the mountains were quaking and all the hills moved to and fro' (Jer. 4.26). In ordinary language this means 'the foundations of our society are shaking. There is danger of a complete breakdown'. In Psalm 30.7 a mountain is a symbol of the foundation of an individual's life.

4. The Israelites also thought of mountains as symbols of the pride and self-assertion of nations and of the rich and powerful groups of people who form the established social order.

When Isaiah spoke of God's day of judgement 'against all that is proud and lofty', he said that God would bring down 'all the high mountains, and ... all the lofty hills' (Isa. 2.12, 14). He did not mean that God would tear down the actual physical mountains. He meant that God would shake the established leaders who were in rebellion against His will. The story of the

Tower of Babel (Gen. 11.1–9) tells how a people built an artificial mountain reaching to the heavens. Their purpose was to establish their own strong social order, and dominate other peoples. For that reason, God destroyed the tower. One writer called Babylon a 'destroying mountain' (Jer. 51.25). By this he meant that Babylon was a very strong nation which destroyed other nations. Amos spoke of the 'mountain of Samaria' as the place where the rich and powerful people oppressed the poor (Amos 4.1). The Canaanite shrines of Baal worship were on the mountains and hills, and these symbolized Israel's rebellion against God (Jer. 3.2, 21, 23). When a poet said that in the future 'the mountain of the Lord's house shall be established as the highest of the mountains' (Isa. 2.2; Mic. 4.1) he meant that all nations and their social institutions would become foundations of the sort of society which God intends.

5. In Isaiah 40—55 the prophet spoke of the physical mountains which God put in place as the foundations of the earth (40.12; 48.13). He was also thinking of them as symbols of the foundations of a good social order willed by God. But from time to time, when people become rebellious, the established institutions may shake and totter (54.10). God will bring them low (40.4; 45.2). He will thresh and winnow them like a harvester threshing grain (41.15), and will lay them waste (42.15).

The prophet also thought of mountains as symbols of God's new creation. He said that the herald should proclaim the good news from a high mountain (40.9; 52.7). People living on the distant mountains would shout for joy when they saw signs of the new age (42.11). The way to the new Jerusalem would be along the mountain ridges (49.11), and the mountains would join the chorus of heaven and earth in the joyful song of the new creation (44.23; 49.13; 55.12).

To summarize: the foundations of a good earth and a good social order were shaking so badly in the time of the Babylonian exile, that a complete breakdown was soon coming. Nations and institutions were under God's judgement. But God was at work laying new foundations (51.16), and Israel had an important part in this work.

Nations: This word relates to the political, economic, cultural, and sociological structures of human society. Synonyms or related terms in Isaiah 40—55 are 'peoples', 'coastlands', 'ends of the earth', 'inhabitants of the earth', and 'all flesh'. Generally, whenever the author of Isaiah 40—55 speaks of the non-Israelite world, he seems to have been thinking of clans, tribes, language groups, nations and all the complex social groupings of his day. Today we would also include such structures as labour unions, political parties, corporations, as well as the political groups we know as 'nations' or 'states'. The author spoke of the nations in five ways:

1. Part of God's original design of creation (40.15; see Glossary:

Justice) living together as a family or 'people' under God's covenant (Glossary: *People*).

2. As part of the world in rebellion against this design of creation and therefore under God's judgement (40.23–24; 41.2, 26).

3. As oppressors of God's people (49.7; 41.11–12; 49.24–25; 51.23).

4. As those to whom the mission of God's people is addressed (Glossary: *Ends of the earth,* numbered paragraph 2). The nations will wait expectantly for the teaching of God's people (42.4) and God's rule (51.5).

5. As participants in the community of salvation and members of the covenant federation, the restored 'people' of God (44.3–5; 45.14–17; 49.7; 49.12, 14–21; 49.22–23; 51.4–5; 53.5; 54.3; 55.5).

For details see interpretation and notes on these verses in the appropriate chapters.

Offspring, descendants: Two Hebrew words are translated by these two English words. One means 'seed' and the other 'growth'. In Isaiah 40—55, both were used to mean that the descendants of Israel would include the nations.

1. The Israelites in exile were descendants of Abraham (41.8). This meant that: (1) they inherited the mission of Abraham as a light of blessing to the nations (Gen. 12.3); (2) they were to become 'a multitude of nations' (Gen. 17.5; this is related to their mission as 'covenant of the people'; Glossary: *People*).

2. God will gather the descendants of Israel from the four corners of the earth (43.5). But in vv. 6–7 God commands His servant community to bring new 'sons and daughters' from the nations (see discussion of 43.6–7, pp. 47, 48).

3. God will pour out His Spirit and His blessing like water on the descendants of Israel, and they will grow like grass from the well-watered ground (44.3). But according to v. 5, other peoples also will join themselves to the community, and accept the name of Israel and the name of the Lord.

4. 45.19 is a straightforward reference to the Israelites themselves as descended from Jacob.

5. God had invited (45.22) the peoples of the whole earth to turn to Him and be saved, and had given His sworn word (45.23) that all will bow to Him and swear in His name. So it is clear that representatives of the nations must be included in the term 'offspring of Israel' (45.25).

6. 48.19 is either a reference to a promise of God in the past which was not fulfilled, that the descendants of Israel would be too many to count, or a hope that the promise would be fulfilled in the future. In the context of the exile in Babylon, and in the light of other references, it seems probable that this was a reference to the 'multitude of nations', descendants of Abraham.

7. The servant of the Lord will see His descendants as the fulfilment of

the purpose of the Lord (53.10 Glossary: *Purpose*). This seems to refer to a continuing Servant community composed of the 'many' who are 'accounted righteous' (53.11), whose sin the Servant bore (53.12), and who are thus related in some way to the 'many nations' of 52.15.

8. The descendants of Israel will inherit the nations (54.3). That is, they will bring the nations into the peaceful family in covenant with God, as the 'people' according to God's design of creation (Glossary, *People*).

People: The Hebrew word (*'am*) means a kinship group with a common ancestor, a common bond. It is something like a tribe or clan. For example, we might say that the nation of Burma is made up of several different peoples, such as the Karen, Chin, Kachin, Lahu, and so forth. The kinship tie may be by blood descent, or by adoption. At the covenant ceremony at Mount Sinai, many non-Israelite groups were received as members of the people of Israel. (Notice the difference between the two possible meanings of the word in English: '*This people* has a long history.' '*People* can be very unkind.' Only the first is used in the Old Testament.)

In Isaiah 40—55, as in the rest of the Old Testament, the word 'people' in its singular form almost always refers to God's people, as in 40.1, 'Comfort my people'. In four verses, however, the prophet used 'people' to mean all mankind:

In 40.6–7, he said in one line, 'all flesh is grass', and a few lines later, 'the people is grass'. In both cases he meant all mankind. But by using the word 'people' he wanted his hearers to think of mankind as a peaceful family of nations. He probably got this idea from Genesis 9 and 10. According to Genesis 9.9, God made a covenant with Noah and his descendants after the flood. The term 'all flesh' is used four times in 9.15–17 to include Noah's descendants. Then, in Genesis 10 there is a list of 'the families of the sons of Noah according to their genealogies, and in their nations' (Gen. 10.32). This is an accurate description of a 'people', as a peaceful family of nations, descended from Noah, and bound together by God's covenant.

In Isaiah 42.5 the prophet spoke about God creating the earth and mankind on it. Again he used the word 'people' to convey the message that God intended all mankind to live together as a peaceful family of nations.

Twice, in 42.6 and 49.8, the prophet told Israel that God had commissioned them as a 'covenant of the people'. This phrase probably meant that Israel was to be a sign of God's intention, and an invitation to the nations to rejoin the new family of nations. We think of the word about Jesus Christ, who 'has broken down the dividing wall of hostility . . . to create one new man . . . . so making peace' (Eph. 2.4–5).

Purpose, will, pleased: Each of these words is used in the RSV to translate a single Hebrew word, *chefets*. Although the prophet used it only six times in Isaiah 40—55, it expresses one of his most important ideas: the purpose of God which directs the process of history. The prophet said that God's word was like rain coming down on dry ground which made the field sprout with grain and bear food and seed. God's word would also work in the hearts of people like Cyrus or the Israelites to bring about results according to His purpose (55.10–11; 46.10). For example, in 41.21 the prophet specifically described God's purpose (RSV: 'He was pleased') as being 'to magnify His law and make it glorious'. It was for this purpose that God put His 'law' in the hearts of His people (51.7), so that they could take it to the peoples of the whole earth (42.4). Cyrus would accomplish God's purpose by defeating Babylon (44.28; 48.14). The Servant of the Lord would suffer in order to fulfil God's long-range purpose (RSV: 'will', 53.10). See also, *word, law, righteousness, justice, salvation.*

Redeem, redeemer: The author of Isaiah 40—55 used these words more often than any other Old Testament writer. He called God the 'Redeemer' of Israel ten times (41.14; 43.14; 44.6, 24; 47.4; 48.17; 49.7; 49.26; 54.5, 8). He used the verb 'to redeem' to describe God's action for Israel eight times (43.1; 44.22, 23; 48.20; 50.2; 51.10; 52.3, 9). The words come from the practice of Hebrew tribal and family law. 'Redeemer' was a legal term for a near kinsman whose duty it was: (1) to buy back ('redeem') family property which had been lost through debt (Lev. 25.25); (2) to pay the redemption price in order to free a member of the family who had become a slave (Lev. 25.47–49); (3) to marry ('redeem') a widow of a relative in order to raise up children for her husband's family (Ruth 3.12–13; 4.3–6); (4) to avenge the murder of a relative (Num. 35.9–27; the word 'avenge' in the RSV translates the Hebrew word which means 'redeem').

The prophet used this word to tell the Israelites that God, as their covenant Lord, was their 'kinsman' by adoption. As their kinsman, God rescues His people from slavery (43.14; 51.10). He forgives their sins (44.22). He takes them back as His covenant people once again (54.5, 8). He raises up many new descendants for them (48.17–19; 54.1–3) from all over the earth (54.5). All of these meanings are summed up in 52.9. The Redeemer of Israel is also God of the whole earth (54.5). Therefore, the redemption of Israel is the beginning of a new creation (44.23). For this reason, it is the central message of Israel to the whole world (48.20). (See notes on 44.6–23 and 48.1–22 for a discussion of key passages dealing with the meaning of redemption.)

Righteousness, righteous, deliverance, victory, vindication, truth, right, triumph: All of these words are translations in the RSV of the one Hebrew word *tsedeq,* or its feminine form, *tsedaqah.* In order to understand what the prophet meant when he used this word, we need to find some definition that will cover its various meanings. Of the twenty-two times that he used it, sixteen refer to God's activity, five refer to human activity, and one is not clear.

Perhaps the best definition is this: *'God's righteous resolve* in action to sustain His creation according to His design'. The prophet used the word to explain: (1) why God acts, (2) how God acts, and (3) the effect of God's righteous resolve on human beings.

1. *Why God acts:* God's saving acts are a part of His righteous resolve (RSV 'righteous God', 45.21). The prophet said that God called His servant people, and aroused Cyrus, in order to accomplish His righteous resolve (RSV 'in righteousness', 42.6; 45.13, and possibly 41.2, where the RSV translation is 'victory'). His purpose 'to magnify His law' was His way of accomplishing His righteous resolve (RSV 'for the sake of His righteousness', 42.21). The same righteous resolve was behind His oath that 'to me every knee should bow and every tongue swear' (RSV: 'in righteousness', 45.23).

2. *How God acts:* According to this prophet, God's righteous resolve in action will deliver His people from Babylon (RSV: 'deliverance', 46.12, 13). This same righteous resolve will be at work among the 'nations' in every generation (RSV: 'deliverance', 51.5, 6, 8), and in particular communities (RSV: 'righteousness', 45.8). The 'offspring of Israel' will know the victories of God's righteous resolve (RSV: 'righteousness', 45.24) in their own lives. When God speaks, it will happen because the spoken word is His righteous resolve in action (45.19, RSV: 'truth').

3. *The effect of God's righteous resolve:* Human beings respond by working for the accomplishment of God's righteous resolve ('triumph', 45.25; 'pursue deliverance', 51.1). They recall the past victories of His righteous resolve (RSV: 'know righteousness', 51.7), and act accordingly ('righteousness will spring up', 45.8). Their whole society will be full of such actions (RSV: 'your righteousness like the waves of the sea', 48.18), which will form the very foundations of their life (RSV: 'established in righteousness', 54.14). The Servant of the Lord is called 'the righteous one' because God has chosen him to fulfil His righteous resolve, and he will cause many to be accepted as 'righteous' (53.11). However, when human beings depart from God's righteous resolve, their action is 'not right' (4.1).

In conclusion, this is one of the words which the prophet used to explain how and why God was present in the world. See also: *purpose, word, hand, salvation, justice, create.*

Save, Saviour, Salvation: The Hebrew word most often translated 'save' means to liberate from external evils, such as enemy attack, wickedness, disaster, and personal or social breakdown.

The prophet used various forms of this word 24 times to refer to the saving word of God, and its effect on Israel and all the 'nations' of the world. In the time before the fall of Babylon, he referred to God's work of delivering the Israelites from exile in Babylon, and the 'nations' from the disorders of human existence.

When the prophet used these words for 'save' he was thinking about God's saving work in:

(a) conquering the forces of disorder and chaos which oppress human beings ('drying up the deep', 44.27);

(b) creating new breathing space ('stretching out the heavens', 41.22), and new living space ('spreading out the earth', 42.5);

(c) restoring the 'wilderness' of the earth as a 'garden' (44.1–5; 45.8; Glosssary: *World picture, Wilderness*).

For him, to be 'saved' meant to inherit God's gift of freedom, security, and wholeness of life, and to share in God's saving activity among the 'nations' in each generation (51.6, 8, 16).

The prophet believed that God used both Cyrus and His chosen Servant people Israel in His saving work, in Israel itself, and among the nations.

1. *God's saving work in Israel:* The prophet told the exiles that God was their Saviour (43.3) as shown by (a) His past acts of deliverance (43.11), (b) His saving acts during the coming crisis of the fall of Babylon (49.26), and (c) in the future when they would be serving God among the 'nations' (49.8).

2. *God's saving work among the nations:* The prophet also told the exiles that their Saviour was *the only Saviour* (43.11), so that they could be witnesses to the true Saviour among the nations. The community demonstrating the effects of God's saving activity (45.8) would be so convincing (45.17) that the nations would come to believe that the 'God of Israel' was the only Saviour (45.15). Shortly after that passage comes the Saviour's invitation to 'all the ends of the earth' to 'turn to me and be saved'. In order to make this invitation heard and understood God would send out His Servant people (49.6), to carry out His saving work among the nations (51.5) in every generation (51.6, 8).

Finally, in chapter 52 the prophet brought both strands together. In his vision of the future, he saw the herald (God's servant community) announcing the fulfilment of God's saving work of peace, redemption, comforting, and restoration of the garden land, in the sight of all 'nations', so that they might at last 'turn and be saved' (52.7–10).

See: In Isaiah 40—55 this means not only physical seeing with a person's eyes, but seeing with understanding, and even belief. The worship of idols blinds the 'eyes' and dulls the understanding (44.18). But people looking at Israel will have their eyes opened to '*see* and know . . . consider and understand' that God is at work making a garden in the wilderness (41.20). The prophet said that when kings (i.e. the leaders of the people) *saw* the glory of God in Israel they would arise and bow before Him (49.7). These kings would *see* how God had exalted His suffering Servant (52.13; 53.1). Finally, all mankind would *see* God's glory (40.5). This would be a fulfilment of the words of Isaiah 29.18, that 'out of their gloom and darkness the eyes of the blind shall *see*'. In the New Testament, these prophecies are related to the coming of Christ, who was 'a light for revelation to the nations' (Luke 2.32). At the festival of Epiphany, held on January 6 each year, Christians remember the revelation of Jesus to the magi (Matt. 2.10–11). We say, in the words of John 1.14, 'We have beheld His glory'.

Servant: This word occurs 21 times in Isaiah 40—55 and, the idea of the Servant is one of the prophet's most important themes. Many of the Old Testament writers used it to describe the covenant relationship between Israel and her covenant Lord. They called worship a 'service' (Deut. 6.13) – as we still do today. They called the members of the Israelite community (Ps. 90.13), the patriarchs (Deut. 9.27), and the prophets (Amos 3.7), the 'Servants of the Lord'. Particular individuals who accepted and obeyed God's will were called His 'Servants'. Some of these were Abraham (Gen. 26.24); Jacob (Ezek. 28.25); Moses (Josh. 1.7); David (Sam. 7.5); Elijah (2 Kings 9.36); Jonah (2 Kings 14.25), Isaiah (Isaiah 20.3).

In Isaiah 56—66 the 'Servants of the Lord' are the worshipping community. These passages will help us to understand the background of this term in Isaiah 40—55.

In Isaiah 40—55, the term 'Servant of the Lord' (in the singular) expresses the intimate relationship between Israel and the Lord. God 'chose' (41.8, 9; 42.1; 43.10; 44.1–2) His Servant 'from the ends of the earth' (41.8), forgave his sins, though he was blind and deaf (42.19; 44.21–22), redeemed him from slavery (48.20), and exalted him (52.13).

The Servant on his side had a service to perform for his Lord:

(a) he was to fulfil God's promise to Abraham that all families of the earth would share in God's blessing through him (41.8; Gen. 12.3);

(b) he was to make 'justice' (see Glossary, *Justice*) a part of the life of the nations (42.1–4);

(c) he was to bear witness to the one true God (43.10);

(d) he was to glorify God (49.3);

(e) he was to carry the light of salvation to the nations (49.6);

(f) he was to be a covenant to the people (49.8; Glossary, *People*), and

(g) he was to give himself as a sacrifice for the sins of the nations (53.11).

The prophet used the term in a flexible way.

1. He applied it to *all the Israelite exiles in Babylon,* who were themselves a 'remnant' of the larger nation (41.8, 9; 42.1–4). In 49.6 this remnant was given the task of gathering Israelites who were scattered among the nations. Perhaps Jesus had this verse in mind when He spoke of His mission to 'the lost sheep of the house of Israel', (Matt. 10.6).

2. Isaiah 50 probably reflects a division that grew up within the community of exiles in Babylon. One group decided to return directly to rebuild the temple and city, and to restore the dynasty of David. The *group of 'disciples'* was the 'Servant'.

3. Finally, in 52.13; 53.12, the prophet described the Servant as an individual.

Thus, the term 'Servant of the Lord' can apply to individuals, to the whole community, or to a part of the community. This is because who or what the Servant is, depends on the service carried out. Those who have the relationship to God, and carry out the mission of Israel, are both 'Servant' and 'Israel'. For this reason, early Christian writers were correct when they saw Jesus as fulfilling what the author of Isaiah 40–55 said about the Servant of the Lord. Jesus carried out the mission of the Servant. Likewise, those who follow Jesus are a part of the Servant community. Therefore, we should study Isaiah 40—55 very carefully; many of its words are for us.

Some scholars believe that the prophet of Isaiah 40—55 had an actual person in mind when he wrote some of these passages, especially 52.13; 53.12, but they are not agreed as to who that person was. Some have suggested it was Moses, or King Jehoiakin who was in exile in Babylon, or even the prophet himself. Probably he did not have any particular person in mind, but was trying to prepare the Servant community for its mission when the rule of Babylon was ended. In any case, it is more important for us to look for what the Servant should *do*, than to wonder who the Servant *was*.

Some scholars believe that four of the passages about the Servant of the Lord (42.1–4; 49.1–6; 50.4–9; 52.13—53.12) were not at first a part of the poems in Isaiah 40–55. They believe that the prophet, or perhaps someone else, composed these passages at a different time, with a different idea of the Servant, and that they were later inserted into the collection of poems. In this Guide we take the view that these passages were a part of the poems from the very beginning.

Wilderness, desert: 1. The ordinary meaning of these words is barren, dry, uninhabited land, in contrast to the fertile cultivated land with its houses, towns, gardens, and fields.

2. The Israelites thought of the wilderness as (a) the place where God and Israel made covenant together, and (b) the land through which the Israelites travelled on their way to Canaan. It was full of danger, not fit for human habitation. There God guided them and trained them.

3. The story of the garden of Eden in Genesis shows that the garden land is the place of blessing and life. The man and woman were given the task of maintaining the blessing by caring for the garden. When they disobeyed, they were sent to live in a cursed land. This is an actual

description of what happens to a land when there is social breakdown, broken covenant, injustice, and immorality (Hos. 4.1–3; Jer. 4.26).
4. 'Wilderness' can thus be a symbol for separation from God (Ps. 63.13), attack by enemies (Ps. 102.8), or spiritual dryness (Ps. 22.14–15).
5. In Isaiah 40—55, the wilderness is both a picture of the uninhabitable land of curse, and the place where God reveals Himself, not only to Israel but also to all mankind (40.3, 5). But God will change the wilderness to a garden by streams of water (41.18; 43.19, 20), and beautiful trees (41.19).

The prophet does not tell us where the wilderness is, or where the transformation will take place. It seems to be somewhere on the way to the new Jerusalem. But in 51.3 he states clearly that the wilderness is Zion, which will be changed to the garden of Eden. Perhaps he meant that 'wilderness' is a condition rather than a place. Wherever people are when they separate themselves from God is 'wilderness', wherever they are when they try to live according to God's laws becomes a garden. This is the way in which many Christians have understood the prophet's words. What is your opinion?

The Word of God: This phrase has various meanings in Isaiah 40—55:
1. God's purpose at work in human life and society (40.8; 45.23; 46.11; 55.11).
2. God's words in the mouth of His messengers (51.15; Jer. 1.9). The messengers must receive God's Word for their own time. They have an important task to carry out in the accomplishment of God's purpose.
3. The words spoken by the messenger, confirmed by God (44.26). The messenger must express God's Word in a way his hearers can understand – in their language and thought-forms, and taking their situation into account.
4. The Word of God in the words of the messenger, heard by people (48.1, 6, 12). Sometimes the people cannot hear what the messenger has to say because their hearts are hard (48.8; 6.9).
5. The Word of God in the words of the messenger recorded in a book for future generations (30.8; 42.23).

World-View, Heavens, Earth, Sea, Waters, Deep: In ancient times people believed that the universe really was something like a three-storey building. According to this picture, human beings and other forms of life lived on a *flat earth* which was the 'ground floor'. Above the earth was either a solid dome, or a tent-like curtain, called *'heavens'*. The purpose of this 'upper floor' was to keep out *the waters* stored above the heavens. Without the protecting dome, people thought that the waters above the heavens would come down to drown or suffocate all life. The dome of the heavens thus protected *the living space* for human beings and other forms of life on earth.

Beneath the earth was a sort of 'basement'. This lower floor was mainly a body of water called *the deep,* but in a cavern just under the earth, and surrounded by the waters of the deep was *Sheol,* also called *the Pit* or *Abaddon.* The waters of the deep which surrounded the earth on all sides, were called *the sea.* The sea was an enemy of the life on the earth. The ridge of land or coastal mountains around the flat earth ('*coastlands*') kept out the waves of the sea, and made the earth *a living place* for human beings and other forms of life.

It is necessary to keep this picture in mind when we read Isaiah 40—55. Seven times the prophet said that God '*stretches out the heavens*' (40.22; 42.5; 44.24; 45.12; 48.13; 51.13, 16). He did not mean that God actually used His hands to do this, but that God *protects the living space* of human beings, and other forms of life, from forces of chaos and disorder that overwhelm or suffocate life. By this protecting dome, God maintains the earth as a place where life is possible.

When the prophet said that the heavens 'would vanish like smoke' (51.6), he meant that the protective covering would break down. In other words, forces of disorder – also called 'the waters of Noah' (Isa. 54.9) – would destroy living space.

When the prophet said that God '*spread out the earth*' (42.5; 44.24), or formed, or created it (45.18), he meant that God drove back the forces of disorder (the 'sea') to *make the earth a living place* for human beings and other forms of life. When he said that the earth would 'wear out like a garment' (51.16,), he meant that the earth would become so disordered that life would no longer be possible.

According to God's design of creation, 'the sea and all that fills it' would join the chorus of praise to the creator (42.10). When the prophet said that God would 'stir up the sea so that its waves roar' (51.15), he meant that God would use the forces of disorder against His enemies on the earth. When he said that God would 'dry up the sea' or 'the waters of the great deep' (50.2; 51.10), he meant that God would overcome the forces of chaos and disorder in order to make the earth a living place once again.

Sometimes the prophet used the 'sea' as a symbol for God's particular enemy, like Egypt ('Rahab', 51.9) or Babylon (50.2). When he said that God's people would 'pass through waters', or that He would make way for them through the sea (43.16; 51.10), he meant that God would make it possible for them to find a way of escape from the powers of disorder and death to salvation and peace.

Note: The world then known to the Israelites extended from the river Indus in the East ('the rising of the sun'), to the Straits of Gibraltar in the West, and from the cataracts of the river Nile at Aswan ('Syene', Isaiah 49.12) in the south, to the mountains of Armenia in the North. When the prophet spoke of two (45.6), three (49.12), or four directions (43.5–6), he was thinking of the earth as flat, and he meant 'the whole created earth'. Although he did not know much, if anything, about peoples and countries beyond the lands bordering on the Mediterranean Sea and Western Asia, his *intention* was to include all peoples on the whole earth.

Of course, this view of the universe, and of our place within it, is very different from what scientists have since discovered about the nature and shape of the earth and its atmosphere, and outer space. But this fact does not diminish the importance, for us as well as for the Israelites, of what the writers of the Bible were *using* this earlier picture of the universe to say. Those writers were not giving a geography lesson. They were trying to describe God's loving care which always provides living space and living place for His creatures on earth.

A 'prophet' today might *use* modern scientific knowledge about the immensities of space, and about man's political strengths and weaknesses in just the same way. The extent of human knowledge and of man's power over nature has changed and increased since the Book of Isaiah was written and is likely to change and increase still further in the future. But this does not affect our understanding of the living relationship between God and His world and His people. We need to remember this as we study the beliefs held by the writers of the Bible and try to interpret them in our own teaching.

Key to Study Suggestions

40.1–11

1. See p. 7, line 1 to p. 8 line 5.
2. See pp. 7, 8, Interpretation, section 1.
3. See p. 8, Interpretation, section 2
4. See p. 9, section 2, para. 4.
5. See p. 9, section 2, para. 5.
6. See p. 9, last para., and p. 11, paras 1 and 2.
7. See p. 13, note on 40.7.
8. See p. 12, para. 1.

40.12–31

1. See p. 16, last 2 lines, and p. 18, lines 1–12.
2. See p. 18, lines 14–18.
3. See p. 18, lines 19–29.
4. See p. 19, lines 8–12.
5. See p. 19, second numbered para. 2.
6. See p. 19, last 2 lines, and p. 20, lines 1–26.
7. See p. 21, lines 1–14.
8. See p. 21, numbered paras 2 and 3.
9. See p. 22, para. 4.
10. See p. 21, para. 3, p. 24, lines 14–33, and Isa. 40.21, 31.

41.1—42.4

1. See p. 26. para. 1.
2. See p. 27, paras 2 and 3.
3. See p. 25, last 2 paras, and p. 27, paras 5 and 6.
4. See p. 28, numbered paras 1–3.
5. See p. 30, lines 3–20.
6. See p. 30, lines 21–34.
7. See p. 30, last 2 lines, and p. 31, lines 1–5 and 26–28.
8. See p. 32, note on 41.22.

42.5–17

1. See p. 34, Background, para. 2, and Isa. 21.16; 60.7; Ps. 120.5; Jer. 49.28, 29; 2 Kings 14.7.

2. See p. 35, Interpretation, 1st para.
3. See p. 37, lines 1–27.
4. See p. 38, para. 3.
5. See p. 38, para. 4.
6. See pp. 38, 39, numbered paras 1 and 2.
7. See p. 39, lines 5–12.
8. See p. 37, last line, and p. 38, lines 1–4.

42.18—43.7

1. (a) See p. 44, last 2 lines, and p. 45, lines 1–5.
   (b) See p. 45, para. 2.
   (c) See p. 45, lines 10 and 11.
2. See p. 45, paras 4 and 5.
3. See p. 45, paras 7 and 8.
4. See p. 45, last 3 lines, and p. 47, lines 1–4.
5. See p. 47, para. 3, and remainder of section on 43.1–4.
6. See p. 47, last 7 lines, and p. 48, lines 1–4.

43.8–13

1. See p. 51, Interpretation, para. 1.
2. See p. 51, Interpretation, para. 2, lines 1–5.
3. See p. 51, Interpretation, para. 2, lines 6–10.
4. See p. 51, last 3 lines.
5. See p. 52, paras 2 and 3.
6. See p. 52, para. 4.
7. See p. 52, last 6 lines, and p. 53, lines 1–6.
8. See p. 53, last 2 paras, and p. 55, lines 1–10.
9. See p. 55, lines 11–15.

43.14—44.5

1. See p. 57 and p. 58, para. 1.
2. See p. 59, section on 43.14–45.
3. See p. 60, para. 1.
4. See p. 60, paras 3 and 4.
5. See p. 60, para. 5.
6. See p. 62, note on 43.22.
7. See p. 63, note on 44.2.
8. See p. 63, note on 44.5.
9. See p. 58, para. 2.

44.6–23

1. See p. 65, paras 1 and 2.
2. See p. 65, last para.
3. See p. 67, numbered para. 1.
4. See p. 67, para. 3 from foot.
5. See p. 67, para. 2 from foot.
6. See p. 67, last para.
7. See p. 68, paras 3 and 4.
8. See p. 68, numbered para. 1.
9. See p. 68, last line, and p. 70, lines 1–6.
10. See p. 70. para. 5.

44.24—45.13

1. See p. 74, Interpretation, para. 1.
2. See p. 74, last 2 paras, and p. 76, numbered paras 3, 4, and 5.
3. See p. 76, numbered para. 1.
4. See p. 76, last 4 lines.
5. See p. 77, numbered para. 3.
6. See p. 77, numbered para. 4, and 2 following paras.
7. See p. 79, note on 44.25.
8. (a) See p. 78, 3rd para.
   (b) See p. 78, numbered paras 1–3.
9. See p. 78, last 5 lines, and p. 79, lines 1–3.

45.14–25

1. See p. 81, Background, para. 1.
2. See p. 81, Background, para. 2.
3. See p. 81, last line.
4. (a) i. See p. 83, para. 3, and Glossary note on p. 204.
      ii. See p. 83, para. 4, and Glossary note on pp. 214, 215.
   (b) See p. 83, para. 5.
5. See p. 83, lines 9–2 from foot.
6. See p. 84, para. 1.
7. (a) See p. 84, paras 3 and 4.
   (b) See p. 84, para. 5.
8. See p. 84, last para.
9. See p. 85, numbered paras 1–6.
10. See p. 85, lines 18–21.
11. See p. 85, para. 7.
12. See p. 85, last 5 lines, and p. 86, lines 1–9.

46.1–13

1. See pp. 94, 95, note on 46.1, 2.
2. See p. 93, Interpretation, 2nd para.
3. See p. 93, 1st numbered para. 1.
4. See p. 93, numbered para. 2.
5. (a) See p. 93, lines 6 and 5 from foot.
   (b) See p. 94, lines 9 and 10.
6. See p. 94, 1st numbered para. 2.
7. See p. 94, section on 46.12, 13.
8. See p. 95, line 7.
9. See p. 95, lines 12–18.
10. See p. 96, notes on 46.10 and 46.11.

47.1–15

1. See p. 98, Background, para. 2.
2. See p. 98, Background, para. 1.
3. See p. 99, Interpretation, numbered para. 1.
4. See p. 99, line 4 from foot.
5. See p. 100, para. 3.
6. See p. 100, numbered para. 4.
7. See p. 100, numbered paras 5 and 6.
8. See p. 100, last 2 lines, and p. 102, lines 1–7.
9. See p. 102, numbered para. 8.

48.1–22

1. See p. 105, Background, para. 3.
2. See p. 106, numbered paras 1–6.
3. See p. 107, numbered paras 1–3.
4. See p. 108, 1st para.
5. See p. 108, numbered para. 1, sub-paras (a), (b), (c), and (d).
6. See p. 108, numbered para. 2 and last para.
7. See p. 110, 1st para. (numbered para. 3).
8. See p. 110, numbered para. 1.
9. See p. 110, numbered para. 1, sub-paras (a), (b), and (c).
10. See p. 110, last 2 lines, and p. 111, lines 1–8.
11. See p. 111, sub-para. (c).
12. See p. 111, numbered para. 3.
13. See Isa. 48.20 and p. 111, numbered para. 4.

Special Note B

1. See p. 115, last para., and p. 116 to end of numbered para. 2.

2. See p. 116, lines 10–16.
3. (a) See p. 115, lines 5–3 from foot.
   (b) Based on p. 115, last 3 lines.
4. (a) and (b) See p. 116, numbered paras 1 and 2.
5. See pp. 116, 117, numbered para. 3 and 2 paras following.

49.1–26

1. See p. 119, lines 6–10.
2. See p. 120, note on key themes and Interpretation, para. 1.
3. See p. 120, Interpretation, para. 2.
4. See p. 120, section headed 'The Mission'.
5. See p. 120, last 5 lines, and p. 122, lines 1–19.
6. See 49.1–6, p. 120, last line, and p. 122, lines 1, 2 and numbered para. 2.
7. See p. 122, last 5 lines, and p. 123, lines 1–6.
8. See p. 123, numbered para. 3, and section on 49.8–9a, 2nd para.
9. See p. 123, section on 49.8–9a, 3rd para.
10. See p. 123, last 4 lines, and p. 124, lines 1–13.
11. See p. 124, paras 5 and 6.
12. See p. 124, last 2 paras.
13. See p. 125, para. 2, last 2 lines.
15. See p. 120, Interpretation, para. 1.

50.1–11

1. See Jer. 27.7–19, 24, and p. 129, numbered para. 2.
2. See p. 129, lines 10–22.
3. See p. 130, Interpretation, and p. 131, lines 1–6.
4. See p. 131, Interpretation, para. 2, and p. 135, section on 50.10, para. 1.
5. See p. 131, Interpretation, numbered paras 1 and 2.
6. (a) See p. 131, numbered para. 1, sub-paras (a) and (b).
   (b) See p. 131, lines 20–33.
7. (a) and (b) See pp. 132, 133, section on 50.4–6.
8. See p. 134, lines 12–2 from foot.
9. See p. 134, lines 6–2 from foot.
10. See p. 135, section on 50.10.
11. See p. 136. section on 50.11.

51.1–16

1. See p. 139, Background, para. 1.
2. See 50.7, 13, 14 and p. 139, Background, paras 2 and 3.
3. See p. 140, Interpretation, para. 1.
4. See p. 140, last 7 lines.
5. See p. 141, numbered paras 1–4.

6. See p. 141, numbered para. 2.
7. See p. 143, lines 1–18.
8. See p. 143, section on 51.7, 8.
9. See p. 143, section on 51.9–11, lines 3–5.
10. See p. 144, lines 6–8.

51.17—52.12

1. See p. 146, para. 1.
2. See p. 147, Interpretation, lines 3–14.
3. See p. 147, last 6 lines, and p. 148, lines 1–7.
4. See p. 148, section on 51.17–23, 2nd para.
5. See p. 148, section on 51.17—52.12, 1st para.
6. See p. 148, last 4 lines.
7. See p. 149, lines 1–5.
8. See p. 149, lines 6–8.
9. See p. 149, numbered para. 4.
10. See p. 149, section on 52.9, 10, numbered paras 1–3.
11. (a) and (b) See p. 151, lines 1–5.

52.13—53.12

1. See p. 152, Background, lines 3–7.
2. See p. 153, Reading Suggestions, lines 1–16.
3. See p. 154, sub-paras (a), (b), (c), and (d)
4. See pp. 154, 155, section on 53.13–15.
5. See p. 155, section on 53.1–9, lines 8–11.
6. See p. 155, last 11 lines, and p. 156, paras 1 and 2.
7. See p. 156, paras 3–5.
8. See p. 156, para. 6.
9. See p. 156, last 2 lines, and p. 157, lines 1–5.
10. See p. 157, para. 2.
11. (a) See p. 157, para 3.
    (b) See p. 157, paras 4 and 5.
12. See p. 157, para. 6.
13. See p. 157, last para.
14. See p. 159, paras 1 and 2.

54.1–17

1. See p. 162, Background, para. 1.
2. See p. 163, Interpretation, paras 1 and 2.
3. See p. 163, Interpretation, para. 3.
4. See pp. 163, 164, sub-paras (a), (b), and (c).

226

5. (a) See p. 164, last para., and p. 165, lines 1 and 2.
   (b) See p. 165, numbered paras 1–3.
6. See p. 165, section on 54.9–17, para. 1.
7. See p. 165, section on 54.9–17, para. 1.
8. See p. 165, last 2 paras, and p. 166. lines 1 and 2.
9. See p. 166, section headed 'Response to Hope'.

55.1–13

1. See p. 168, Background, paras 1–3.
2. See p. 169, Interpretation, para. 1.
3. See p. 169, last para., and p. 170, 1st para.
4. (a) See p. 170, numbered para. 1.
   (b) See p. 170, numbered para. 2.
   (c) See p. 170, numbered para. 3.
5. See p. 170, section on 55.3–5, para. 1.
6. See p. 171, lines 1–13.
7. See p. 170, last 3 lines.
8. See p. 171, para. 4.
9. See p. 171, section on 55.6–9, sub-paras (a), (b), (c).
10. See p. 172, lines 3–7.
11. See p. 172, lines 8–20.
12. See p. 172, section on 55.12, 13, para. 3.

56—59

1. See p. 177, para. 1.
2. See p. 178, para. 2.
3. See p. 178, lines 6 and 5 from foot.
4. See p. 179, paras 1 and 2.
5. See p. 179, numbered para. 1, and p. 180, numbered paras 2 and 3.
6. See p. 181, last 2 paras, and p. 182, lines 1–12.
7. See p. 182, numbered paras 1–3.
8. See p. 182, last 13 lines.

60—62

1. (a) See p. 184, Background, para. 1.
   (b) See p. 184, last 2 lines, and p. 186, lines 1–5.
2. See Isa. 60.4; 61.4; 61.9, and pp. 186, 187, Interpretation, section headed 'God's Intention'.
3. See p. 187, lines 15–19.
4. See p. 187, lines 7–2 from foot.
5. See p. 187, last line, and p. 188, lines 1–4.

6. See p. 188, lines 5–12.
7. See p. 188, paras 4 and 5.
8. See p. 188, para. 5.
9. See p. 188, para. 5.
10. See p. 189, lines 3–7.
11. See p. 189, para. 3.
12. See p. 189, para. 4.
13. See p. 189, paras 5 and 6.

63—65

1. See p. 191, Background.
2. See p. 192, paras 1 and 2.
3. See p. 192, para. 3.
4. See p. 193, numbered para. 3, sub-paras (a), (b), (c), and (d).
5. See p. 194, section on 45.1–25, para. 2.

66.1–24

1. See p. 196, last 2 lines.
2. See p. 197, section on 66.1, 2, para. 1.
3. (a) See p. 197, section on 66.1, 2, para. 2.
   (b) See p. 197, section on 66.1, 2, para. 3.
4. See p. 198, para. 3.
5. See p. 199, lines 3–8.
6. See p. 199, section on 66.7–9, 18–22, paras 2, 3, and 4.
7. See pp. 200, 202, numbered paras 1–7.

Index